Building a Profitable Online Accounting Practice

Critical Praise for
Building a Profitable Online Accounting Practice

"*Building a Profitable Online Accounting Practice* does an excellent job of articulating the evolutionary changes accounting professionals are facing in order to better serve the small business market. I highly recommend it to all CPAs who are searching for innovative strategies to build a more effective practice, develop partnerships, and enable their small business clients to capitalize on e-business opportunities."

> —Stephen King, CPA
> CEO and Co-Founder
> Virtual Growth, Inc.

"The way our profession will service our clients in the future is taking a dramatic turn for the better. Jack Fox understands this new paradigm of service and, like a coach, takes you step-by-step through how to prepare your firm to profit in this new age of online services."

> —Charles R. McCann, CPA
> Former Managing Partner
> of Mayer Hoffman McCann

Also by Jack Fox

Starting and Building Your Own Accounting Business, Third Edition
Accountants' Guide to Budgetary Automation
GOD's Business Gamebook and Business Planning Guide
Selling Skills for Client/Server Accounting Software Professionals
Accounting and Recordkeeping Made Easy for the Self-Employed
How to Obtain Your Own SBA Loan

Building a Profitable Online Accounting Practice

Jack Fox, MBA

John Wiley & Sons, Inc.
New York • Chichester •Weinheim • Brisbane • Singapore • Toronto

Library of Congress Cataloging-in-Publication Data:

Fox, Jack.
    Building a profitable online accounting practice / Jack Fox.
      p. cm.
    ISBN 0-471-40308-3 (pbk. : alk. paper)
    1. Accounting firms—Computer networks. 2. New business enterprises. I. Title.
  HF5625.7 F69 2001
657′.068′1—dc21   00-049645

Printed in the United States of America

10 9 8 7 6 5 4 3 2 1

To all who have lived with, loved,
and been loved by an animal.
They teach us how much better our business world would be
if it were more like the animal kingdom.

Acknowledgments

I take this opportunity to acknowledge and express my gratitude to some of those who have contributed to this project and my life.

God, who makes all things possible.

My parents, for fostering an entrepreneurial spirit and optimism tempered with realism.

My wife, Carole Olafson Fox, and her wonderful children, Danny, Troy, Theresa, and Trisha.

My teachers, students, friends, clients, associates, and competitors who demonstrated what Samuel Goldwyn so aptly said, "No person who is enthusiastic about his work has anything to fear from life."

Yorky, our beloved Yorkshire terrier, who shared his too brief life with my wife and me. He demonstrated how such a very small dog can fill an enormous place in every aspect of our activities and leave an even larger void in our hearts. We will always cherish his memory.

Contents

Preface   xxi

1 ONLINE VIRTUAL E@CCOUNTING™   **1**

Implications of the Internet for Accounting   1
Accountants' Primary Issues   2
Staffing Strategies and Issues   5
Technology Vendors' Issues   6
Accounting Client Concerns   8
Changing Market Conditions   9
Financial Planning Internet Market Implications   10
Accounting-Related Internet Newcomers   12

**2 THE SMALL TO MEDIUM-SIZED
ACCOUNTING SERVICES MARKET OPPORTUNITY**   **15**

Market Overview   15
   Chasing the SMB Market   16
   Strategies That Pursue Opportunities   18
ASPs   21
ISPs   22
Transitional Factors   25
Evolving into an E-business   27
Unlocking the Market   28
Summary   29
   Findings from Recent Demographic Studies   30
   What the Numbers Mean   30

3 BUSINESS PLAN DEVELOPMENT AND IMPLEMENTATION   **37**

Your Business Plan—A Key Practice Development Tool   37
   What Is a Business Plan?   37

The Narrative	37
Suggested Business Plan Table of Contents	38
The Plan Summary	38
Background	39
Accounting Practice Description and Analysis	39
Potential Clients	40
Market Size and Trends	40
Competition	40
Matrix	41
Management and Staff	41
Organization	41
Key Managers	41
Compensation and Ownership	42
Markets and Marketing Strategy	42
Target Markets	42
Client Analysis	43
Competitive Analysis	43
Pricing	44
Advertising and Promotion	44
Summary of Markets and Marketing	44
Accounting and Consulting Services, Facilities, and Processes	44
Financial Information	45
Risk Factors and Rewards	46
"SWOT" Analysis	46
Timetables and Benchmarks	47
Plan Appendices/Exhibits	47
Practical Advice and Considerations	47
Writing and Organizing the Plan	48
Don't Use Professional Jargon	48
Don't Repeat Yourself	49
Support Your Claims	49
Confidentiality Considerations	49
Don't Be Selective in Your Disclosures	49
Obtain an Objective Review	50
First Impressions Count	50
Four Do's and One Don't	50
How The Accounting Guild Can Help	51
4 THE ONLINE VIRTUAL ACCOUNTING PRACTICE	**53**
Structuring Your Accounting Practice	53
Fulfilling Promised Purposes	53
Orientation of Material	54

Profit Motivation   55
Professional Prognostications   55
  Goals   55
Components of an Online Accounting Practice   57
  Categorical Organizational Listing
     of Accounting Firms' Menu of Services   57
Basic Core Accounting and Compliance Services   57
  Accounting Software Resources   58
  Write-Up Software Resources   59
  Fixed Asset Management   61
  Fixed Asset Management Resources   61
  Web-Based Payroll Processing   61
  Service Bureaus Ally with Accountants   63
  Payroll Software and Service Provider Resources   63
  Online Tax Preparation   64
  Future of Tax Preparation   64
  Tax Return Preparation Software Resources   64
Financial Planning Services   65
  Financial Planning and the Internet   65
  Financial Planning Software   65
  Financial Planning Software Resources   66
  Extensive Employee Benefits Consulting   66
  Employee Benefits Market Niche   67
  Employee Benefits Niche Services   67
  Third-Party Administration   68
  Third-Party Resource   68
  Internet Implications   68
Specialized Areas of Expertise   69
  Making Your Professional Dreams Come True   69
  What Do You Really Want?   69
  Turning Your Dream into Reality   70
  Accounting Success Comes in Different Flavors   70
  Internet Consulting Relief   71
  Are CPAs Serious about the Internet?   71
  Specialized Market Niche Resources   72
  Professional Associations   72

5 GETTING CONNECTED AND OTHER LOGISTICS
   OF PROVIDING ONLINE SERVICES   75

What Is the Internet?   75
Change   75
Infrastructure   76

e@ccounting All Starts with a Web Site 76
Choosing the Server 77
  Reliability 77
  Performance 77
  Function 78
  Cost Considerations 78
Connections, Bandwidth, and Internet Service Providers 78
  Internet Technology Value Proposition 79
  Dial-Up 79
  Integrated Services Digital Network (ISDN) 80
  Digital Subscriber Line (DSL) 80
  T1 and Other Advanced Services 81
  Cable 82
  Satellite 82
  Summary 83
  Bottom-Line Footnotes 83
Information Technology 84
Start-Up and Ongoing Costs 84
The Human Element 85
  Training the Staff 86
Questions to Ask 87
  ISPs 87
  Telcos 87
  Other Providers 87
Jargon of the Trade 87
  Information Sources 90

6 **INTERNET NETWORKING OPERATING SYSTEMS** **93**

Network Integration 93
Talent Retention 94
Constant State of Change 95
Web-Enabling Software Integration 95
  Oracle Corporation 95
  Sun Microsystems, Inc. 96
  Microsoft Corporation 96
  Cisco Systems, Inc. 97
Achieving End-to-End Management 97
Middleware Demystified 98
  Why Use It? 99
  Middleware Benefits 99
  Basis of Middleware Confusion 100
  Types of Middleware 100
  Prognosis 103

Open Source UNIX and Linux   103
    Time-Tested Model   104
    Natural Progression   104
    Viable Business Models   105
    Business Benefits   106
    Applications Adoption Preferences   108
    Disruptive Technology   110
    Open Source Requires Community   110

7   ACCOUNTING SOFTWARE ONLINE AND OFF   113

Accounting: Every Business's Mission-Critical Application   113
Accounting Software Categories   114
    Example of Software Programs by Category and Costs   114
    Typical Client Business Revenue   115
    Difference between Categories   115
    Foundational Database Listed by Popularity   116
    Leading Client/Server Accounting Software Programs   116
    High-End Accounting Software   117
    Leading Mid-Range Accounting Software Programs   117
Accounting Software Partnering   118
    Application Hosting   118
Beyond Accounting   118
    Practice Management   118
    Market Prognosis   119
    Accounting Software Vendor Resources   119
    Application Software Providers (ASPs)   121
    Other Software Resources   122

8   APPLICATION SOFTWARE PROVIDERS   131

The ASP Market   131
    What Is an ASP?   131
    Background   131
    Characteristics   132
    Advantages of Using an ASP   133
The ASP Market Holds Plenty of Promise   133
    The Promises   134
Advising a Client about Choosing to Use an ASP   135
Negotiating an ASP Deal   135
    Questions to Be Asked and Answered   136
ASPs' Contract Checklist   136
ASPs from A to Z   138

Aggregators, BSPs, MSPs:
    The Next Generation Service Providers   140
    Prognosis and Accounting Profession Implications   141

**9 INFORMATION TECHNOLOGY: THE CURRENCY
OF ONLINE PRACTICE DEVELOPMENT   143**

Strategy   143
   Dichotomy of Strategy   144
   Internet Time   144
What Do Prospective Clients Want from an Accounting Firm?   148
 E-business Goals of Most Clients   150
   "E-active" Clients   150
   Clients' Differing Perceptions of the Internet   150
Electronic Data Interchange (EDI)   151
   History   151
   EDI Evolution   151
   EDI Prognosis   152
Enterprise Resource Planning (ERP)   152
   What Is ERP?   152
   How Does ERP Work?   153
   Why Do I Want ERP?   153
   Where Do I Get ERP?   154
   ERP Vendors   154
   Other Significant ERP Vendors   154
   ERP Prognosis   155
Extensible Markup Language (XML)   155
   XML Is Not a Glorified HTML   155
Extensible Business Reporting Language (XBRL)   157

**10 DATABASES, DATA WAREHOUSES,
AND DATA MARTS   159**

Databases   159
   Background   159
   Database Definitions and Jargon Clarification   160
   "Relational" Defined   162
   Database Knowledge   163
   Choice of Database   164
   Using Databases   165
   Association and Market-Basket Analysis   165
   Segmentation and Classification   165
   Caveat   165

Decision Trees   166
Neural Networks   166
Drill Down or Blast?   166
Privacy Issues   167
Data Warehouses   167
Tour through a Data Warehouse   167
Accounting Professionals in High Demand   168
Partnering with Database Vendors   169
Data Modeling   169
Data Warehouse Solutions and Prognosis   169
Accountants' Opportunities   170
Data Marts   170
Target Your Database Market   171
Data Mart Tools' Necessities   171
Clients' Hopes and Fears   172
Your Best Shot   172

11   DATA MINING, DOCUMENT MANAGEMENT, AND STORAGE   173

Data Mining   173
Definition   174
Data-Mining Algorithms   174
Procedure   175
Data-Mining Project   175
Mining Your Accounting Firm's
    and Your Clients' Web Statistics   176
Document Management and Business Intelligence   176
What Does Document Management Do?   177
Document Management Is More than Simply Imaging! 177
What Document Management Relies On   177
Managing Information as a Corporate Asset   177
Document Managing Requirements   178
Planning Is Critical to Success   178
Define the Economic Life   178
Who Is Responsible?   179
Once a System Is Selected   179
Enterprise Reporting and Data Mining   179
End-to-End Report Management   180
Storage   180
Beyond Terabytes   181
Storage Trends   181
Consolidate and Manage Data   181

Explosive Data and SAN Benefits   182
Reality Check   183
Rules for Dealing with Vendor Propaganda   183
Network-Attached Storage (NAS)   184
Fibre Channel Overview   185
Other Types of Imaging   186
Total Cost of Ownership   186
Get It on Tape for Business Preservation   187
Targeted Applications   187
Outsourced Storage   188

**12 BUSINESS INTELLIGENCE
AND KNOWLEDGE MANAGEMENT   189**

Business Intelligence   189
Customization   190
Aligning with Your Client's Information Technology Functions   190
Client/Accountant IT Consulting Brokerage   191
Prognosis   192
Online Analytical Processing (OLAP)   192
The OLAP Market   193
Business Intelligence as a Market Niche   194
Vendors Seek Your Expertise   194
Knowledge Management (KM)   195
Tacit Knowledge   195
Intangible Assets   196
Two Faces of Knowledge Management   197
Insight   197
Knowledge Management Market   198
Accounting: Acquiring and Analyzing Client Information   199
Selecting a Robust Internet Platform   199
Start with Data Integration   200
Scalable Storage, High Performance, and Data Mining   200
Relational Database   200
Multidimensional Database   201
Data Mining   201
Summary   201
Suggested Further Reading   202

**13 ASSESSING THE POSSIBILITIES AND PLANNING
FOR A SUCCESSFUL ONLINE ACCOUNTING PRACTICE   203**

Basic Preparation   203
Balancing Our Professional and Personal Lives   204
E-entrepreneurship   205

Consider a Part-Time Consulting Foray   205
Launching the Part-Time Consulting Venture   206
Covering Your Professional Assets   207
Make Lemonade when Dealt a Lemon   207
Personal Finances   208
Pay Attention to Details   208
Virtual Opportunities   209
Overcoming Obstacles   209
Failure Factors in Starting an Online Accounting
     Consulting Practice   209
Success Factors in Starting an Online Accounting
     Consulting Practice   211
     Focus   211
     Marketing and Selling   211
     Success Building Blocks   212
     Success Indicators   212
Your Business Plan   213
     Adapting to Change   214
     Planning Pitfalls to Avoid   215
A Model Online Accounting Practice Business Plan   215
     Navigating the Minefield   215
Finding Your Optimum Fit   217
Protecting Your Future Investment   218
Software Tools   218
Resources   219
     Small Business Administration (SBA)   219
     The Accounting Guild   220

**14 IDENTIFYING GOALS:
LAYING THE PRACTICE FOUNDATION   221**

Prospectus   221
     Mission Statement of the Practice   221
Strategic Goals   221
     Steps to Identifying Goals   222
     Formulate Specific Goals   223
Business Structure   223
     Online Accounting Consulting Market Demographics   224
     Who Do the Clients Call?   224
     Why Make the Move?   225
     Classic Consulting Model   225
     Elevating the Position   225
     Accountant's Consulting 101   225
     Practice Lifeblood   226

The Partnering Option 227
Transition 228
Use Tax Season to Probe Clients' Technology Plans 229
Probing Questions 229
Taking the Next Step 230
Consultant or Contractor? 231
Communication 231

15 PRACTICE STRATEGIES AND STRUCTURE 233

Introduction to Strategic Planning for an Online Practice 233
    Questions Concerning Future Plans 233
    Client Demographic Study 234
    Pruning Clients That No Longer Fit 234
    Where Do You Want to Go? 234
    Practice Management Internal Financial Reporting 235
    Staffing Strategy 235
    Alliances 235
    Written Strategic Plans 236
    New and Improved Skills (How Do You Get There?) 236
    Strategy Process 237
The New Rules of Engagement 237
Full Service Providers (FSPs) 237
    Strategy #1: Move Beyond E 238
    Strategy #2: Avoid the IT and CIO Functions 239
    Strategy #3: Invest What's Necessary 239
    Strategy #4: Choose Your Partners Wisely 240
    Strategy #5: A Foot in the Door Isn't Very Important 240
    Strategy #6: Partner at Your Peril 241
Successful Practice Building Strategies and Policies 242
Step-by-Step Guide 244
    Appoint a Practice Evangelist 244
    Publish Your Vision 244
Discovering the Path from Compliance to Reliance 245
Real-Time, Online Accountants 246
Technology: Boon or Bane? 246
The Road to Somewhere 247
Client Feedback 247
Core Competencies 248
    Key Performance Indicators (KPIs) 248
    Computing Technology Competencies 248
Credibility 249
Competitive Edge 249

**16   MARKETING FOUNDATIONS:
DEVELOPING AN ACCOUNTING FIRM BRAND   251**

Marketing Misconceptions   251
   Marketing Ineptness   251
   Consistency and Relevance   252
Types of Marketing   252
Effective Professional Accounting Services Marketing   253
Selecting Clients   255
   Show Me the Money   255
   Good Client/Bad Client   256
Courting Clients   256
Communicating with Your Prospective Client   259
Communicating with Your Active Clients   259
Client Turnoffs   261
The Waiting Game   262
   Keep the Fire Burning   262
   Know the Difference Between "No" and "Not Now"   262
The Concept of Branding as a Competitive Online Advantage   263
   Your Accounting Services Brand   263
   Why Brand Your Accounting Firm?   263
   What Can You Expect Your Brand to Do?   264
   Do You Know You Already Have a Brand?   264
   But What Does Your Brand Mean?   264
   Is Your Brand an Opportunity?   264
   How Do You Stamp a New Brand on Your Firm?   265
   How Do You Promote Your Brand?   265
   Your Good Brand Is Good Business   266
   Developing Your Brand   266
Winning Profitable New Business   267
Marketing Strategies   267

**17   INTERNET, DATABASE, AND TARGET NICHES:
MARKETING GUIDE   271**

Database Marketing   271
   Good Marketing Begins in Your Database   271
   Database Marketing   272
   Definition of Database Marketing   272
   Designing Your Database   272
   Relational Database   274
   Building a Better Database   274
   Client Profiles   274

Database Marketplace Mining   275
   Accounting Marketplace Data Mining   275
   Database Mining/Marketing Technologies   275
Database Marketing Requirements   276
   Easy Access to Data   276
   Easy Manipulation and Viewing of Data   276
   User-Friendly Analysis   277
   Easy Use of the Results   277
Reaping the Rewards   277
Database Marketing Buzzwords   278
Success in the Accounting and Consulting Profession   278
Winning Clients by Asking and Answering Vital Questions   281
   Communicating with Prospective Clients   282
   Decision-Making Questions Prospects Ask Themselves   283
Target Niche Marketing Plan   283
Investigate Methods of Promoting Firms' Niches   284
   Internal Marketing   284
   External Marketing   284
   Create a Specific Niche Market Database   284
   Individual Partner/Team Member Marketing   285
   Speaking Opportunities   285
   Niche Marketing Benefits   285

**18 PARTNERING: PROFILES IN PROFITABILITY:
ACCOUNTING PARTNERSHIP RESOURCES
COMPENDIUM**   **289**

Partnerships Pave the Way   289
   Components of E-commerce   289
   Technology Gap   290
   Critical Success Factors in E-commerce Services   291
   Stages of E-commerce   291
   Lack of Vision and Commitment   291
E-commerce Is Coming to a Firm Near You   292
   Action Steps   292
   Intuit   292
   Bizfinity   293
E-commerce Specialized Technology Requirements   293
E-commerce Prognosis   293
Partnering Compatibility   294
Make Yourself Visible   294
Due Diligence   294
Online Accounting Profitability Partnerships   295
   Virtual Growth   295

Becoming an Online Accounting Success Story   295
Technology as a Strategic Asset   296
Small Business Client Accounting Practice   296
Online Accounting Software   297
   The Online Accounting Software Value Chain   298
   Small Business Internet Accounting Software Issues   298
   Online Accounting Value Proposition   299
Accountant Affiliation Programs   299
Online Accounting Services Business Models   299
Accounting Professionals' Strategies   300
   Evaluation Criteria   301
Accountants' Professional Implications   301
Accounting—The Language of Business   302
Accountants' Client Training Courses   302
Accountants' Client/Customer Relationship Equation   303
   Accounting Partnership Resources Compendium   303

19 TEAM BUILDING AND RETREATS   **307**

Vision and Mission   307
Building a Winning Team   307
   Team Members   307
   The Partners   308
   Services   308
   The Accounting or Consulting Firm   308
Implementation   308
   Increase the Net Financial Worth of Its Clients   308
   Aggressive, Professional, and Focused Marketing Posture   309
   Maintain the Highest Standards of Ethical Conduct   309
   Become the Preeminent Practice in Its Chosen Niches   309
Team Member Implementation   309
   Professional Advancement   310
   Personal Growth   310
   Involvement in Decision Making   310
   Trust and Mutual Respect   311
   *Team Members to Understand and Support Firm's Vision
      and Mission*   311
   Team Member's Role   311
Partnership Issues   311
Services   312
Retreats   312
   Partner Retreats   312
   Unsuccessful Retreats   313
   Retreats Must Lead to Action   313

Varieties of Retreats   314
Retreat Structures   314
Partner Relations, Problems, and Solutions   315
Retreats Should Provide Opportunities for Partners to Be
   Open and Honest   316
The Outside Facilitator   316
What to Look for in a Facilitator   317
Retreat Bottom Line   317

**APPENDIX: THE ACCOUNTING GUILD
AND E@CCOUNTING™: SEMINARS, CONSORTIUM,
TRAINING, AND CONSULTING**   **319**

Retreat Facilitation   319
Continuing Professional Practice Development   319
The Accounting Guild   320
   e@ccounting Client Acquisition Marketing Seminars™   320
   e@ccounting Marketing Alliance Consortium™   320
   e@ccounting TeleSeminars™   321
   TeleSeminar Class Agenda   322
   e@ccounting ABC's Accounting Basic Concepts™
      Training Centers   323
   Accounting Practices Assessment Tools   323
   Contacting The Accounting Guild   324

Glossary   325
Index   333
About the Author   337

Preface

There can be no business without clients. One of the key things I have learned in my accounting business journey is that the type of clients you attract and serve, and the caliber of associates with whom you partner, determine the kind of accounting or consulting business you build.

In earlier books, I chronicled how I managed to build a profitable and quality practice that provided excellent service and counsel to many smaller business clients. Perhaps my success was due in great part to my lack of a certified public accountant (CPA) certificate. I had opted to forgo the examination despite possessing all of the prerequisite educational course requirements.

The stringent restrictions placed on the profession at that time by the AICPA and tradition-bound state accounting societies would have prevented me from serving the small to medium-sized market niches I had chosen in the way I knew to be most effective. It is interesting that the manner in which I practiced is now permitted if not encouraged. Enrollment in CPA preparatory courses is down, with many of the brightest and most capable entering Internet-based businesses rather than public accounting. The Big Five are losing partners and managing partners to dot.com enterprises.

With the success of my first edition of *Starting and Building Your Own Accounting Business,* I sold my six-year-old accounting business to concentrate on providing accounting practice development services. I have since been professionally devoted to the development and advancement of accountants' practice development, which includes marketing and Internet accounting and training skills.

After conducting hundreds of seminars, I searched for ways to share my knowledge with the personalized, in-depth attention so beneficial to new and growing accountants and consultants. Each entrepreneurial accounting and consulting professional has specific skills, interests, personality traits, hopes, and dreams that no seminar or book, no matter how good, can completely address.

During my more than 20 years in the accounting and consulting industry, I have learned a great deal about what does and does not work. The latest developments of Internet-based, application software providers have brought the industry to a threshold of opportunity and prosperity never imagined in the past.

The Accounting Guild was launched with the publication of the third edition of *Starting and Building Your Own Accounting Business* by John Wiley & Sons in 2000. It empowers entrepreneurial accounting and consulting professionals to affiliate with a virtual organization, yet remain very much in business for themselves.

I appreciate your readership. For just as there can be no business without clients, there is no purpose for books without readers.

I wish you Godspeed on your exciting journey. Your questions and comments are most welcome and will receive a response. Please e-mail at: jfox1961@aol.com.

Jack Fox, MBA
Las Vegas, Nevada
January 2001

CHAPTER 1

Online Virtual e@ccounting™

IMPLICATIONS OF THE INTERNET FOR ACCOUNTING

Members of the accounting community who want to succeed must walk a fine line between stability and change along the brink of chaos. Many accountants shy away from that brink and so are uncomfortable with regard to today's complex environment, where change is rapid and success uncertain. Accountants must accept the paradox that the only thing permanent in business is *change*.

To achieve success, an accountant or professional accounting services firm depends on adaptive skills in three areas:

1. An adaptive accountant or firm understands its competitive space, or landscape, and is capable of measuring that landscape's ruggedness, its risks and opportunities.
2. An adaptive accounting organization is, at heart, a learning organization, one that stays in touch with clients and rewards innovation.
3. The leadership of an adaptive organization not only welcomes change but nurtures it.

An organization with such attributes will be able to embrace change and function effectively in our frightening, yet exhilarating, economy. The Internet economy requires constant work to shape an environment where change is always possible and usually occurring. It is an environment finely balanced between surprise and order. The Internet has the potential to transform the profession—not merely augment or refine business practices, but lead the industry in entirely new directions.

Accounting is the language of business but information is the currency. Manufacturers, distributors, retailers, and all other accounting services clients that excel at sharing information — about customer demand, inventory, shipments, even defects — stand to be the lowest-cost, highest-profit suppliers. The financial brokers and analysts with the fastest access to the most complete market and company information will make the most money. Transportation, logistics, and other service companies that can create bonds with their customers by linking them directly to their information systems are the most likely to be serving those same customers a decade from now.

In the end, the accountants who are the most efficient financial information handlers, processors, and manipulators will be the ones that come out on top. It's an easy enough concept to comprehend. Embracing and implementing it is far more difficult. The Internet may reinvent the marketplace through the ways computer and electronics providers do business, but it doesn't reinvent the businesses themselves. Accounting professionals must start thinking how to apply the Internet outside their traditional organizational or professional boundaries. Your competitors aren't sitting still. They can't afford to. Neither can you. What Internet risks are your firm taking? Are you competing against types of competitors that didn't exist or that you never dreamed of facing five years ago? Exhibit 1.1 describes the leadership attributes necessary to develop an adaptive management style.

ACCOUNTANTS' PRIMARY ISSUES

A massive restructuring and reordering of the accounting business is under way. The days of your parents' independent CPA firm handling only tax and audit work are almost gone. Changing the good old days' way of doing business has been a primary issue for tax and audit professionals.

In retrospect, the good old days of accounting, with manual spreadsheets and key-punched data entry cards, were not that good for those of us who detest tedium and can't type. Has it really been only 10 years ago that the operating system of choice was an eight-column pad in easy-on-the-eye pale green? Affordable computers and easy-to-use software have emancipated us from the drudgery of repetitive work in which many of us were mired for years. Computers have become fully integrated into our work and leisure lifestyles.

ADAPTIVE STYLE LEADERSHIP ATTRIBUTES

Build and manage a network of personal relationships.

- Ask
- Encourage
- Cajole
- Praise
- Reward
- Demand
- Motivate

Study the landscape.

- What are the developments, patterns, and trends among competitors (both current and potential)?
- What about customers? Or suppliers?
- Constantly ask "What if"?
- Get constant exposure to insiders and outsiders who can help improve your understanding of the landscape.

Set high expectations.

- Replace detailed agendas with broad goals or targets.
- If you know how to get there, it's not a stretch goal.
- It is essential for you to believe the goals are attainable.

Let go.

- Managing partners must set goals, then get out of the way.
- The management role is one of providing associates with whatever is needed to serve the clients.

Be available.

- Be available to help others, especially clients and staff.
- Ask questions and share information.
- Listen to others and let them know how to reach you when they need help.

(Continues)

Exhibit 1.1 Checklist of Leadership Attributes

Choose the measures on which to focus.

- What you can measure you can manage.
- Be wary of measuring everything and understanding nothing.
- The three most important things you need to measure in an accounting business are client satisfaction, staff satisfaction, and cash flow.

Communicate a direction.

- Describe the business direction and goals clearly to interested parties, both internal and external to the firm.
- The more forums management can hold, the better.
- Clients and staff come and go, people forget, and circumstances change. If the direction is not communicated clearly and often, people in the firm will get lost in fairly short order.

Be decisive.

- Debate and study must lead to action.
- The three things you have to remember in battle: shoot, move, and communicate.
- Survival begins with action.
- Decisions have to be made before things start to happen.
- One never has all the information one would like to have.

Act with urgency and energy.

- You can't do it fast enough.
- Work on the razor's edge.
- If you can't energize others, you can't be a leader.

Exhibit 1.1 *(Continued)*

This latest generation of accounting professionals can't fathom the time we previously spent manually footing, cross-footing, and accounting for historical transactions to prepare financial forecasts, multi-year cost-benefit analyses, and other prospective planning and decision-making tools. The computer, and now the Internet, have propelled the profession from the arcane and mundane to the advisory, valuably proactive, and infinitely more profitable.

The accounting profession has been keeping pace with the attitudes and work styles resulting from the increasing use of technology and the dramatic changes in the economy. The path for the future has torn away a dependence on the older perceptions of the profession in the same way Excel and Lotus eliminated our need for 13-column pads.

STAFFING STRATEGIES AND ISSUES

Small and large accounting firms are being forced to adapt and be creative in dealing with today's staffing shortages. Developing existing personnel, working with local school districts, and offering higher than competitive salaries are some of the strategies these firms use to attract people in a technology field where talent is in particularly short supply. The shortage of qualified staff has forced some accounting firms to rein in their growth, rather than spread limited staff too thin by taking all the available engagements.

It is highly improbable that you will find the perfect candidate, with a mixture of financial, management, and technical skills, short of cloning yourself. Many firms are looking within to develop the talent they require through in-house training programs. A technical background is very important, but management skills, along with loyalty and reliability, are far more important than a perfect technical match. Some accounting firms put their newly hired consultants on a formal training track to fill any gaps in their backgrounds and to help them develop a specialty.

The training approach is an effective way for professionals to immerse themselves without becoming overwhelmed. With the shortage of qualified technology professionals, it would be counterproductive to lose a skilled business consultant because of poor training. Teaching Internet technical skills produces mixed results. No matter how good the training, some CPAs are just not cut out for Internet technology consulting. Not everyone has the personality to deal with the range of issues and problems found in the field. The solution is to continue to look for qualified people and develop the existing staff.

Accounting firms are continuing to see increasing value in offering flexible work options and innovative compensation packages to attract and retain the best staffs. Job flexibility, generous pay based on performance, and promotions from within the firm are among the favored tactics. Sometimes it's the little things that matter most, like a compli-

- Developing talent from within
- Offering flexible work arrangements
- Offering higher pay
- Networking with local schools and colleges
- Restricting growth

Exhibit 1.2 Staffing Strategies

mentary refreshment area, a freshly ground coffee or cappuccino machine, and fresh flowers in the offices. Exhibit 1.2 summarizes staffing strategies.

TECHNOLOGY VENDORS' ISSUES

The technology services segment of the accounting industry confronts the same daunting, dual challenges of keeping up with the fast-changing software systems that are at the core of their businesses, and, at the same time, redefining exactly what their businesses are. Accountants agree that keeping pace with all the new tools that technology vendors are producing and helping clients put those tools to their full use represent the biggest obstacles facing accounting software resellers and consultants serving the small to medium-sized market.

Industry leaders have noted that their most prominent concern is to redefine their companies' missions in the face of today's new landscape. Technology and accountant client demands are both increasing at quantum speed. Accounting technology has expanded beyond just financials. Accounting technology providers are challenged to define who they are, separate from their competition.

The vendors have migrated from accounting software to enterprise resource planning systems — which integrate accounting with distribution, manufacturing, electronic commerce, and other applications — all too quickly for some end users in the middle market. Service firms must be able to educate clients on what these broader enterprise systems mean — a task that can include getting clients to view their organization differently — and automate systems that have been managed manually.

The changes are also occurring too quickly for the accountants as well as their vendor partners. As soon as a system is installed at a client site, it's already out of style because it's no longer the latest and greatest although it is fully functional. Most important is the ability to make the connection between the business processes of a client and marketplace dynamics — using technology to improve the business as a whole, rather than just automating basic accounting functions. The goal that remains steadfast throughout all of the changes is that of redefining the products and services that are provided to clients in order to help them better manage and grow their businesses.

Staying in the forefront of an Internet compliant practice includes making employee training and ongoing education a top priority. Many firms are partnering with software developers to provide the increasingly complex e-commerce solutions that are demanded by their clients. Accounting firms are increasing the initiative to form strategic alliances with complementary providers of needed expertise. Since e-commerce is fast becoming a major component of all accounting system installations, accounting firms are opting to solve the technology issues inherent in e-commerce by partnering and sometime acquiring the needed technical expertise. Exhibit 1.3 is a chart of technology vendors' concerns.

> **First Law of Adapting:** As soon as you start doing what you always wanted to be doing, you'll want to be doing something else.

The core values and core competencies defined for the profession through the Vision Project of the AICPA are being seriously challenged by new and largely unforeseen forces in the marketplace. The challenge to the accountant's role as the primary valued business advisor of choice is being mounted by entrepreneurs who are placing more and more empha-

---

- Keeping pace with new technologies
- Expanding the depth of their products and services
- Migrating to enterprise planning systems
- Becoming application software providers (ASPs)
- Keeping up with professional accountants

Exhibit 1.3 Technology Vendor's Concerns

- Accounting software/systems
- Electronic commerce
- Client/server
- Manufacturing
- Payroll
- EDI (Electronic Data Interchange)
- Internet/intranet
- LANs/WANs/networking
- Human resources
- Enterprise resource planning (ERP)
- Computer hardware/peripherals
- Systems management
- Data warehousing
- Mobile computing
- Telephony
- Unix

Listed in order of increase in business
Source: The Accounting Guild, Las Vegas, Nevada, *Trendsetter Study,* 2000

Exhibit 1.4 Accounting Professional Growth Areas

sis on the use of technology at the expense of providing less and less emphasis on the prudent analysis and counsel of the intelligence provided by the technology. Exhibit 1.4 lists accounting professional growth areas.

Accountants are being buffeted by an onslaught of challenges centered on identifying new ways to add value to client relationships and to generate new revenue as traditional functions become commodity functions and relationships become less personal. Industry vendors of accounting services and products are steadily enhancing their material content and are developing Internet tools that have revolutionized how that information is gathered, prepared, and distributed to the accountant marketplace.

ACCOUNTING CLIENT CONCERNS

Taking advantage of technology, profiting from electronic commerce, and competing in the global marketplace are the biggest challenges facing small and medium-sized business clients. Managing advances in technology is the main concern now confronting business clients. Technology in general and the Internet in particular have changed the face of competition from a local to a global concern.

The biggest challenges these business clients face is adapting and responding to the rapidly changing technology landscape. The questions that keep business owners awake at night are, "Who is my competition?" and "How do I compete against people who are not even in the same locale?" Many small to mid-sized clients in the past had a lot fewer competitors.

Professional accountants are also concerned about how quickly their clients are embracing the Internet to transact business. If their clients move too slowly, they may lose out to competitors located hundreds or thousands of miles away. If they react too late, they may have difficulty catching up with their competitors and potential customers. Exhibit 1.5 lists accounting client concerns.

CHANGING MARKET CONDITIONS

Newer and possibly more innovative services have been battering the gates of a once staid profession. Many accounting services are being "commoditized" by consolidators, who are less concerned about client relationships and instead develop an end-user business approach that is standardized like computer operating systems. The unconsolidated firms must provide more value to compete with the large organizations.

Internet accounting service start-ups are working diligently to steal the traditional small business accounting clients by eliminating the personal services of the accounting professional. Other virtual online

---

- Keeping up with and understanding technology
- Internet capability
- Capital
- Staffing
- Outsourcing
- Developing alliances

Exhibit 1.5 Accounting Client Concerns

accounting services, acknowledging the marketplace value of the accountant, are designing outreach campaigns to enlist accountants into acting as resellers, co-branders, or recommenders. Some combine marketability and motives and offer hybrid programs that will add to the turmoil. Accounting practitioners can fight or join, but will not have the opportunity of ignoring, the new market dynamics.

Becoming expert in an ever-increasing and broader array of accounting and related services that clients require is one of the surest ways for CPAs to provide added value. The accounting profession must focus on helping small business owners run their companies more efficiently and profitably rather than on simply providing compliance services. The supplier component of the accounting industry is responding to the challenges by offering CPAs, who use and resell its products, a meaningful business-building arsenal of courses and tools, new product and service opportunities, and relevant strategies for growth and increased profits.

Among the accountants' greatest allies are the technology services that are becoming increasingly available. Conversely, the greatest drawback is the endemic procrastination to adapt to change. CPAs need to sell and support, or at a minimum recommend (since selling seems to be such an anathema of the profession), packaged or online software to their accounting clients.

> **Fox's Law of Technology:** Any technical problem can be overcome given enough time and money.
>
> **Corollary:** You never are given enough time or money.

FINANCIAL PLANNING INTERNET MARKET IMPLICATIONS

Financial planning is the service area that most concerns those in the accounting profession. Some accountants maintain that the very survival of the profession relies upon the acceptance of the all-in-one tax preparer/financial planner as a viable entity.

Vendors of financial planning products and services have long identified the accounting profession as its most-likely-to-succeed marketing channel. They claim that financial services will prove to be the CPA's best ticket to success. Indeed, with the enactment of regulations permitting CPAs to accept commissions, financial planning has become a much larger part of the industry and financial planning software a significant segment of the accounting market. Accountants are streaming into financial planning, drawn by the surge of baby boomers approaching retirement and seeking financial consulting assistance.

Practitioners should be prepared to offer clients the nontraditional services that the market is demanding. Adapting to the technologies that are required to increase efficiencies will allow the accountants to brace themselves for the challenges that may result from the ever-changing regulation of the industry.

CPAs place a high value on client relationships. They must strengthen these by expanding upon their consultative role and improving their use of available technology. Accountants seeking to survive and thrive in these turbulent times must, above all else, be prepared to adapt to change. The paramount issue facing the accounting business is change — change in the form of market demands, regulation, technology, and the Internet.

The Internet and other technologies mean that the ways CPAs interact with clients is radically changing to a new platform. The scope and speed of change is altering how the public interacts and communicates with the tax, accounting, and consulting professional. New knowledge is necessary and new tools are required by all practitioners in the field, regardless of practice size, focus, or ownership. Practitioners must reevaluate their entire approach to business. In order for CPAs to be the professionals businesses continue to turn to for leadership, they must reinvent how they think and how they work. Today's pace of change is forcing the profession to become more agile than ever before. Accountants have to develop and maintain more finely tuned systems in order to respond quickly and intelligently to change.

Often, the more that things change, the more they stay the same — even for accountants. Amid all the change and the carnage, CPAs still must be concerned with maintaining the hard-earned respect of the public that has long been an industry hallmark. Yet, CPAs must understand that they cannot be all things to all people. Although they must continue to acquire and enhance their consulting skills and value-added services, the accounting profession must be vigilant to guard their independence, integrity, and objectivity.

ACCOUNTING-RELATED INTERNET NEWCOMERS

Some of the new Web start-ups have been extremely aggressive about launching into accounting services and are looking for CPAs and other accounting professionals to become partners. Accounting services are not the only verticals wooing the accountants and their trusting smaller business clients. Purchasing services and savings are touted by officedepot .com, onvia.com, staples.com, and works.com — to name but a few of the better-known vendors.

Another category of newcomer to the small business marketplace may best be categorized, at least for now, as small business portal. These new entrants are not much more than online magazines, or e-zines in the virtual vernacular. They include allbusiness.com, bcentral.com, bigstep.com, digitalwork.com, eCongo.com, hotoffice.com, office.com, and cpavenue.com. In addition to promised lower prices, a few offer extras such as business planning tools and libraries of legal and other forms.

At the higher end are such specialists as agillion.com offering customer management, adp.com and employease.com with payroll and benefits, and Bizfinity.com in e-commerce systems. What almost all these entrepreneurial accounting services ventures have in common is that they have appropriated the strategies and technologies developed by companies such as America Online and amazon.com. Their primary strategy is to seize customers without regard for costs and hope that profits will follow. Although the stock market at times appears to reward this profitless prosperity, one cannot help but remember the California gold rush when the only ones to make a profit were the purveyors of tools and work clothes. Accountants, consultants, and the manufacturers and resellers of Internet equipment and knowledge should profit immensely by delivering the necessities.

The small business market casts a siren's spell with the tantalizing prospect of providing needed services to the nation's approximately 23 million small businesses. To make matters even more irresistible, more than three million new businesses are launched every year, 800,000 of whom have employees. Often overlooked is the sorrowful fact that about 80 percent of these new businesses will cease operations within five years. This phenomenon has not escaped those professionals who profit as the undertakers of lost ventures. A market niche specializing in the accounting needs of the unsuccessful is a consistent revenue producer, by providing creditors' accounting, bankruptcy filings, and final corporate tax returns.

Quick calculations reveal that start-ups account for about 15 percent of the existing small business base, a 2 percent net growth each year. Waiting in the wings are a little over 8 percent of the United States' adult population (or approximately 16 million people) who are trying to start their own businesses. One third of this group are women.

The many challenges confronting the accounting industry represent a major opportunity of watershed proportions for accountants to develop relationships with software vendors that will enable both to succeed. The major challenge is one of redefining roles in a time of unparalleled growth. This is compounded by the reality of consolidation, small businesses' need to obtain much needed additional services from their "trusted advisor" CPAs, and the perils inherent in expanding into nontraditional service areas.

Electronic commerce is turning the business world on its ear while the accounting community ambivalently embraces and resists the change. While pondering the enormous possibilities that the Internet is offering, they evaluate a business world with virtually no limits to business growth. Whether the accounting profession is ready or not, the Internet is here to stay. Exhibit 1.6 lists technology solution providers who may augment areas of expertise.

TECHNOLOGY SOLUTION PROVIDERS

The following solution providers are recognized as trendsetters. The information is provided as a list for further investigation and market research. No inference is intended as to references regarding ability or any other criteria.

- **ABS Solutions, Schaumburg, IL**
  http://www.absusa.com
- **Affinity Technology Group, Hoffman Estates, IL**
  http://www.affinitytechgroup.com
- **AKA Computer Consulting, Staten Island, NY**
  http://www.akaconsulting.com
- **AmEx Tax and Business Services, Rolling Meadows, IL**
  http://www.americanexpress.com

(Continues)

Exhibit 1.6 Trendsetting Accounting Solution Providers

- **Anderson ZurMuehlen & Co., Helena, MO**
  http://www.azworld.com
- **Brunswick Integrated Computer Solutions, Akron, OH**
  http://www.bicsoft.com
- **Burch Group, Houston, TX**
  http://www.burchgroup.com
- **Business Management International, New York, NY**
  http://www.bmiusa.com
- **Catalyst Software Evaluation Centers, Dallas, TX**
  http://www.catalysteval.com
- **Charon Systems, Toronto, Canada**
  http://www.charon.com
- **Client Server Solutions, Atlanta, GA**
  http://www.css-sql.com
- **Computer Counselors, Indianapolis, IN**
  http://www.computercounselors.com
- **CRM Solutions, North Canton, OH**
  http://www.crmsys.com
- **Desmond & Ahern, Chicago, IL**
  http://www.desmond-ahern.com
- **Kerr Consulting and Support, Fort Dodge, IA**
  http://www.kerr-consulting.com
- **Kissinger Associates, Centerport, PA**
  http://www.kissingerassoc.com
- **Murdock & Associates, Santa Clara, CA**
  http://www.murdocknet.com
- **Olive, Indianapolis, IN**
  http://www.olivellp.com
- **Plus Computer Solutions, Coquitlan, B.C., Canada**
  http://www.plus.ca
- **SA Consulting, Miami, FL**
  http://www.sacg.com
- **Second Foundation, Waterloo, Canada**
  http://www.second-foundation.com
- **Select Systems, San Mateo, CA**
  http://www.select-systems.com
- **Silverware, Phoenix, AZ**
  http://www.silverw.com
- **Soltech Group, Charlottesville, VA**
  http://www.soltechgroup.com
- **Stanley Stuart Yoffee & Hendrix, Maitland, FL**
  http://www.ssyh.com
- **Toback Technology Group, Phoenix, AZ**
  http://www.tobacktech.com

Exhibit 1.6 *(Continued)*

CHAPTER 2

The Small to Medium-Sized Accounting Services Market Opportunity

MARKET OVERVIEW

The small to medium-sized business (SMB) market for computer hardware, software, consulting, and related services is $175 billion and growing at 15 percent each year, according to IBM research. There is still no shortage of potential customers: Some 23 million small businesses populate the nation, according to the Small Business Administration (SBA).

The accounting industry has always tried to go after the low-hanging fruit — the larger the client, the better — but the reshaped market landscape is causing accountants to take another look at where the opportunities are. What accounting firm can afford to pass up an opportunity the size of SMB? Everybody is focused on SMB now, from very small sole practitioner practices to the Big Five (accounting/consulting firms). They are following the siren song of the 40 percent of SMB IT (Information Technology) spending — or $70 billion annually — that goes straight to accounting and consulting services.

Midsize businesses are defined as clients with 500 to 1,000 employees. Accounting firms have achieved a lot of success in the midsize market, providing accounting services, consulting, systems integration, and outsourcing. The dilemma is that 80 percent of the $175 billion market is spent by small businesses (50 to 500 employees) and very small businesses (VSBs — fewer than 50 employees). The Big Five and other top 100 consulting firms such as IBM's consulting unit cannot scale their services down to clients with fewer than 50 employees. The titans of the industry recognize that they are not going to get to the VSB market by themselves. This presents enormous opportunities for accountants who specialize in the market or who partner with the giants.

Small businesses have remained largely untouched by the Internet. According to the Small Business Administration, 7.5 million businesses in the United States have fewer than 100 employees each, and they collectively employ over 70 million people. In addition, there are 23 million income-generating small office/home offices (SOHO) that employ an additional 40 million people. The SBA estimates that these two groups, together called "small businesses," will spend over $107 billion online by 2002. Despite the size of these business markets, the larger accounting firms and the enterprise software industry have ignored them for the most part for several reasons:

1. The cost of selling and implementing accounting and software services into small business has been too high relative to the revenue potential of small business clients.
2. Small businesses lack the IT resources and infrastructure to maintain or operate Internet-related software.
3. Internet-based online software had been designed with the assumption it will be deployed in a large and complex enterprise with several specialist departments, including a sophisticated IT department.

In a small business, the manager or owner is responsible for managing the day-to-day operations of the business. This manager may be the owner, a controller, or an office manager. The small business manager buys products and services for the business, and is usually responsible for managing these services. Typically, this manager has little or no IT expertise, and has limited financial and technical resources, which are severely constrained.

Chasing the SMB Market

The smaller business client or prospective client is unwilling or incapable of either paying for or implementing larger scale software and services. Therefore, small business managers often rely on low-end accounting software packages like QuickBooks to maintain their accounts, and do the other administrative tasks (purchasing, benefits, hiring) manually.

Smaller businesses have been hit with a double whammy in competing with larger businesses: Their business processes are less efficient because they lack automation. Procurement and marketing costs are higher because they lack buying power.

The masters of the industry (Big Five and Smaller 95) are working furiously to figure out just what it will take to succeed in the SMB market. They are reevaluating and reassessing the SMB marketplace and opportunities. IBM and others have launched a number of initiatives targeting the SMB space. One of those efforts was the creation of a new breed of business partnerships called service providers. IBM provides leads and access to its intellectual capital to the service providers, which are experts in core areas and will attempt to resell IBM-branded services, such as e-business. IBM certifies its partners at various levels, ranging from large to small accounting and consulting firms.

"Dot.comming" SMBs could become gold mines. Fewer than 15 percent of U.S. small businesses have e-commerce capabilities, according to market researcher Access Media International Inc., New York.

Another approach to gain market share in the SMB market is to host applications. Instead of buying applications, an SMB would pay a monthly subscription fee and access applications over the Internet. Network-delivered services are the offerings that are going to be key to addressing the SMB and VSB markets. At least 75 to 100 application-hosting programs are under way that are targeted directly at SMBs. A variety of applications (including accounting, financial, human resources, and enterprise resource planning) are offered by vendors, including ACCPAC International, Computer Associates, Great Plains Software, J.D. Edwards Corporation, and Oracle Corporation.

Hewlett-Packard Corporation estimates that 25 percent of its $50 billion plus revenue now comes from SMB and believes that figure is growing. HP makes a "consultive selling" training module available to business partners.

Most clients prefer to deal with similarly sized service providers. You won't find the seven-person accounting firm on the Accounting Today's Top 100 Firms List because it didn't make the cut, but you will find it doing box office hit business with schools, law offices, and real estate developers. Such firms work with a great many of 5-, 10-, and 25-person business clients. The smaller clients may be delighted to have IBM or PricewaterhouseCoopers call on them, but they quickly learn that they don't get the personal attention they would get from an accounting firm that's the same size as their business.

The Big Five and coterie do not present a formidable threat to small accounting firms, who may fear losing business to the behemoths. There is no magic formula for dominating the SMB market. Millions of small businesses in vertical markets require a knowledgeable accountant who understands their particular needs. A 10-person travel agency has very different needs than a similarly sized legal or medical practice or a smoothie shop chain. No gargantuan CPA firm can possibly handle every kind of SMB need single handedly.

Strategies That Pursue Opportunities

The accounting industry's larger and smaller participants must begin to realize their opportunity and assert the proper role as the ultimate guide for electronic commerce among America's small to medium-sized business communities. The rapid growth of the Internet and business-to-business (B2B) e-commerce provides interesting opportunities for e@ccountants™ to provide services to smaller businesses that enhance their productivity and increase their buying power. Individual suppliers, like American Express and OneCore (finance), Office Depot (office supplies and equipment), NetLedger (accounting), and Bizfinity (basic business services), are reaching out to businesses by creating Web-based offerings for small businesses.

The really interesting development is the emergence of a number of B2B hubs that are defined as neutral Internet-based intermediaries. They focus on specific industry verticals or specific business processes, host electronic marketplaces, and use various market making mechanisms to mediate any-to-any transactions among businesses. These hubs create value by aggregating buyers and sellers, creating marketplace liquidity, and reducing transaction costs.

Such hubs provide Web-based tools, products, and services to the accountants focused on building and operating an online practice. The accountant partnering with B2B hubs can fulfill the promise of creating significant value for small businesses by aggregating demand among a large base of small businesses, and by facilitating the sharing of infrastructure costs across this same large base.

Internet-related services, barely a blip on accounting professional's radar screens before 1998, have now become a growth niche for most firms. Electronic commerce-based companies, characterized in the industry vernacular as "dot.coms," are one of the fastest-growing accounting client sectors.

CPAs and other accounting professionals are learning that they can leverage the reputations they enjoy as businesses' most trusted advisors to facilitate their clients' conduct of business online. Advising clients on the most profitable places to do business in a digital commercial arena is another rewarding endeavor.

Avoiding the dilemma of the fabled cobbler's children, accountants should be able to garner a fair share of the great revenues to be earned. The market for e-business integration services is forecast to reach $100 billion by 2004 and is growing by 500 percent year-to-year, according to Las Vegas, Nevada-based industry researcher, The Accounting Guild.

Exercise caution—e-commerce is an extremely competitive field. Everyone wants a piece of the opportunity.

The Big Five accounting firms, while quickly spinning off into separate management consulting operations, dominate the large-enterprise consulting segment. The market composed of small to medium-sized businesses is the bailiwick of rank and file accounting services providers.

Accounting firms have originated effective strategies designed to win their share of the available opportunities. Some have become ISP (Internet Service Providers), offering businesses physical access to the Internet. Other accountants have formed full-service operations combining a technical practice with an e-commerce services specialty firm. Finding financing for fast-growth dot.com start-ups is a lucrative practice specialty. Accounting firms are even becoming a part of alliances so that they may offer various client services that would otherwise be beyond their own limited resources.

The commonality of these accounting firms is that they all offer the e-commerce market whatever is needed to build viable, profitable, and sustainable businesses. Those offerings range from advising a client on whether e-commerce is the optimum strategy and assisting them with obtaining financing, to integrating, implementing, and managing the necessary technology.

Assisting your clients to digitize their businesses is a major trend that has far-reaching implications for you and your accounting firm. As an accounting professional, you don't necessarily require the technical expertise to fill specialized niches. One can offer a needed service for e-commerce start-ups such as constructing business plans and locating seed capital. Teaming with technically proficient partners to provide the solutions to the client's technological needs in a virtual partnership enables each service provider to play to their strong suit. There are tremendous opportunities available that many of your competitors are ignoring.

The Big Five have built the e-commerce industry's first business models and have written the manual for accounting's consulting role on e-business. PricewaterhouseCoopers (PwC) has even formed a "Knowledge Alliance" with six of the leading graduate business schools. The alliance will pool findings on trends among e-commerce enterprises in significant areas such as labor, marketing, and specific vertical industries. The graduate schools for their part are using materials from the collaboration to develop electronic commerce courses for their MBA programs. The purpose of the program is to disseminate the knowledge that e-commerce does not merely happen but must be planned and executed.

PwC has significantly contributed to the accounting consulting industry by having created an "e-business maturity model," a consulting tool that measures the e-commerce maturity levels of businesses and determines how to properly advance the maturity that is measured. This program, known as Emma, features best-practice standards for more than 700 specific e-commerce business areas.

In your rush to embrace the Internet, you and the CPA profession as a whole must be aware that all are playing serious catch-up to other e-business service competitors. There is a strong public perception that the Big Five lag behind the e-commerce specialist consulting firms, that smaller accounting firms have traditionally lagged in technology in general, and that e-commerce will not be the exception. The idea of participating on a level playing field without the protection of a CPA license and its aegis of limited competition is alien to many accounting firms. Some accountants believe that because many of their clients are not involved in e-commerce to any significant degree they will continue to watch what impact e-commerce will have and not take any proactive action. This is another example of the business adage that some business people make things happen, others watch what has happened, and some don't even know that anything has happened.

Small and medium-sized business market perception is a major factor for participating consultants. Analysts of the high-end consulting industry have noted that the consulting areas of the five largest accounting firms have done little to distinguish themselves from the consulting companies that are known exclusively for e-business, such as Scient, Viant, and Lante. The Big Five and other traditional consultancies have an image problem in the SMB area. E-business is new and operating in uncharted waters. The firms winning the headlines now are fresh and innovative. It is now perceived that relatively small, newcomer specialist firms have an edge in this market.

The two most prevalent strategies for launching and initially growing an SMB practice are as follows:

- Hiring a specialist (evangelist) to guide the e-commerce services within a firm's management advisory service practice
- Referring clients to third-party electronic commerce service specialists

Note that some accountants urge clients to examine the feasibility of e-commerce strategies and then go on to refer them to third-party vendors.

ASPs

Applications software providers (ASPs), which lease software that users access over the Internet from remote servers, have also emerged as an e-commerce entry point for accounting firms. Most of the software vendors with reseller channels that include accountants are actively recruiting CPAs to also resell ASP versions of their products. Accountants are joining alliances with vendor ASPs that provide for Internet delivery of accounting and payroll administration services.

Establishing alliances with, or referring clients to, electronic commerce service specialists appears to be the currently preferred e-commerce passageway. Accounting firms are either partnering with, or directly referring clients to, third-party specialists in key e-commerce areas, such as Web site design and systems integration. Making e-commerce referrals is particularly crucial for firms that lack the internal service skills and want to ensure that clients receive excellent service. Take every precaution that appropriate sets of controls are in place to reduce the possibilities that the client may suffer from any unexpected outcomes.

You have virtually unlimited opportunities within the small to medium-sized business universe because the e-commerce area is hot and becoming torrid. The constraints placed upon your activities center around capital and qualified personnel.

ISPs

An accounting firm can receive significant assistance in growing an e-commerce practice from Internet Service Providers (ISPs). The ISPs are national and locally based companies that provide businesses and private individuals with access to the Internet. The explosive growth of the Internet coupled with bandwidth-hungry, timing-sensitive, and mission-critical network applications presents a formidable challenge to all Internet users and providers who must provide reliable bandwidth and guaranteed service levels to users in a finite resource environment.

Accountants and Internet service providers must tailor services to clients based on their individual requirements. Tiered service offerings, bandwidth on demand, usage-based billing, and service level guarantees are all ingredients that permit service providers to remain competitive. These ingredients as well as the terminology are for the most part alien to the majority of practicing accountants. The entrepreneurial accountants must get up to speed at the same time they are pursuing a moving target.

Your small business clients must accept the fact that e-commerce will affect their business and they must have a clear strategy in place. Before conceiving an e-commerce business strategy, the accounting professional must assist the client in steering clear of the common misconceptions about e-commerce that could lead to poor business decisions and economic disaster. Exhibit 2.1 addresses frequent misconceptions concerning e-commerce strategies.

A recent study conducted by The Accounting Guild of 350 CEOs of small to medium-sized businesses produced two revealing statistics:

- Over 55 percent of the 350 CEOs said Internet e-business start-ups represent a "meaningful competitive force" in their industries.
- Almost 60 percent predicted that more than 25 percent of their business's revenues would come from e-commerce in the next five years.

Advise your clients to consider e-commerce as high risk when appraising any proposed efforts. They should closely analyze their e-business goals, objectives, funding, and implementation plans.

The rush to get online has caused many otherwise level-headed business professionals to turn reckless. Whether your client is building an e-business from the ground up or expanding an existing enterprise

1. **"Our business is too small to be impacted by e-commerce."**
   This is the business equivalent of burying one's head in the sand. It is just not true. Many small to medium-sized business owners and managers believe that if they are not engaged in a technologically driven business their business is immune to the vagaries of digital revolution. Other business managers think that e-commerce only applies to large scale business-to-consumer situations. The reality lies more in the business-to-business areas of customer self-service and supplier access to information that are the vital lifeblood of any business. Your clients must accept the economic reality that e-commerce will affect their business and that they must have a clear and viable strategy in place.

2. **"E-commerce is identical to e-business."**
   E-commerce was the initial step in the evolution of the Internet business channel. The majority of e-commerce applications dealt with the utilization of the Internet and their business applications in the buying/selling transaction process. The primary goal of e-business should be to optimize a business's value proposition and processes by the use of information technology coupled with the Internet as the primary communications medium. This will include both the models of business-to-business (B2B) and business-to-consumer (B2C) applicability. Merely adding an "e" to a business does not make it an e-business.

3. **"E-commerce is such a popular trend, we couldn't fail in developing our business model."**
   One can fail in any business, regardless of the state of the market if certain core competencies are not addressed. Every Internet success is countered by 100 businesses that do not survive.

4. **"Our business has sufficient existing resources to transform into an e-business."**
   The essence of e-commerce requires Internet activities to act and react quickly and display a high degree of creativity. Most businesses have been unable to internally develop a team or otherwise acquire the resources with the experience to conduct e-commerce.

(Continues)

Exhibit 2.1 E-commerce Misconceptions Q & A

---

5. **"We'll jump into the e-commerce arena later when the risk decreases, after others develop the channel."**
   The phenomenal successes of pioneering organizations at the expense of their brick and mortar competitors is directly related to their early market entry. Many businesses triumphed against larger and more established rivals by virtue of their willingness to innovate. Even as some businesses are outspending e-businesses on their advertising and branding in a brick and mortar presence, their e-business competitors are taking over market share.

Exhibit 2.1 (Continued)

from brick-and-mortar to online, there is probably only one chance to get it right before the window of opportunity closes.

As an entrepreneurial accountant you can advise your client that getting it right means building on the strengths of the business and remedying any weaknesses. Together, you must work with technology and business partners that know the business and the industry. Most importantly, it requires a thorough understanding of what e-business is in general and specifically how it can benefit the business in a cost-effective manner.

Follow the same basic business principles that one would prudently apply when venturing into any new business opportunity. Your role as the accounting professional requires you to keep your client focused on the ultimate goal—to build a successful business. The "e" part does not exempt the advisor and the client from due diligence. The business model of the e-business must be clearly focused. A properly grounded understanding of the business processes that should be improved, eliminated, or implemented is necessary to design a successful e-business. A checklist of key process issues that clients should focus on before developing an e-business strategy appears in Exhibit 2.2. Exhibit 2.3 provides a checklist of questions to ask business clients before creating an e-business strategy.

Remember that a successful brick-and-mortar business has at least one major advantage over a competitive dot.com: experience and success in the business. Many dot coms have executives with very strong business backgrounds at the helm. They may be gifted at garnering venture capital funding or cleverly marketing their product or service, but

- **Capitalization.** Initially, the business should focus on marketing and gaining new customers. This begins with a basic, simple, static Web site. Activities such as online advertising, Webcasts, and online recruiting can be included in very basic Web sites.
- **Customization.** Now, the pace can accelerate. The business begins to interface with customers, adapting offers in real-time and providing true one-to-one marketing. An example is information repositioning, such as turning internal knowledge networks into salable information.
- **Economization.** The most potentially beneficial and challenging e-business opportunities lie in economizing. This is truly where the e-business rubber meets the road, whether it involves selling product online, conducting business-to-business e-commerce, or taking advantage of online procurement. A fundamental method of economization includes the integration of all the systems and departments in the business, and potentially the systems and departments of the business's partners and suppliers.

Exhibit 2.2 Key Process Issues Checklist

may lack knowledge of the inner workings of the business. The online part is simply a new channel for your client. Your client already has a successful business. Counsel your client to remain calm, focus on the core business, and find ways to make that business more successful. They are already one step ahead of their dot.com competition.

TRANSITIONAL FACTORS

The choice of the right technology—whether in the form of properly installed software or outsourced services—is a critical issue for the accountant to address, and a potentially profitable one as well. Enabling your clients to select and implement more cost-efficient and cost-effective business solutions will benefit both you and the client as well as create an excellent revenue stream for yourself.

Although every client will have individual needs, Exhibit 2.4 lists specific factors that may prevent you from overlooking considerations that might impair the maintenance of needed information, such as an audit trail and other components of the traditional business systems.

- **Why should we become an e-business?**
  Your client's primary goal should not be to set up an e-business just because everyone else has one. The need to have some degree of e-business strategy is prevalent in small to medium-sized businesses, but the "why" must be answered to create a strategy that will ensure success. For some, the traditional ways of conducting business will be dramatically altered. For others, an elementary system of contacting customers and facilitating sales via an email server will suffice. Determine the compelling reasons for going "e" before proceeding any further.

- **Do I understand what I wish to achieve by establishing an e-business?**
  Implementing an e-business requires a well-constructed plan. Be very clear on the client's goals, quantify the benefits, and weigh the costs as part of your research. Know the specific benefits for each function and business process. This will help you to introduce the system to partners (customers, suppliers, and affiliates) and motivate them to use it effectively.

- **Should the client maintain or outsource the work?**
  Evaluate whether the client has adequate staff and expertise in-house to take on and maintain the project. Does the client need to hire someone to manage the system, or will maintenance be minimal? Would the client prefer to have their ISP or ASP handle most of the maintenance? If a third-party is engaged, how will they interact with the internal staff, and who will oversee this relationship? These are important questions to answer because the appropriate resources are critical to a successful transition into e-business.

- **Will the client's employees be able to use an intranet? What training is needed?**
  In the event the client has a large number of employees who are not Web-literate, moving into an e-business becomes a larger and more difficult project. The client will want to distibute important information such as benefits data to all employees, so all employees must be able or trained to use the new business tools effectively.

(Continues)

Exhibit 2.3 Business Client Pre-e-business Creation Questionnaire

- **What type of information technology investment has the client already made?**
  Assess the client's types of computers, networks, and servers that are already in place. Discuss the existing infrastructure with the client's IT professionals who will implement the e-business. Determine which of the existing applications can be extended to the e-business processes. It is generally more cost-efficient to use technology that's already in place, provided it's compatible with the new system.

- **Are all elements involved in the e-business project defined?**
  Examine the basic issues: Complexity, implementation timing, and upkeep requirements. Study and evaluate other solutions that have been implemented at similar businesses, especially in the same industry, and consult with business partner professionals who are experienced with e-business design and implementation.

Exhibit 2.3 (Continued)

EVOLVING INTO AN E-BUSINESS

Evolving into an e-business can be particularly difficult for clients that have not previously focused on working directly with customers. Your client's staff—particularly the executive—must be willing to accept the fact that the Internet will now either drive or at least be a significant part of their business, and they must support the transition.

Internet strategy and business strategy must become one and the same. They cannot be developed separately, or one or both will fail. Your client must be prepared to profoundly adjust the traditional model if necessary. For example, the e-business may take business away from the traditional channel.

Today's small to medium-sized business client is much smarter, has more available choices, is better informed, and must never be underestimated. Your client and prospective client must be educated to provide as much information to assist with the buying decision as possible and be willing to work harder to convince customers to choose their products or services. Service on your part and on the part of the client remains the key to success. Neither of you must lose that focus.

1. **Educate** yourself thoroughly on all the tools and services available, and learn how to charge properly for your services. You are working in an area that can contribute significantly to your professional services revenue stream. Prepare for it.

2. **Choose** e-business software that is fully integrated with the accounting/business management packages you resell and/or service. The back office must integrate with the online portion, or you will be creating havoc for everyone concerned.

3. **Partner** with those who run online servers with whatever software you want to offer your client. The advantage to using these partners is in running larger database applications or applications that require administration or expert support, not in smaller applications that are easy to use and support.

4. **Host** your services when appropriate. Smaller clients will need the most assistance, but they can often gain the most from e-business. On the Web, even the smallest client business can offer the same products and services as their larger competitors and with your assistance, just as effectively. The advent of hosting permits your clients to rent an inexpensive service from you that provides the same solutions as what historically had been only within the means of much larger businesses.

Exhibit 2.4 Transitional Factors

Recommend outsourcing when warranted. Most of your clients lack an IT staff that can handle their internal needs now, much less an Internet strategy. Many lack an IT staff entirely. If you cannot implement or maintain the entire project, use an expert partner. Collaborative computing solutions accounting practices are resulting in an overwhelming acceptance of the Internet and e-commerce. Smaller clients now enjoy the connectivity amenities only larger companies could previously afford.

UNLOCKING THE MARKET

Your key to unlocking the smaller to medium-sized business market is to show prospective clients how they can increase productivity without increasing staff. Does the prospective client have sticky notes hanging from the computer monitors? Are there several fax machines in the office? How are internal memos disseminated? The answers to these questions will reveal whether the client is a viable candidate for an Internet solution. The cost can often be easily justified by the reduction of wasted labor used to distribute paper-based communications.

Conducting a careful needs analysis may still leave the client resistant to making the initial investment required for an enterprise-wide Internet solution. The best approach in such a situation may be to suggest a modular solution that solves major inefficiencies in their current mode of operations.

There aren't many applications more mission-critical than accounting. A challenge is to have your client overcome the common misconception that there hasn't been much development or change to accounting applications. In the minds of business people, large and small, accounting is shifting from being merely a means of reconciling the business checkbook to a more powerful business management tool. This places accounting applications in the same arena as other new technology tools such as data warehousing. Directly linking accounting systems to the business's e-commerce system will reduce the unnecessary expenses of rekeying inventory levels to account for Web-based transactions.

Before selling a new accounting system or an upgrade, check the following:

- Software can be customized as the needs of the client change.
- The program offers a clear path toward e-commerce interoperability.
- The application offers multicurrency and multilingual capabilities.

SUMMARY

Smaller to medum-sized clients and prospective clients are particularly sensitive (since they often operate on the slimmest of margins) to increased competition and the relentless pressure to reduce ballooning costs, improve lagging productivity, and increase responsiveness to the general market and key customers in particular. This market is being bombarded by change from simultaneous revolutions in business and technology. Your opportunity is to proactively step in and help keep the two in sync. The commitment of a small firm's precious assets for technology must be in the pursuit of solid business goals. Technology is not valuable because it is new and flashy. It is valuable because it provides the smaller business client with the robust means to forge newer, more innovative, and more effective profitable business solutions.

Findings from Recent Demographic Studies

A recent Dun & Bradstreet study shows that an impressive 72 percent of small businesses expect to expand during 2001, with new or enhanced computer capabilities being central to their growth programs. Tapping into this burgeoning market should be the aim of every market-wise accountant.

The U.S. Small Business Administration, using data supplied by the U.S. Department of Labor, recently announced that small businesses employ 53 percent of the private work force, contribute 47 percent of all sales in the nation, and are responsible for 50 percent of the private gross domestic product. Even more importantly, small business-dominated industries produced an estimated 75 percent of the 3.5 million new jobs created during 1999.

Since 1993, 17.5 million new jobs have been created across the entire economy. According to the U.S. Department of Labor Office of Advocacy Research, the fastest-growing sectors of small business-dominated industries during the past several years include the following:

- Restaurants
- Outpatient care facilities
- Physicians' offices
- Special trade construction contractors
- Computer and data processing services
- Credit reporting
- Medical and dental labs
- Day care providers
- Counseling and rehabilitation services

What the Numbers Mean

The previously cited figures demonstrate the size and viability of the vibrant small to medium-sized business marketplace. Small businesses are also in the forefront when it comes to employing technology, too. How do the numbers affect the accountant and accounting services integrator and consultant? Regardless of the type of small business, modern computer technology (and the proactive accountant who provides it) succeeds with this market because it empowers results.

A small company that makes and sells high technology equipment has just as much need for computerized business tools that access the Internet and enable e-commerce as the local dental clinic. People who have been trained as electronic engineers may have no more of a clue about how to run a spreadsheet than someone in a "low-tech/no-tech" small business.

Your competitors, large and small, continually announce their intention to target small business, your client base. And one by one, they will fail to make a dent in your growing practice. The reason is not that smaller clients lack accounting services. Small businesses need technology solutions as much as their larger counterparts — maybe even more, given their need to compete with the larger businesses. Large companies can always shift one or more people to wherever the work piles up. The larger businesses can afford to pump up temporary hires when the need arises. This is not the case in smaller businesses, where cash-flow management can vary from month to month. Providing services to a small client may present serious headaches because you may be working in a highly technical area with nontechnical people. They may require solutions that reach far beyond their ability to comprehend the issues and the solutions.

Making matters worse, there are no easily replicable solutions because the market is too diverse. You cannot easily apply the same technology to a medical office and a convenience store. That is why most of your competitors have lumped small business with midsize business, and casually refer to it as the SMB market. The two have really nothing in common, other than the misconception that it's easier to manage both markets together because not much effort is needed for small businesses. Yet, no back-end solutions have penetrated what is known in some circles as the last, great, untapped market.

You are going to change the perceptions of the market. Your efforts will be driven by data hosting and a shift to selling software as a service rather than as an application a small business client buys along with a PC.

It's up to the entrepreneurially minded accountant service-provider marketers to put together solutions for specific vertical markets that can be tapped nationwide. Accounting application providers will slice particular segments out of the market at large and will focus on providing that segment with a monthly service offering that can be profitably provided to smaller clients.

Profitable accounting practices must drill down to create meaningful solutions. That will make the sale much simpler for the practice developers when working with prospective clients who are not involved with technology on a daily basis. To win in small business, you have to be small and broad at the same time. How appropriate for accountants, that this is a numbers game. You need volume and space to make it work. Exhibit 2.5 is a compendium of resources focused on the SMB market.

GOVERNMENT

- **U.S. federal government**
  gov.us.fed
- **U.S. Department of Commerce**
  gov.us.fed.doc
- **Department of Commerce announcements (moderated)**
  gov.us.fed.doc.announce
- **Commerce Business Daily**
  gov.us.fed.doc.cbd
- **Contract awards in Commerce Business Daily (moderated)**
  gov.us.fed.doc.cbd.awards
- **Surplus property sales in Commerce Business Daily (moderated)**
  gov.us.fed.doc.cbd.forsale
- **Small Business Administration announcements (moderated)**
  gov.us.fed.sba.announce
- **Electronic commerce/services with government**
  gov.us.topic.ecommerce
- **Issues involving foreign trade, importation, customs (moderated)**
  gov.us.topic.foreign.trade
- **Information on trade opportunities collected by U.S. government (moderated)**
  gov.us.topic.foreign.trade.leads
- **Detailed reports on economic and demographic statistics (moderated)**
  gov.us.topic.statistics.reports
- **The Securities and Exchange Commission provides its online database of filing information, called EDGAR. The database can be searched by keyword to bring up filings like 10-Q, 8-K, and proxies**
  http://www.sec.gov/edgarhp.htm
- **Internal Revenue Service**
  http://www.irs.gov
- **United States Postal Service**
  http://www.usps.gov

(Continues)

Exhibit 2.5 Resources for Building a Small to Medium-Sized Business Presence

PUBLICATIONS

- **Accountancy**
  http://www.accountancymag.co.uk
  Great Britain
- **Accounting Guild**
  http://www.accountingguild.com
  Targeted Market Niche Reports
- **Accounting Professionals Product News**
  http://www.cpanews.com
- **AccountingWeb**
  http://www.accountingweb.com
- **AICPA**
  http://www.aicpa.com
- **American Accounting Association**
  http://www.rutgers.edu/Accounting/raw/aaa/
- **Association for Computers and Taxation**
  http://www.taxact.org
- **Bottom Line (The)**
  http://www.butterworths.ca/tbl.htm
  Canadian
- **Business Finance Magazine**
  http://www.businessfinancemag.com
- **Business Funding Directory**
  http://www.businessfinance.com
  Provides potential sources of funding based on type of financing and business characteristics. Includes both government and private-sector sources.
- **Business Journals**
  http://www.amcity.com
  The American City Business Journal publishes business journals in 28 cities in the United States.
- **CA Magazine**
  http://www.cica.ca/cica/camagazine.nsf/eCurrent/toc
- **Census Bureau (U.S.)**
  http://www.census.gov/
  Wide selection of databases with social, demographic and economic information that can be searched by county. The site also provides links to other sources of federal statistics, including the Bureau of Labor Statistics.
- **CFO Magazine**
  http://www.cfonet.com
- **Corporate Finance Network**
  http://www.corpfinet.com/Small_Bus.html
  Links to lenders actively seeking to lend to small businesses.

(Continues)

Exhibit 2.5 *(Continued)*

- **CPA Journal**
  http://www.cpajournal.com
- **CPA Software News**
  http://www.cpasoftwarenews.com
- **Dun & Bradstreet**
  http://www.dbisna.com
  Dun & Bradstreet enables you to search through its business database of U.S.-based businesses and provides online access to its Business Background reports with a charge for each report. It offers news and business management tips at no cost.
- **Electronic Accountant**
  http://www.electronicaccountant.com
- **ExpoGuide**
  http://expoguide.com
  Detailed information about industry trade shows.
- **Faulkner & Gray**
  http://www.faulknergray.com
  Faulkner & Gray publishes an array of publications including the areas of accounting and business strategy. Familiar titles include Accounting Today (twice a month) and Accounting Technology and Practical Accountant (monthly). Trial subscriptions are available.
- **Inc. Online**
  http://www.inc.com
  Online version of Inc. magazine.
- **Institute of Management Accountants**
  http://www.rutgers.edu/Accounting/raw/ima/
- **IOMA Business Page**
  http://www.ioma.com
  The Institute of Management & Administration (IOMA) page is a marketing center for IOMA's newsletters directed at business, accounting and other industries. The IOMA guide to business resources is an exhaustive guide to business-related websites.
- **Journal of Accountancy**
  http://www.aicpa.com
- **National Association of Enrolled Agents**
  http://www.naea.org
- **National Foundation of Women Business Owners**
  http://www.nfwbo.org
  Reports, news, and trends affecting women business owners, focusing on the special characteristics of women-owned businesses and how they compare to other businesses.
- **National Society of Accountants**
  http://www.nsacct.org

(Continues)

Exhibit 2.5 *(Continued)*

The 19,000-member National Society of Accountants is a leading trade group and professional association for practitioners serving small businesses.

- **OSHA**
  http://www.osha.gov/
  Information about OSHA regulations, compliance assistance, OSHA publications, programs, services, statistics, and technical information.
- **Pro2 Net**
  http://pro2net.com
- **SmallbizNet**
  http://www.lowe.org/smbiznet
  A service of the Edward Lowe Foundation allows users to search an enormous database of articles and books about all aspects of starting and running a small business. Some items are provided without charge and others can be downloaded for a fee.
- **Small Business Adminstration**
  http://www.sbaonline.sba.gov
  SBA's services include counseling by international trade experts, training sessions and publications, and services to link U.S. firms with potential foreign customers.
- **Small Business Advancement National Center**
  http://www.sbaer.uca.edu
  Contains directories of Small Business Institutes, Small Business Development Centers, SBA offices, and other small business resources. Also provides access to publications, financial planning software, and industry profiles.
- **Tradeshow Central**
  http://www.tscentral.com
  Trade show and convention information.

Exhibit 2.5 (Continued)

CHAPTER 3

Business Plan Development and Implementation

YOUR BUSINESS PLAN—A KEY PRACTICE DEVELOPMENT TOOL

A well-conceived business plan is essential to the success of your online virtual accounting practice. It is an excellent way for a potential partner, associate, or alliance vendor to review your firm's potential. The quality of your plan can be a major factor in attracting, enrolling, and retaining the people and companies that will contribute toward your success.

A business plan is also a management and development tool. It can help you focus, in a logical and organized manner, on the future growth of your firm. The process of planning helps you to anticipate and meet the inevitable changes of the future. A business plan is a control tool that permits you to monitor and assess progress.

What Is a Business Plan?

A business plan is a document that discusses your practice's plans, shows that the plans can be achieved, and demonstrates that the outcome satisfies the reader's requirements.

THE NARRATIVE

Although the financial projections may be at the core of the business plan, the reader's perception of their achievability depends on the detailed plans set out in the narrative. It is important that the narrative and the figures be consistent and support each other. They are both equally important — on its own, neither tells the complete story. The narrative provides the opportunity to argue your case and justify the assumptions you have made in arriving at the forecasts.

SUGGESTED BUSINESS PLAN TABLE OF CONTENTS

When writing any report, it is essential to plan in advance what it will look like. This specimen plan is for a proposed online virtual accounting services practice. It is important that your business plan be tailored to the unique concerns of your particular accounting firm. A great deal of the focus will depend on your particular purposes for the business plan. It may not always be necessary to include all of the suggested sections — some could be combined and new sections added as required. The typical table of contents for this example would be as follows:

1. The Plan Summary
2. Background
3. Accounting Practice Description and Analysis
4. Management and Staff
5. Markets and Marketing Strategy
6. Accounting and Consulting Services, Facilities, and Processes
7. Financial Information
8. Risk Factors and Rewards
9. Timetables and Benchmarks
10. Plan Appendices/Exhibits

THE PLAN SUMMARY

Your goal in the plan summary is to quickly and concisely provide an overview (within one to three pages) that convinces the readers to continue reviewing your plan. Although a plan summary appears first, it should be the last part you write.

The plan summary should highlight key elements of the entire business plan, and indicate why this business plan is different — the "success ingredient." Do not forget that you are trying to attract the attention of a busy reader and convince that person that it would be worthwhile to read the rest of your business plan. The summary should be designed to do just that and should include the following:

- Your objectives for the practice
- The rationale for writing the business plan
- Brief descriptions of services, resale products, and markets highlighting the benefits to your clients
- Your estimate of market potential and assessment of the competition
- Your practice's management team's experience, expertise, and talent
- How the services will be performed and the products resold
- Projected financial highlights
- A statement of how much money is required and for what purpose
- Return expected and when, showing how the partners will benefit

BACKGROUND

This section of your practice's business plan describes the following:

- The practice you are in or plan to be in
- The professional services, resale products, and current and/or potential clients
- The history of your practice, including when it was started, highlights of its progress, and the roles of key management and staff
- An outline of the firm's present financing, including details about its present stakeholders and any security given to lenders or suppliers
- The current ownership of the firm and a description of partnership profit agreements and future options granted

ACCOUNTING PRACTICE DESCRIPTION AND ANALYSIS

This section is typically one of the most difficult for the entrepreneurial accountant to prepare. Here is where you show how you will turn your ideas into services and products that clients will want to buy. Your objective is to convince your intended reader of the following:

- There is a marketplace need for your services and products.
- You understand your potential clients' needs, and your services and/or products will fulfill those needs.
- You can market your services and products at a profit.

Potential Clients

Discuss the major current and potential clients of your practice by responding to the following questions:

- Who are your major clients?
- Why do they remain clients?
- What are their billings, cycles, and types of services purchased?
- What are their expectations for fee range, timeliness, and services?

Market Size and Trends

Your readers want to know the current and potential size of the market. How big will the market be in five years? Ten years? Support growth estimates with industry trends, technological developments, changing client needs, and other marketplace factors. Your sources and assumptions should be clearly stated, and they must be realistic. If you overstate the size of the market or your potential share, the credibility of your entire business plan will be questioned.

Competition

Describe the accounting firms and any other providers of similar accounting services that are your current or future competition. In addition to local competitors describe regional or national competitors that impact upon your market. Assess their respective strengths and weaknesses, including the following:

- The market share potential for each competitor
- How your services and products compare with competitors' in price, service, and other features
- Your competitors' strengths and weaknesses in the financial, marketing, and operational areas of management

Matrix

A matrix is an excellent way to present comparative data on the competition. An objective appraisal of your competition will add significant credibility to your business plan. Be sure to include all possible competition.

MANAGEMENT AND STAFF

One of businesses' major concerns is a firm's key management team players and their supporting staff.

Organization

Explain how your firm's management team is organized, and describe the primary role each team member plays. Demonstrate how team members' skills complement each other. Evaluators are looking for a team with a balance of marketing, professional, financial, management, consulting, and implementation skills, as well as experience and expertise with the products and services you are developing. Show the number of people supervised by each manager. Make an assessment of the need for additional managers and staff in the future; explain how they will be selected. If appropriate, use an organization chart. Include in an appendix the existing organization chart as well as a three-year projected growth chart.

Key Managers

Briefly profile each key manager, including the following:

- Duties and responsibilities, demonstrating you have a balanced team
- Career highlights
- Significant past accomplishments that demonstrate ability for the tasks required. Their past track record and how it affects your future plans. Mention the size of their previous companies and the tasks they've undertaken.
- Detailed resumes should be included not in this section but in an appendix. Resumes should include sufficient detail for an evaluator to evaluate each key manager.

This section should also discuss any apparent weakness in your management team. Are any critical skills missing? If so, how will this be overcome? By training? Recruiting? Outsourcing? Prepare an honest appraisal of vacant positions and your plans to rectify the situation. Describe previous mistakes. It is a strength to show that you have learned from these.

Compensation and Ownership

State how each person will be compensated (by salary, incentive bonus, or profit sharing), and what investment each has in the firm. How many of the key managers have performance-related packages? How many have service contracts? Include a list of key stockholders, with the number of shares each owns. Discuss the relationship between ownership and management and the long-term aims and objectives of key individuals.

MARKETS AND MARKETING STRATEGY

This section of the plan must demonstrate that your firm understands how its market should be segmented, and that it has the ability to sell and deliver its services and products effectively to the correctly targeted clients. This is the place to show why clients will buy from your firm.

Target Markets

Identify your firm's target market(s). It is important to segment and target the marketplace properly — something that many accounting firms frequently overlook. Concentrating your resources on the needs of a specific segment and carving out a market niche may mean the difference between success and failure.

Clearly define your particular niche in the marketplace in terms of services, products, territories, clients, and so forth. Include summaries of the statistical data available on your particular market niche(s). Justify your decision to target that particular niche and outline the prospects for that niche in comparison to the marketplace generally. It may be cost-effective to outsource the expertise for a market research study to obtain this information.

Estimate the market share and revenue volume that you think your firm can achieve over the next two, three, four, and five years. Identify which components of your estimate represent "hard" engagement commitments, and present this information in tabular form.

Client Analysis

- Who are they?
- Where are they?
- Why do they buy accounting services?
- When do they buy?
- Do they buy specific engagements or retainer agreements?
- Who are the decision makers?
- What is the typical fee?
- What are the requirements of each client? For example, 80 percent of your particular niche may be dominated by only 20 percent of your prospective clients. You must demonstrate that you recognize this factor.
- Who are the ultimate customers and what influences on their purchasing habits are beyond your control? One influence consists of the banks or lenders that specify what accounting services your prospective clients must obtain.

Competitive Analysis

An analysis of your competition would include the following:

- Who are they?
- Where are they?
- What is their size and potential?
- How much of the marketplace do they serve?
- What are their strengths and weaknesses?
- How will you compete successfully against them?
- What is the anticipated response by competitors to your market plans?

A realistic and honest appraisal of your competition adds significant credibility to your business plan.

Pricing

Discuss the pricing strategy and policy for your services and products and compare it to that of your competition. Explain your credit terms. Show how your pricing approach will enable you to accomplish the following:

- Penetrate the marketplace
- Maintain and increase market share in a competitive environment
- Make a profit

Advertising and Promotion

What are your proposals for advertising and promotion? What percentage of anticipated billings does this cost represent? When will the costs be incurred and what are the anticipated benefits?

Discuss how you will generate awareness of your firm among prospective clients. Which promotional activities will you use?

- Public relations?
- Advertising?
- Trade or professional shows?
- Sales incentives?
- Promotional literature?
- Internet-based promotion?
- Professional articles?

Summary of Markets and Marketing

Your accounting firm must measure and show the market(s) for its professional services and products. The firm must demonstrate that it understands the needs of its clients and prospective clients. Above all, the firm must convince any evaluator that its services and products meet the demonstrated needs.

ACCOUNTING AND CONSULTING SERVICES, FACILITIES, AND PROCESSES

In this section, describe how and where your accounting firm plans to process, perform, and deliver its services and products. Consider these factors:

- **Location.** Discuss the location of your accounting firm. Consider the most important cost components: labor and material cost and availability, proximity to clients and outsourcers, taxes, local laws, and real estate (rental) costs.
- **Facilities and Equipment.** Describe the facilities that the firm currently occupies and the equipment it currently uses. Discuss future needs. What will these cost? Will you lease or buy?
- **Production, Service, Training, and Sales Operations.** Describe the following processes and methods of performing the various services:
  - Production and/or operating processes
  - Production and/or operating advantages
  - Quality control procedures
  - Breakdown of costs (fixed and variable)
  - Organization and operation of various departments
  - Production and/or operations capacity
  - Outsourcing decisions
  - Potential suppliers and contractors
  - Availability of skilled staff

FINANCIAL INFORMATION

You will need to include financial statements and projections for the next three to five years including:

- Projected statement of operations
- Cash-flow projections
- Pro forma balance sheets
- Breakeven analysis

Your projections should correlate with your market expectations. It is important to state clearly the assumptions you used when preparing the pro formas and projections. Include a commentary on the forecasts to explain, in layman's terms, what the data mean. This commentary should address any early losses or sub-par performance, if appropriate, as well as the transition to profitability. It should also relate the timing of any investments from initial outlays to the generation of revenues, profits and finally, to cash. It should comment on the strength of the balance sheet and draw attention to any off-balance sheet assets (e.g., intellectual property rights or licenses) that might affect a valuation.

Your financial analysis should identify and support the amount of investment you are seeking. As a professional accounting services firm you will be held to a higher standard than would be expected from a company of lay people.

RISK FACTORS AND REWARDS

Do not conceal the problems! Remember that you and the recipient of your plan share common aims and concerns. All participants are risking money and effort on the same project.

Highlighting the risks adds to the credibility of your firm's business plan. It shows that you have recognized the risks in advance and have given thought to how you propose to either overcome them or minimize their effect. State the risks inherent in each part of your business plan and your opinion of the likelihood of their occurrence. Also show what steps you have taken, or propose to take, to minimize any impact these risks might have on the performance of your firm.

Assuming the risks cannot be overcome altogether, you should also include an analysis of the effect on both profit and cash. Include only a summary of the results. However, it is important to include your comments on the analysis.

While you must exercise the tenets of full disclosure, don't be all doom and gloom. The business plan is a selling document in addition to a plan and you should maintain a sense of proportion in discussing the risks. Demonstrate how your firm plans to overcome the particular risks of its business.

"SWOT" Analysis

S—Strengths
W—Weaknesses
O—Opportunities
T—Threats

As part of the "Opportunities" section, mention the rewards to participants if the plan is achieved. Demonstrate the worth of the firm in three to five years' time and the resulting return on investment.

TIMETABLES AND BENCHMARKS

Summarize your firm's objectives. Not all of them need be financial. A business plan prepared for management's own internal use might contain far more detail than a business plan being presented to an outside entity. The report should also deal with the sub-objectives to be met to attain the main objectives. You should include the objectives set by each department, the timetable for major events, and the resources needed to achieve them. It is often helpful to represent this information graphically. Your timetables and benchmarks not only show that you have carefully planned the steps of your proposal, but also aid subsequent monitoring.

PLAN APPENDICES/EXHIBITS

Include appendices and exhibits to provide any additional details that help tell your story. These might include the following:

- Glossary of terms used
- Marketing and technical literature
- Organization charts
- Resumes of key management
- Marketing surveys and studies
- Licensing information
- Reseller agreements
- Financial forecasts:
  1. Profit and loss
  2. Cash/funding
  3. Balance sheets
  4. Assumptions
- Most recent audited financial statements
- Most recent internal financial statements
- Third-party confirmations, when applicable

PRACTICAL ADVICE AND CONSIDERATIONS

Following are several questions commonly asked by practitioners when writing business plans for the first time and suggested ways of dealing with them:

- *Who should write the business plan?*
  If the business is to be effectively managed, it is important for the management to have a thorough knowledge of plans for the future. The business plan should not be written by an outside advisor. It needs to put across management's enthusiasm and determination to succeed, and it should, therefore, be written by that group.

- *How long should it be?*
  This is a difficult question to answer because it will depend on the stage of the firm's development and the purpose of the plan. It should be comprehensive, tailored for a specific reader, and as short as possible. There is a tendency today to write shorter business plans. Remember your proposed reader is likely to be a busy person and you will need to retain his or her attention. Any supporting detail should be relegated to an appendix. However, as an example, a business plan for a $15 million high tech practice start-up project might run to 80 pages whereas a $3 million expansion project for an existing accounting firm might be adequately covered in 20 to 35 pages.

WRITING AND ORGANIZING THE PLAN

Organize your plan so it is easy for the intended readers to find specific sections. Many readers will read only selected sections according to their needs and preferences for specific information.

- Your plan should have a table of contents.
- Consider using tabs to identify major sections.
- Decide who is to coordinate and write the plan.
- Agree on who is to provide the necessary information.
- Gather information for each topic and note all ideas.
- Organize the information logically.
- Start writing.
- Challenge the assumptions.
- Expect revisions. Business plans are not written, they are rewritten.

Don't Use Professional Jargon

Your proposed readership may know very little about an accounting practice and its market. Your business plan should, wherever possible, be written in lay terms and avoid the use of jargon. Should this prove to be impossible, because of the nature of the accounting industry, a glossary of the terms used should be included as one of the appendices.

Don't Repeat Yourself

In order to keep your business plan as concise as possible, try not to repeat yourself. For example, try not to repeat what you have said in the background section in the section dealing with marketing.

Support Your Claims

Where you have made claims in your business plan, or have made assumptions that may not be readily accepted by your intended reader, include copies of any third-party confirmations that you may have. It also helps if you are able to include copies of endorsements by your clients and confirmations of appropriate parts of your plan.

CONFIDENTIALITY CONSIDERATIONS

Your plan will contain sensitive and confidential information. You may be concerned that sending your business plan to a potential investor or lender might result in your firm's trade secrets becoming known to your competitors. However, provided you are dealing with reputable organizations, there should be no need for worry. Such investors and lenders see details of companies' secrets daily and are used to keeping confidences.

If you are not prepared to reveal your secrets at an early stage, one option is to send only the Summary to your potential investor or lender and disclose the remainder of your plan if serious interest is expressed. You should, in any event, mark your business plan "Confidential" and carefully control its distribution.

Don't Be Selective in Your Disclosures

Analyze the risks facing your firm or project. Ensure that all known risks are discussed and that you did not just select those for which you have a ready answer. If your readers subsequently discovered other risks, your proposal might suffer a serious loss of credibility.

OBTAIN AN OBJECTIVE REVIEW

After you have completed your business plan, have others review it before sending it to potential investors or lenders. Individuals in the best position to provide you with constructive comments include knowledgeable members of The Accounting Guild, your trusted business colleagues, and your attorneys. If possible, have at least two people not directly involved with your accounting firm be involved in the review.

The reviewers should put themselves in the place of the readers, to ensure that the business plan is credible, and that it meets the known criteria of the proposed reader. The reviewer should suggest improvements to the contents of the business plan and to the presentation of the case to make the proposal as attractive as possible to the proposed reader.

FIRST IMPRESSIONS COUNT

The reader should be attracted by the appearance of the plan. The business plan should, therefore, look good, but not too good — the expensively packaged plan might be considered wasteful extravagance. A suggestion is some form of loose-leaf or spiral binding that would allow any subsequent updating.

FOUR DO'S AND ONE DON'T

- Do provide an index.
- Do provide a summary.
- Do number each copy.
- Do show who the business plan is submitted by. It is surprising how many do not!
- Do not produce too many copies. If an investor were to receive copy number 75, she might consider that your plan had already been rejected by 74 others, or that 74 other parties were currently looking at your plan. In either case, she is unlikely to give it much attention.

HOW THE ACCOUNTING GUILD CAN HELP

As stated previously, a business plan should be written by the accounting firm's own management; however, The Accounting Guild can play an important role in the preparation of your business plan. The Guild believes it can be particularly helpful to your accounting firm in the following areas:

- Planning the business plan and advising on the format and content
- Assisting in the preparation of the forecasts and sensitivity analysis
- Arranging and facilitating partner/management retreats concerning the business plan
- Evaluating and designing budgets and forecasts
- Challenging your assumptions and generally acting as a sounding board for your proposals
- Reviewing the completed business plan
- Identifying a suitable merger or consolidation partner

Once the business plan is completed, the Guild can also arrange for the introductions to potential sources of financing and generally assist with initiating potentially profitable affiliations for your accounting firm. These services can be tailored to help your accounting firm achieve its potential. The Accounting Guild's Internet address is http://www.accountingguild.com.

CHAPTER 4

The Online Virtual Accounting Practice

STRUCTURING YOUR ACCOUNTING PRACTICE

This chapter will enable you to convert your ideas and desires into your ideal accounting practice. The section on significant accounting practice components contains techniques for discovering and exploiting specific market gaps (those which will support a practice) and transforming those gaps into operational services with real product deliverables. Mastering the material will help you avoid the abundant misinformation, rumors, and bad counsel and facilitate your entry and success in a business that has so much to offer so many.

Exhibit 4.1 is a fictitious note of regret from a nonexistent managing partner of a non-entity. Had it been from an actual person at a large firm, it is highly unlikely any regrets would have been felt or expressed.

FULFILLING PROMISED PURPOSES

The five key requirements of identifying and fulfilling your promised purposes for satisfaction in your entrepreneurial accounting adventure are as follows:

1. Know yourself
2. Know the business and specific components you want to operate and build
3. Know marketing
4. Know financial management
5. Know accounting

Subj: **Regrets on Starting a Practice of Your Own**
Date: 5/21/00 3:25:26 PM Pacific Daylight Time
From: JFox1961
To: accountingentrepreneur@accountingguild.com
cc: JFox1961

Dear Accounting Entrepreneur and Former Associate,

We regret that you have chosen to leave our firm to start a practice of
your own.

We feel that this move is ill-advised because the future of small firms is
tenuous at best, and they will soon be absorbed by larger practice units.

Managing Partner
Big Five Firm
Soon to be part of the Gigantic One

Exhibit 4.1 Regrets on Starting a Practice of Your Own

ORIENTATION OF MATERIAL

This material is directed and written to the person who is not wealthy
(yet) and who must make every dollar do $15 worth of work. Being
financially well off is a significant handicap in operating an accounting
business, at least in the early formative stages. Almost all of the large and
well-run enterprises were created by people who could not afford failure. Since they could not afford failure, they did not tolerate it and therefore succeeded. You should not have a "Plan B" mentality concerning the
success of your practice. The hungrier the owner, the less he is willing to
accept half-hearted attempts at achieving success.

Every strategy, every plan, every tactic, every step, every product,
every component, every business partner or affiliate, and every formula
must make complete sense with specific regard to an accountant's particular goals or it is probably wrong for that particular situation. Since
there is a plethora of misinformation, bad counsel, half-truths, false
rumors, and generally incompetent advice available to anyone who is
working to break new ground, the reader must be extremely vigilant. If

something appears to be illogical, then it is probably part of that mass of misinformation.

An accounting practice must be the image of what the business community needs. The business community will not conform and become the image of what an accounting practice needs.

PROFIT MOTIVATION

A primary pillar of a profitable accounting practice, off- or online, is the principle that there is no such thing as an unjust profit. Profits are merely the difference between the sales price (a price set on the value of your services and products to the clients) and the costs incurred in procuring, producing, and marketing services and products and in doing business. There is certainly nothing unethical, illegal, immoral, or improper in achieving the highest difference (profits) possible. Profits are the name of the game. An accounting practice is a business.

PROFESSIONAL PROGNOSTICATIONS

The accounting profession is being stretched out, and now is the time to scramble to fill the voids. Scramble ahead, but not in a helter-skelter fashion. Sharpened aggressiveness and competitiveness are the keys.

Goals

If it hasn't already been done, you and any partners should determine what goals you wish to attain. Some of the specific individual goals listed may include the following:

- To retire
- To increase or decrease the number of hours worked
- To specialize in a particular area
- To increase individual earnings

The listing will include broader firm objectives, such as the following:

- Growth of the practice
- Expansion of the capabilities of the firm

- Adequate management of the practice
- A preferred organizational structure
- Preferred client service and industry specialties

Goal Achievement Factors—Once the firm's management agrees upon the direction it will take, the factors to be employed are relatively easy to determine.

Aggressiveness—Once the goals are known, do not relax and become complacent. Protect your firm at all times from the potential of losing clients. Act more aggressively as you head toward the set goals. Aggressiveness is defined here as *"bold and active; enterprising."*

Competitiveness—Other firms are still professional contemporaries and colleagues, but they are also competitors and rivals. To reach the goals of accounting services and industry specialties, accounting firms must become prominently visible in the marketplace. There must be no guess-work on the part of the prospective clients as to what your firm does.

Mergers and other consolidations of accounting firms are so preva-lent that potential clients will choose to turn elsewhere for needed ser-vices. Those firms that have the ability to provide such services, or have chiseled out specialties through experience, will benefit. While many potential clients focus on a decision whether to change to another firm, the successful firms will be those that are most visible in the marketplace.

Your firm may also encounter a fallout of small business clients from medium-sized firms as they zero in on larger clients. If your firm has prepared itself with industry specialties and expertise in quality ser-vice—and the potential clients are aware that your firm exists—your firm will benefit.

It is important for your firm to transition into the marketplace now before the Internet environment of change dissipates, while the larger firms are preoccupied with merger plans and the medium-sized firms are looking into consolidations. Before the commotion abates, smaller firms have the opportunity to expand their client base. They should not allow it to pass without taking advantage of it.

So, what does the future hold? It is up to every individual account-ing entrepreneur and accounting firm to decide its own future. The voids in the professional marketplace are stretching, and the business commu-nity is demanding that they be filled. The smaller firms can get their share, if they earn it.

COMPONENTS OF AN ONLINE ACCOUNTING PRACTICE

The Menu of Services that follows is a categorical listing of most services that are offered by accountants in public practice. Only the largest and most comprehensive accounting firms may offer every category, but they probably will not offer every service within each category. The categorical listing attempts to guide your selection by offering a wide exposure to possible areas of concentration. Bear in mind that you can never be everything to everybody.

Categorical Organizational Listing of Accounting Firms' Menu of Services

The Accounting Guild conducted an Accounting Market Characteristics Study 2000. The study identified the "menu of services" offered by accounting firms. The findings of the study are contained in Exhibits 4.2, 4.3, and 4.4.

Exhibit 4.2 is a chart of Basic Core Accounting and Compliance Services. Exhibit 4.3 is a chart of Financial Planning Services. Exhibit 4.4 is a checklist of Specialized Areas of Expertise.

BASIC CORE ACCOUNTING AND COMPLIANCE SERVICES

The Internet has had a heavy impact on basic accounting, which hadn't changed much for many years. The accountant can choose from a vast array of inexpensive accounting packages for small and mid-range businesses. Several new accounting packages designed for use over the Web do not require software other than an Internet browser.

Every professional accounting package covers General Ledger, Accounts Receivable, Accounts Payable, and Payroll; has a range of predefined reports; and can print sales invoices, purchase orders, and several kinds of checks. Accounting professionals expect to find accounting software that has good documentation and is easy to use. Accounting software, to be competitive, must have features such as to-do lists, import and export data in commonly readable formats, and take advantage of the Internet with transmission of data and updated tax tables.

Accounting Write-up
Audits
Bankruptcy/Insolvency
Budgetary Processes/Cash Flow Forecasting/Management
Compilation and Review
Cost Accounting Systems
Expert Witness Testimony
Financial Planning (Business)
Financial Statements
Financing Arrangements
Fixed Assets Accounting
Forensics/Fraud
International Tax
Lease *versus* Buy Analysis
Litigation Support
Operations Planning
Payroll Processing Services/Consulting
Pro Forma Statements
Receivables Management
Representation Before Taxing Authorities
Tax Work
Trusts

Source: The Accounting Guild, Las Vegas, Nevada, *Accounting Market Characteristics Study,* 2000

Exhibit 4.2 Basic Core Accounting and Compliance Services

Accounting Software Resources

Bizfinity
Bizfinity, Inc., Cupertino, CA
www.bizfinity.com

Howell Client Accounting Software
ABS Systems, Lake Mary, FL
www.mrasystems.com

Compensation/Benefit Planning
Employee Benefit Extensive Consulting
Employee Stock Ownership Planning (ESOP)
Estate Planning
Pension Plans
Personal Financial Planning
Profit Sharing Plans
Trusts

Source: The Accounting Guild, Las Vegas, Nevada, *Accounting Market
   Characteristics Study,* 2000

Exhibit 4.3 Financial Planning Services

Simply Accounting v.7.0
Accpac International, Pleasanton, CA
www.accpac.com

NetLedger
NetLedger, Inc., San Mateo, CA
www.netledger.com

Write-Up Software Resources

EasyAcct
Tax and Accounting Software, Tulsa, OK
www.taascforce.com

GL 32
UniLink, Jackson, WY
www.unilink-inc.com

WinCabs
Client Accounting System, Culver City, CA
www.clientaccounting.com

Write-up Solution
Creative Solutions, Dexter, MI
www.creativesolutions.com

Accounting Outsourcing
Bankruptcy/Insolvency
Business Coaching
Business Management for Small to Medium-Sized Businesses
Business to Business (B2B) E-commerce Consulting
Business Valuation
Buy/Sell Agreements
Collection and Credit
Computer Systems/Client-Server Systems/Accounting Software
Customer Relationship Management (CRM) Consulting
Database Consulting
Data Mining
Disaster Recovery Planning
Document Management Consulting
E-commerce Consulting
Electronic Data Interchange (EDI) Consulting
Employee Search
Enterprise Resource Planning (ERP)
Financing Arrangements
Industry Specializations
Inventory Management Consulting
Knowledge/Information Technology (IT) Consulting
Legal Practice Financial Management
Medical Practice Financial Management
Mergers/Acquisitions
Nonprofit Organizations
Risk Management Consulting
Software Development
Software Reselling/Implementation and Service
Training Provider

Source: The Accounting Guild, Las Vegas, Nevada, *Accounting Market Characteristics Study,* 2000

Exhibit 4.4 Specialized Areas of Expertise

Fixed Asset Management

Selling and using fixed asset software probably isn't on the accounting professional's list of exciting new specialties, but it does deserve serious consideration. More and more clients are being forced to invest in expensive technology—while also controlling costs—in order to remain competitive. There is a strong market opportunity available as mid-size businesses driving for cost-efficiency seek better control of their equipment, factories, and real estate. As a result, clients are focusing on fixed asset management software and services. Dataquest predicts the market for asset management tools and services will expand from $2.5 billion in 2000 to $4.9 billion in 2003.

Fixed Asset Management Resources

Blackbaud Fixed Assets
Blackbaud Inc., Charleston, SC
www.blackbaud.com

BNA Fixed Assets
BNA, Washington, D.C.
www.bna.com

FAS Encore
Best Software, Reston, VA
www.bestsoftware.com

WorthIT Fixed Assets
WorthIT Software, Mississauga, Ontario, Canada
www.worthitsoftware.com

Web-Based Payroll Processing

The Internet is a valued resource not only for news, investments, shopping, and global communication, but also for a plethora of online services, including payroll processing. Accounting services providers are offering online payroll at a torrid pace and many veteran payroll processors, like ADP and Paychex, are migrating to the Web, enabling businesses to enter data from remote locations any time of the day or night. Often the online services are less expensive than traditional payroll processing, providing small businesses with services once available only to larger companies with larger budgets.

As is the case with most Web-based services, since the system is online, there's no need for users to purchase and install software. For many of the Web-based systems, users need only limited Internet access such as an Internet appliance and a browser.

Once clients find the accountant's Web site, they have all they need as far as an online accounting system. Services to small businesses include direct deposit of employee paychecks; electronic tax filing of federal form 941 deposits; downloadable and printable employee earnings statements and pay stubs; preparation of all state and federal quarterly and annual payroll tax returns; downloadable and printable payroll, management, and payroll tax reports; and automatic filing of all quarterly and annual federal and state payroll tax returns.

National payroll processors that have designed Web-based systems include Automatic Data Processing (ADP), and Paychex. With Automatic Data Processing's EasyPayNet, users can submit payroll information to ADP via the Internet. The only requirement is a browser and Internet access. Clients can do same-day payroll processing, reporting and tax filing; background checks and drug screening; retirement plan administration; and optional employee benefits programs available through payroll deductions.

Paychex is expanding its Internet-based service capabilities to keep pace with competition. Paychex's remote-entry system, Paylink, enables clients to enter payroll data, add and change employee information, and produce reports via a modem at any time.

Barry Star was a small business owner in Boston, Massachusetts who found himself frustrated with payroll, bookkeeping, and banks. In 1998, Star launched OneCore.com, a broker/dealer of financial services for small to mid-size businesses. Clients need only Internet access and a browser to set up a OneCore.com (Bedford, MA) account, which is a money market account with check-writing privileges. They can then choose from a suite of financial services including bill payment, 401K, merchant card processing, and payroll processing. Every OneCore service operates within this single account.

OneCore's payroll services are administered by payroll service provider and Intuit subsidiary Computing Resources of Reno, Nevada. Full-service payroll processing includes tax reporting and W-2 generation. Clients enter the employees' hours, the dates, and any changes from their computer. Within three days, clients receive checks, check stubs for those using direct deposit, and the payroll report.

Service Bureaus Ally with Accountants

CPAs have long referred their clients to payroll processors, primarily ADP and Paychex. The competitive climate and the processor's increased recognition of the value of the referrals have goaded many processors to set up programs that financially reward the recommending accountants.

Automatic Data Processing (ADP), of Roseland, New Jersey has instituted its Accountant Advantage Program. Not only can accounting professionals benefit from referring clients, they can also resell ADP's EasyPayNet service. Private labeling is a service offered by several processors that enables the accounting firm to build its own brand image. Reselling a payroll processor's services allows the accounting firm to learn from experience while avoiding the capital expenditure of creating a service bureau from scratch. However, the capital expenditure is not that great at this time of falling technology prices.

The revenue share for the accountant is generally 15 percent in a private label program. Recommendations generate a 10 percent fee. For an accounting firm that is considering offering a payroll processing service, it would be prudent to learn about the business by reselling private label services as the initial marketplace foray and evolve into offering a full service in-house payroll service.

There is a growing trend among the accounting community to offer the full range of payroll services, including timekeeping and check-writing. This extension of services is well beyond the traditional bailiwick of after-the-fact (ATF) payroll services such as ensuring compliance with ever-changing government regulations, performing tax deposits, and filing quarterly reports. A driving force behind this trend is the increasing functionality of the software, the pervasiveness of the Internet, and the dramatic price drops for equipment and software.

Payroll Software and Service Provider Resources

Automatic Data Processing, Roseland, NJ
www.adp.com

OneCore, Boston, MA
www.onecore.com

Paychex, Rochester, NY
www.paychex.com

Online Tax Preparation

Preparing tax returns now involves heavy-duty Internet surfing during tax season as practitioners avail themselves of a trove of Web-based services developed by software publishers. The Internal Revenue Service is launching new initiatives aimed at expanding the opportunities for taxpayers to file or pay taxes electronically.

A heated price war is being waged by more tax software publishers offering online tax preparation amid a continuing trend in vendor consolidation through merger and purchase. As a result, or because of the situation, tax return preparation is fast becoming a commodity. If accounting professionals act as tax advisors who provide valuable service, they will not be tainted by the spectre of commoditization. If they merely prepare the forms, they will be hurt in the process.

Besides the comparatively low prices, Web-based tax preparation services have many features. Each service stresses the security and confidentiality of client data and most target filers that actually prepare their own taxes with paper and pencil. Many Web tax programs provide users with an easy-to-use questionnaire that walks them through the preparation.

Future of Tax Preparation

With the Internet, tax preparation can now be faster, easier, cheaper, and less profitable for the accounting practitioner. Does this mean that the days of needing a professional preparer will soon be over? The consensus is no.

Preparers who rely on simple returns are going to find a lot more competition from computer-based and Internet-based programs. For those professionals who do more complicated returns, there will still be ample work. The trend will have a more severe impact on the store-front operations than on the professional preparer.

The writing is clearly on the wall. The profession must wake up to marketplace realities. If professionals want to be in the ranks of the viable and prospering practitioners, they can't be doing what they've done for the past 20 or 30 years.

Tax Return Preparation Software Resources

ATX Forms, Caribou, ME
www.atxforms.com

Creative Solutions, Dexter, MI
www.creativesolutions.com

Orrtax, Bellevue, WA
www.orrtax.com

Petz Enterprises, Tracy, CA
www.petzent.com

Research Institute of America (RIA), New York, NY
www.riagosystem.com

Tax and Accounting Software, Tulsa, OK
www.taascforce.com

FINANCIAL PLANNING SERVICES

Financial Planning and the Internet

Financial planning represents a particularly robust opportunity for accounting professionals. The loss of tax and audit revenue has forced many accounting firms to expand their repertoire of services in order to keep clients. For many accountants, financial planning provides a close fit to existing services, the capabilities of the firm, and the needs of its clients.

Professionals seeking the software tools to perform financial planning services face a mixed market with many options. Each year of software development brings incremental improvements in speed and functionality. However, no one software package, online or shrink-wrapped, has gained enough dominance to consolidate the market.

Financial Planning Software

Financial planning software at a minimum must perform three basic functions:

1. Assist in the collection of financial data from the client
2. Organize the data for comparison to standards or assumptions
3. Create a roadmap for present and future financial assets

Many broker/dealers are actively promoting financial planning services as a practice niche for accounting professionals. Each state has specific licensing requirements. Full information is provided by the financial institutions. In some instances, software is provided to the practitioner. Listed below are the developers of components for a toolkit for financial planning accountants.

Financial Planning Software Resources

M-Plan
Checkfree Investment Services/Mobius Group, Research Triangle Park, NC
www.mobius.com

Distribution and Estate Planning, Accountant Specialists
Cowan Financial Group, New York, NY
rfrazer@cowanfinancial.com

FPlan Professional Advisor +
First Financial Software, Orlando, FL
www.FPlan.com

MasterPlan 2000
MasterPlan Financial Software, Davis, CA
www.masterplanner.com

Easy Money Suite
Money Tree Software, Philomath, OR
www.moneytree.com

Principia Pro
Morningstar, Chicago, IL
www.morningstar.com

Extensive Employee Benefits Consulting

Employee benefits have risen dramatically to encompass almost 40 percent of an employer's compensation budget, with 80 percent of full-time employees participating in one or more employer-sponsored retirement plans, according to the U.S. Department of Labor. As a result, many employers are turning more frequently to accounting professionals to show them how to reduce expenses in this area.

To make money from this niche, the accountant must fully understand all aspects of employee benefits. A practitioner with tax knowledge differs significantly from one with specific expertise in ERISA. The major responsibility of a practitioner in this area is to ensure that all of the client's plans remain qualified.

Accounting benefits specialists usually draft and analyze a survey of employees' attitudes toward employer-sponsored plans. Once the facts have been gathered, the specialists then provide the following consulting services:

- ERISA reporting requirements for various benefit plans, including self-insured medical and profit-sharing plans
- Executive compensation packages including nonqualified stock options, phantom stock, golden parachute payments, and non-qualified deferred compensation plans
- Allocation assistance regarding any leveraged employee stock ownership plans, installation of an employer-sponsored 401(k), and other profit-sharing programs

Employee Benefits Market Niche

This area has become so specialized that to make it lucrative, the accounting professional must become totally immersed in employee benefits consulting. To maintain profitability, the accounting firm must provide the broadest possible services to each client, touching on nearly every aspect of employee benefits.

Employee Benefits Niche Services

- Determining eligibility for participation
- Determining which plans
- Allocating contributions
- Reallocating forfeitures and crediting investment gains or losses
- Performing the annual nondiscrimination test for elective deferrals and matching contributions
- Coordinating the activities of the trustee, plan administrator, attorney, accountant, and other advisors
- Advising trustees regarding their fiduciary responsibility and any changes in pension laws as promulgated by Congress, the IRS, and the Department of Labor (DOL)
- Preparing all required IRS, DOL, and Pension Benefit Guaranty Corporation forms as well as IRS Forms 1099R, 1096, W-2P, and W-3 relating to any distributions from a plan

To save the client lots of headaches and money, closely watch that annual additions limits have not been exceeded. Exceeding those limits can be very costly.

Third-Party Administration

Accounting professionals provide the following third-party administration services:

- Defined Contribution/401(k) Plan Administration
- Defined Benefit Pension Administration
- Qualified Prototype & Volume Submitter Plan Documentation
- Section 125 Cafeteria/Flexible Benefits Administration
- Cafeteria Plan Documentation
- Participant Termination Calculation System
- Qualified Plan Minimum Distribution Calculations
- FAS 132 Reporting System
- Data Entry & Review Module

Third-Party Resource

DATAIR Employee Benefit Systems, Inc., Westmont, IL
www.datair.com

Internet Implications

There are close to 1 million private pension plans and more than 4.5 million health and welfare benefit plans covering over 170 million participants and beneficiaries in the United States. These plans own more than $1 trillion in assets, including 25 percent of equity securities and 15 percent of taxable bonds in the U.S. economy. This data was furnished by the U.S. Department of Labor.

As a result, there is great emphasis on providing benefits to employees that will also help the employer's bottom line. The accountant who assists businesses in identifying those benefits that are most meaningful to employees and then counsels the client companies on what specific plans make sense to both employers and employees will be an invaluable asset to the client.

Employee benefits consulting is an exceedingly lucrative area as practitioners have expanded their focus from compliance and audit work to a broad range of benefits consulting that includes not only specific plans but human resources and payroll as well. It is expected that as Internet utilization increases it will bring even more of a concentrated effort in this area.

SPECIALIZED AREAS OF EXPERTISE

Making Your Professional Dreams Come True

Many of us fantasize about what we want in our professional life. Your heart may be set on a specialized practice located in Hawaii with periodic winter assignments in Aspen. For others it could be fame and fortune and guest visits on the Oprah show as the accounting expert everyone wants to listen to. But some of us have absolutely no idea what we want to be or do when we "grow up," we only know it's something other than what we have now.

Our dream may seem out of reach, yet it haunts us. We can't ignore it. Nor should we, because often our dreams are possible, and striving for them helps us reach our highest potential. But how can we bring our dreams down to earth and turn them into reality? How can we breathe life into them? Planning, patience, hard work, and courage are required. It may seem overwhelming, but it can be done.

What Do You Really Want?

The first step is to turn your dream into a clearly defined goal. We may think we know exactly what we want, but in truth it may be what we used to want or what we think we should want. Our choices are often influenced by the values and expectations of others, which, however well-intended, may not be right for us.

To find out what you really want, set aside private time with pen and paper—writing down your ideas forces you to think clearly. Write down all your dreams, even if at first they sound unattainable or ridiculous. Don't be afraid to aim high and stretch yourself. You must then narrow down your list to what really matters most to you, what really excites you. If you are ambivalent about your goal, you won't go after it. To help set priorities, write down the benefits and results of each item on your list.

If you're still not sure about what you value the most, ask yourself what you would do if you had only one year to live. If you're in touch with your deepest needs, this test won't change your list. But if you're ignoring important parts of yourself, you'll get some startling answers. It may take a few weeks of soul-searching before your true priorities become clear. (See also the section in Chapter 13 on "Balancing Your Professional and Personal Life.")

Turning Your Dream into Reality

- Choose your goal.
- Describe it in as much detail as possible.
- Write down everything you can think of that might help you achieve it.
- Break the goal down into a series of smaller steps.
- Brainstorm to loosen your imagination.
- Formulate a plan.
- Set a deadline.
- Exercise flexibility and persistence.
- Make each day count.

Accounting Success Comes in Different Flavors

Accountants are rapidly catching up with today's emphasis on the Internet and are finding a ready market for their expertise. Specialized areas of consulting have become profitable fields for many CPAs, as clients seek advice on choosing and installing an accounting system, while relying on their accounting firm's practical knowledge of how to handle the cash flow.

However, fitting a technology consulting practice into a traditional accounting firm takes some adjustment. Trying to give a client everything on a wish list can cause technology consultants to lose out on the bottom line. One can run into a situation where a lot of unbillable time is spent (and therefore dollars) to get a particular report, although that client is valuable to the firm in other areas.

Bringing up a new accounting system can lead to unexpected costs that the firm could be obligated to bear if it's under contract. Accounting professionals are cautioned to avoid pursuing new business blindly without regard to how much it might end up costing their firms.

Internet Consulting Relief

Rapid technological changes may severely test the business community, but the Internet could prove to be its best friend. The accounting profession's technology leaders have been urging practitioners to seize control of the vast and rapid changes confronting the industry — or face professional extinction.

Those accountants that are open to embracing technology will thrive in the Internet Information Age. Those that cannot make the transition run the risk of being left behind and missing opportunities to grow.

The Internet promises to fundamentally change the way business is done both on a consumer and on a business-to-business level. The professionals that take advantage of it will prosper. The Internet will become the leading mechanism for selling, marketing, distributing, and supporting software in the next three years. Exhibit 4.5 lists the challenges facing the accounting profession from the Internet.

Are CPAs Serious about the Internet?

"Mainstream CPAs are not embracing technology" is a statement coming from various quarters of the accounting software industry. A large seg-

---

- Keeping up with technology
- Client demand for technology consulting
- Attracting, retaining staff talent
- Diversifying into nontraditional services
- Handling rapid growth
- Electronic commerce
- New tax laws
- Overcoming accountants' resistance to change
- Getting Internet-enabled
- FASB fair value accounting standards
- Moving clients to new technologies

Source: The Accounting Guild, Las Vegas, Nevada, *Internet Challenges,* 2000

Exhibit 4.5 Internet Professional Challenges

ment of the accounting profession is definitely failing to recognize the importance of creating new sources of revenue. More than a few predictions call for the dwindling of current profits reaped by accountants from traditional services when economic growth slackens.

The leadership of the American Institute of CPAs sees the Internet as a major business segment that CPAs must develop. The problem is not just that many CPAs aren't embracing the Internet as a new way of bringing in revenue. They also aren't embracing the Internet in their day-to-day lives for internal use. Many CPAs' eyes glaze over when they are confronted with their need to master Internet technology.

What will be the impact on the profession as the more technology-oriented practitioners chaff at the bit while the pace is slowed by leaders of the industry who resist Internet technology? The real risk is that the best and the brightest will desert the profession, leaving it stripped of leadership. Leadership will need to show some masterful skills in pushing, dragging, and kicking their reluctant members into the next century.

Specialized Market Niche Resources

The Accounting Guild, Inc.
www.accountingguild.com

American Fundware, Denver, CO
www.fundware.com

Blackbaud, Inc. Charleston, SC
www.blackbaud.com

ElectronicAccountant
www.electronicaccountant.com

Greatland Corporation, Grand Rapids, MI
www.greatland.com

Great Plains Software, Fargo, ND
www.greatplains.com

H. D. Vest Financial Services, Irving, TX
www.hdvest.com

Professional Associations

Association for Accounting Administration, Dayton, OH,
937-222-0030

American Association of Hispanic CPAs, Rowland Heights, CA, 626-965-0643

Accountants for the Public Interest, Baltimore, MD, 410-837-6533

Affiliated Conference of Practicing Accountants International, North Andover, MA, 978-689-9420

American Institute of Certified Public Accountants, New York, NY, 212-596-6200

American Society of Women Accountants, Northbrook, IL, 800-326-2163

Institute of Management Accountants, Montvale, NJ, 201-573-9000

National Association of Enrolled Agents, Gaithersburg, MD, 301-212-9608

National Society of Accountants, Alexandria, VA, 703-549-6400

CHAPTER 5

Getting Connected and Other Logistics of Providing Online Services

WHAT IS THE INTERNET?

The Internet's predecessor, ARPANET, was created in 1968 by the Advanced Research Projects Agency, for the Department of Defense. During the Cold War, the objective was to create a nationwide network with all sites linked. If a hostile attack eliminated some sites, those remaining could continue to work without interruption. ARPANET had no central computing facility and therefore no single crucial target for a sophisticated enemy's attack.

This bit of history is significant to understanding why there is still no central control or authority managing this "network of networks." The communications protocols developed by ARPANET are still used today. New sites are added continuously, each connected to the other, and there is no interruption of service when new sites are connected (or when inactive sites are disconnected).

CHANGE

In accounting, as in most professions, we are what we experience and learn. The ideas that come from these formative perceptions become comfortable and we can't readily part with them. Change is not about understanding new things or having new ideas, but rather seeing old familiar things with a fresh perspective.

Change can be exhilarating, joyous, and liberating while at the same time terrifying because we are really questioning our identity and sense of value. To change, we must stop what we're doing, step back, look, and then challenge the very thoughts and business practices that perpetuate outdated mindsets, from training programs to Internet systems adoptions.

The accounting profession, as it enters this new century, is an industry that has strength, resilience, creativity, and a vibrant role in the economy. We are riding the crest of a wave of technological breakthroughs, market openings, and new service and product introductions. This wave of change marks the advent of not only a new millennium, but also a global economic revolution.

We learned from the Industrial Revolution of the nineteenth century, that technological change helps create social change. Since we are still in the early stages of the social restructuring that the Information Revolution has set in motion, we must view this positive change as achieving the marketplace's demand for "faster, better, my way." If we can change our mind, we can change the world. We need to combine the courage to be creative with the mindset that having creativity and responsibility is essentially what our business is all about.

If we embrace and run with technology, understand business consolidation, and come to grips with the fact that the 13-column accounting pad may not return, we are positioned to leave our comfort zone. Learning to change as society evolves hasn't always been easy. However, learning to change is vital to continued growth.

INFRASTRUCTURE

The Internet is rapidly changing the way the accounting profession does business. A profitable accounting practice will use the Internet to simplify and automate all of its processes. Internet applications are relatively easy to develop and inexpensive to operate. Complexity is centralized, making it easier to manage. Data is consolidated, making it accessible to analyze, report, and understand.

E@CCOUNTING ALL STARTS WITH A WEB SITE

Web sites are the basic building blocks of Internet online accounting computing. Transforming your accounting firm's information systems for e@ccounting starts with the creation of high-performance Web sites that are easy to configure, update, and manage. Done effectively, the transformation from accounting practice to e@ccounting goes right to the core of a firm's operations, making them more efficient, less expensive, and more nimble than ever before.

Your accounting firm's Web site on the Internet can incorporate text, graphics, images, audio, streaming video, and new features that will be constantly added in the future. From your Web site, visitors can garner key information about your firm.

CHOOSING THE SERVER

You must have a reliable, high-performance system to act as a Web server. Since the system will have network access, efficient security will be paramount. Servers are the foundation for your Internet presence. If the servers fail, the site fails. If they lag, the site lags. Choose wrong, and your entire practice presents a red face to the world while you present a red face to your clients. The following Web server factors should be considered.

Reliability

This is clearly the most important aspect of a Web server. But reliability is tightly integrated with a Web server's function. For instance, a Web server that will serve up relatively static Web pages day after day needn't be as expensive or robust as one that will be providing streaming video to thousands of hits a day. How can you tell which server will be the most reliable? The weak link in reliability tends to be the operating system rather than the hardware, although hardware reliability shouldn't be completely dismissed. Reliability features should include tight integration of hardware components and excellent quality control over the manufacturing process.

Performance

The true measure of performance is how the hardware responds under heavy stress. Tests should be run on the network/bandwidth, not just the Web server application. Run the server that is being evaluated and see if it does what you expect. Obtain loaner programs from the manufacturer or value added reseller (VAR) to allow you to try out different vendors' products before deciding which to install.

Function

Test the functions that the server will perform. If complex functions such a database interactions will be added, this will affect the servers' performance as Web services become more complex. Video, voice, and VRML should absolutely be tested on a variety of hardware platforms before they are installed as these are much more CPU- and disk-intensive than static pages.

Cost Considerations

A significant concern is price. While some lower-priced Web servers may be perfectly functional running Apache to server-static Web pages, their scalability must be evaluated in terms of your present to near future needs. The difference in cost is determined by how many CPUs are in the same box and I/O performance. Typically, the more CPUs added to the box, the less performance per CPU is gained. That is, while adding a second CPU may double the box's performance, adding a third one may increase the unit's capacity to handle requests by only 25 percent.

Some accountants are encouraged to participate in hosting, rather than place cheaper servers onsite. With hosting services steadily decreasing in cost, this could be a better way for firms to experiment with the Web than buying their own. You can partner with a VAR that sells the Internet in a box and Internet service. They would do all the integration for the servers and the front-line support. Working with a VAR can lead to a relationship in jointly providing Internet hardware, software, and accounting services to clients without investing in a sales, integration, and implementation program of your own.

The bottom line is that no magic answers will appear to guide you through the selection and implementation of your server for the Web. Legwork and testing remain the tried and true methods.

CONNECTIONS, BANDWIDTH, AND INTERNET SERVICE PROVIDERS

Every accounting practice, and for that matter every other Internet-connected business needs an Internet Service Provider (ISP) to gain access to the Web. ISPs are the new telephone companies of the Internet Age.

They provide services and support that hold essential parts of any business together.

ISPs provide e-mail, Web site design and hosting, and many other integral business services and support options. Each ISP offers different connection types. If you have a specific "pipe" in mind, be sure to ask in advance if they support it. For the most part, cable connections are only offered from local cable providers. Satellite setups require going through separate vendors as well. However, with all of the mergers and acquisitions going on in this industry, things are changing all the time.

Before shopping for the best package of ISP services and support, first decide the best way to connect your accounting practice to the Internet. There are several different connection types to choose from, with various speeds and performance levels. Prices also vary, and availability of certain connections depends on location. Faster communications, using broadband connections such as a T1 line or DSL service, can save time and boost productivity, but they may also prove costly, complex, and unreliable. It is important to understand clearly how each technology works and what the pros and cons are before making a decision.

Internet Technology Value Proposition

- T1 is cost-prohibitive for most smaller accounting practices.
- DSL has become an excellent alternative, although availability remains a problem.
- ISDN is an alternative where DSL is unavailable.
- Cable modem infrastructure is not that common, and cable is less popular with business customers than with retail customers.
- Satellite service and support have not been widely available to date.
- Analog service is the last resort.

Dial-Up

The most basic of the connection options is dial-up Internet access. With a regular phone line, a modem, and a few minutes to enter an ISP's information into the operating system, you're ready to e-mail and surf the Web. Every accounting firm needs to have several dial-up accounts to support remote access via laptop, if nothing else. However, at a total monthly cost of about $50 per user (about $30 for a phone line and $20 for ISP service), a dial-up connection is not really the bargain it is made out to be, especially for more than a handful of users.

The major drawback of a dial-up connection is that data transfer is relatively slow. Even if phone lines and modems are capable of delivering a 56K connection in many locations, 28.8Kbps (Kilobytes Per Second) is the best available, making serious Web use tedious, and e-commerce impossible. Although it is possible for LAN users to share one or more dial-up connections for Internet access, dividing already slow dial-up transfer speeds will cause a bottleneck. Providing shared access to a single-user modem will maintain speeds and is a better solution. Also keep in mind that simultaneous voice and data services on dial-up are not possible.

Integrated Services Digital Network (ISDN)

ISDN uses digital technology to provide simultaneous, always-on access; advanced voice features; and fast data transmission over regular copper phone wires. Basic ISDN lines are considerably faster than dial-up service, but they can't hold a candle to cable or DSL bandwidth. It's the voice service option that makes ISDN worth considering. ISDN lines can make up to eight phone numbers available on one phone line. In addition, calls are completed faster, and digital connections provide clearer signals. However, the equipment is more expensive.

ISDN service adds an additional charge averaging about $20 per month to basic POTS (plain old telephone service), plus data transfer is charged per minute, per channel. Costs vary widely by telco, and even by state. ISDN is scalable (up to T1 speeds) because its channels can be combined to provide higher speed. An ISDN Primary Rate Interface contains 23 data channels that can provide a bandwidth of 1.544Mbps.

ISDN provides the following features:

- Significant economies in line usage
- Tremendous convenience and flexibility
- Reasonably fast data transfer
- Easy scalability

Digital Subscriber Line (DSL)

DSL is the telephone companies' answer to the threat of cable modems. Like ISDN, it provides always-on digital data service over regular phone lines. Unlike ISDN, voice service is analog. Data transmission speeds are also much higher, and pricing is flat rate with unlimited usage.

Several standards exist within the technology, primarily ADSL (asymmetric DSL), where download speeds are much higher than upload speeds, and SDSL (symmetric DSL), where download and upload speeds are equal. ADSL is considered a consumer service, and is generally priced between $50 and $70 per month, depending on connection speed. SDSL is priced higher than ADSL, generally between $130 and $200 per month, depending on connection speed. Options vary with provider and distance.

DSL is highly sensitive to distance, and can be blocked altogether by fiber-optic cables and analog signal-boosting equipment. As a result, DSL is available primarily in metropolitan areas, and suburban service coverage is spotty at best. DSL is up-and-coming, but it is not recommended for a mission-critical application as it is still a technology without well-established standards and reliable support. It would be sufficient to provide Internet browsing on a LAN, to support telecommuters, or for other applications where lower price and simultaneous voice and data connections make sense, and where reliability problems can be worked around.

T1 and Other Advanced Services

T1 service is provided via a leased digital phone line between an accounting firm and a service provider's hub. The bandwidth of a standard T1 connection is 1.544Mbps, which is totally dedicated to the user. A T1 line, however, is just a big conduit. In order to get the most out of it, "smart" devices such as switches, bridges, and routers are needed to control and direct its capabilities. An even larger conduit called T3 is available, providing 45Mbps bandwidth over dedicated fiber optic cables.

Although a T1 connection by itself is reasonably economical ($300–$500 per month on average, varying by distance), the equipment and personnel needed to manage its usage is much greater. AT&T, Uunet, and larger regional ISPs offer managed T1 services to accounting firms without an internal IT staff, but the price tag is fairly steep. In general, T1 is best suited for a firm with technically oriented personnel and advanced needs, such as providing a mix of Internet access and voice services to a large staff, interconnecting LANs at different locations, or offering extensive Web hosting services.

For the firm with less complex needs a T1 line is a waste of resources and money. A better option for many smaller accounting firms is frame relay service. This is a digital technology that divides data transmissions into large chunks (called frames), then transmits them over "permanent virtual circuits," which connect business locations via mapped pathways on the public telephone network. With many of the advantages of leased-line access at a lower non-distance-sensitive cost, frame relay is a good choice for occasional high-speed access, such as uploading Web pages to an offsite host, or downloading transaction data from a remote LAN.

T1 is a complex service — and one that accounting firms usually evolve into as demand grows. An alternative service like frame relay is usually a better starting point for most smaller firms.

Cable

Cable Internet service is always on, and offers extremely high-speed potential at a flat rate per user, generally around $40 per month. With a download bandwidth of 8Mbps (though 500–1000Kbps is a more realistic expectation) and upload speeds of 128Kbps, a cable connection has more than enough speed for most accounting firm applications.

On the downside, availability is very limited, and even if a local cable company offers data services, wiring may not exist in industrial parks and business districts. Users are also limited to the cable company's choice of ISP, and performance decreases as the total traffic on your node increases. Additionally, cable is commonly considered a consumer service, and e-commerce activities are almost universally prohibited.

Some of these problems will be addressed in the near future. It's only logical that e-commerce and traffic congestion issues will be addressed, if not eliminated. If your local cable provider hasn't announced the availability of Internet service yet, don't wait. The cable market is hugely fragmented, and many local firms are dragging their feet, unwilling to make the investment in required system upgrades. ISPs, CLECs, and telcos are challenging cable Internet's cost and reliability advantages by rapidly expanding DSL availability — perhaps misguidedly.

Satellite

Your accounting firm may not be located near a metropolitan hub. It may not even be in a suburban industrial park. Advanced communications and overnight shipping supposedly make it possible to operate a global accounting business from almost anywhere. But how does one get fast Internet access when the accounting firm is located in the middle of a prairie or on the shore of a mountain lake?

The way you get fast Internet access is the same way many get TV — via satellite. Hughes Network Systems provides Internet information delivery via its DirecPC satellite network. DirecPC, like its DirecTV cousin, is a receiver, not a transmitter. The satellite system handles only information downloads; uploads are done via garden-variety dial-up access. Because browsers are programmed to direct downloads to the satellite instead of the phone network, DirecPC acts like a supercharger.

DirecPC provides more than enough bandwidth to supply a LAN. While Hughes offers several service packages, including a LAN connection, they refer businesses requiring more support to qualified service providers. Satellite service is an excellent tool for the many practices located in areas where dial-up and perhaps ISDN are the only alternatives. It brings some real speed to information gathering, and is particularly good for broadcasting video, multimedia, or other large data files to multiple locations.

Summary

Each technology has enough weaknesses that none of them is a clear overall winner for general accounting firm usage. Because pricing and service availability can vary widely by location, the one universal piece of advice is to summarize your needs as succinctly as possible, then discuss them with several service providers, including local telcos, ISPs, and any other relevant technology providers (cable company, CLEC, satellite provider, etc.). Be specific about costs, and don't be afraid to ask for a package. Reliability and support are key issues, and will make or break any deal.

Bottom-Line Footnotes

- **Dial-up**—Light to moderate use and in remote locations.
- **ISDN**—Advanced voice and data needs and video.
- **DSL**—Up-and-coming technology; not for mission-critical applications.
- **T1**—Best for high volume needs.
- **Cable**—Good for high-speed surfing; more of a consumer option.
- **Satellite**—High speeds in remote areas.

INFORMATION TECHNOLOGY

Building a profitable online accounting practice puts great new demands on the information technology that runs your firm. You need a software foundation that delivers full-featured applications and the scalability to handle fluctuating demand and rapid growth. Ideally, such a platform should also be based on open industry standards to protect your investments and make integration with other systems easier.

In the client/server era, the desktop operating system dictated the choice of development tools and programming languages. In the Internet age, the operating system is reduced to managing systems resources. The choice of development tools and programming languages is determined more by support for higher-level standards, such as HTTP, Java, XML, and XBRL. Perhaps the biggest difference for accountants moving to Internet computing is that applications are now centralized on multi-tier servers that must support hundreds or even thousands of users.

For accounting software application developers, this shift means that the important first decision is no longer which desktop operating system (OS) to standardize on, but rather which platform to use going forward. Because of the centralized nature of Internet computing, that decision has far-reaching implications for an accounting firm's e-business strategy. In the foreseeable future, all business will be e-business and the reliability, scalability, and security of your application platform can determine your firm's success or survival. Changing application architectures or replacing software that won't scale as your practice grows can mean the difference between winning and losing in the ever competitive networked economy.

START-UP AND ONGOING COSTS

Start-up costs will include the server hardware and software, a router, charges from your Internet service provider (ISP), the cost of a data line, and the cost to create your site. Ongoing costs will include monthly charges from your Internet service provider, monthly line cost, and the cost of maintaining your server and Web pages. Be wary of ISPs that are priced below market rates and keep in mind that expensive is not a guarantee of excellent service. Look for a service provider that provides telephone support outside normal working hours.

THE HUMAN ELEMENT

Processes, programs, and procedures are fine, but people fuel your accounting practice. For the past 15 to 20 years, we have seen an avalanche of management fads, techniques, and gurus, all professing to make accounting firms better:

- Total Quality Management (TQM)
- Continuous Quality Improvement (CQI)
- Re-engineering
- Downsizing
- Rightsizing
- Delayering
- Destabilizing
- Management by Walking Around (MBWA)
- Management by Crawling Around (MBCA)
- Management by Whining (MBW)
- One-Minute Management
- Empowerment

Unfortunately, they have one major thing in common: a failure rate of 70 percent or greater. The reason for this high failure rate is that firms forgot the most important element when they abandoned all their methods and processes to start over. They forgot about the people in their organization. Your management and staff are integral to the success of your firm. Accounting firms can get so wrapped up in their procedures, programs, and policies that they neglect the human element—the most important one.

Technology is not the answer. Technology is only a tool. A new application or technology may help accountants do their jobs better and more quickly, but it will never replace people. That's because technology has no mind to take the initiative or address out-of-the-ordinary problems, and no heart to handle the softer issues of client interaction, at least not yet. For the present time only people do. To succeed, firms must go beyond audits, implementations, engagements, methods, and inconsequential cultures to engage, enable, and ennoble their people.

Management needs to focus on employees' emotions, their intrinsic motivation, their commitment to loyalty (always a two-way street), the amount of trust they place in each other and management, and the balance between their work and home life. Every accounting firm must have a fully engaged and totally committed staff. Make sure people are agreeable to learning new technology before you hire them. Part of your recruitment process should be to make certain that the prospective staffer knows he or she will be working with technology. It is important to hire on the basis of a willingness to learn technology.

Get your staff users involved during the selection process. These are the people who will use the system on a day-to-day basis. If they don't see how it's helpful, or at least how it will do no harm, you'll meet a lot of resistance.

Training the Staff

Training is essential to ensure staff acceptance. However, training is a more complex topic than most accounting firms realize. Most small to mid-sized firms do training as an afterthought. Spending a few more dollars to train the staff to use the technology is like buying an insurance policy.

How much should the small to mid-sized accounting firm plan spend on training? In the Big Five and large firms, training often can be between 5 and 10 percent of the MIS budget. Small firms should think about what it costs per person. Is it worth $500 or $1,000 per person to train them properly? The answer is usually a clear yes.

When you do the training, make sure there's enough time to learn it well and keep pressure to a minimum. For the training to be effective, it must help the staff use the technology in their day-to-day work. Your staff may often fear that the new technology will disrupt their lives and hurt their careers. Overcoming that fear and explaining to staff that the new technology will improve their working lives will ease its acceptance. Explain to people why they'll be better off: the world is changing and this technology will provide opportunities for them in the future. The important thing to make clear is that learning the new technology means future employability. Help them understand the inevitability of the change.

QUESTIONS TO ASK

ISPs

- Will you coordinate solving problems with the telephone company?
- What modem/router equipment works best with your system?
- What if I want to change or upgrade technology in the future?
- Does the ISP have the connections I need, where I need them?
- What do I commit to when I sign up?
- How does the ISP enable e-commerce?
- What are the traffic and storage limits?

Telcos

- Can I get a package discount for my data service?
- Do you have a plan or price if I do all my voice, Internet, and wireless services through you?
- Is there a package plan to upgrade my analog voice setup to ISDN?
- Do I have to get phone/modem/router equipment from you? If not, which modems/routers/switches do you support?
- I'm using a CLEC to get SDSL service, but who handles line problems?
- I think I need more bandwidth to do e-commerce, but what alternatives to T1 do you offer?

Other Providers

- What service and performance guarantees do you have?
- How do you handle LAN connections?
- If my needs grow, what options do you provide?

JARGON OF THE TRADE

ADSL: Asymmetric DSL is technology that provides 6Mbps downstream and 640Kbps upstream throughput. It's often used in Voice over DSL (VoDSL).

ATM: Asynchronous transfer mode is a high-speed networking standard used in WANs and often used to connect DSL lines to your Internet backbone.

Bandwidth: The total capacity of a communication link, generally specified as a maximum constant bps capability.

BPS (Bits Per Second): The common measure of data communications speed. Kbps refers to thousands of bits per second, and Mbps refers to millions of bits per second.

CLEC (Competitive Local Exchange Carrier): An independent company providing local telephone service over telco wiring. These were founded after the Telecommunications Reform Act of 1996.

CO: A central office is the consolidation point for the POTS lines in a given area. It's usually owned by the local ILEC.

DHCP (Dynamic Host Configuration Protocol): A protocol for automatically assigning and managing IP addresses on a network.

DNS (Domain Name System): A hierarchical system of servers that exist to maintain databases enabling the conversion of domain names such as youraccountingfirm.com into their IP addresses.

DSL: Digital subscriber line service is the generic term for a family of high-speed data and voice communication standards that can work over ordinary POTS copper-pair wiring.

DSLAM: The DSL access multiplexer is the heart of any DSL solution. It brings together multiple DSL lines to the CO's WAN ports.

Ethernet: A protocol for sending packets of information over local area networks.

FTP (File Transfer Protocol): An Internet client/server protocol that allows the exchange of files between computers.

G.Lite: is a DSL standard for 1.5 Mbps downstream and 384 Kbps upstream bandwidth. This standard is expected to be widely deployed in 2000.

IAD: Integrated access devices deliver both DSL voice and data services.

ILEC: Incumbent Local Exchange Carrier: Alphabet soup for the local telco.

IP address: IP addresses are not the same as e-mail addresses or URLs. An IP address is a 32-bit number assigned to individual computers and/or network interfaces in a TCP/IP network. Every client and server station must have a unique IP address.

ISDN: Integrated service digital network is an older broadband data/voice technology.

ISP (Internet Service Provider): A business selling access to the Internet.

ITCP/IP (Transmission Control Protocol/Internet Protocol): A series of network protocols used on the Internet for communication between computers.

LAN (Local Area Network): A computer network in a small area, such as a firm or department, connecting users through wires, hubs, and network interfaces.

Points of Presence (POPS): A POP is a local number for dialing into an ISP's network; the more POPs, the more ubiquitous the ISP's coverage.

POTS (Plain Old Telephone Service): Analog voice and transmission over a pair of copper telephone wires.

RBOC (Regional Bell Operating Company): One of the local telephone service providers that resulted from the breakup of AT&T.

SDSL: Symmetric DSL tops out at 768Kbps both upstream and downstream, and is the most popular flavor of DSL for VoSDL deployment.

Service Level Agreement (SLA): Many ISPs offer a contract that details exactly the reliability you can expect and specifies how the ISP will compensate you if performance falls below that level.

Static and dynamic IP addressing: With static IP addressing, your account always uses the same address code. Dynamic IP addressing assigns a different code each time a user logs on.

Dynamic IP addressing is fine for e-mail and Web surfing, but in order to host a Web site, your service provider must offer the more-expensive static IP addressing.

Telco: Local telephone service provider.

Virtual Private Network (VPN): A system for linking scattered telecommuters and branch offices into a unified corporate network. VPNs are expensive, but the efficiency and security they provide are worth the cost.

VoDSL: Voice over digital subscriber line.

WAN (Wide Area Network): Two or more local area networks connected to allow data to flow between the networks.

Information Sources

ISPs

    http://www.ameritech.net

    http://www.bellatlantic.net

    http://public.pacbell.net

    http://www.att.net

    http://www.earthlink.net

    http://www.us.uu.net

DSL Providers (CLECS)

    http://www.covad.com

    http://www.northpointcom.com

    http://www.rhythms.com

Telephone Companies (ILECS)

    http://www.ameritech.com

    http://www.bellatlantic.com

    http://www.bellsouth.com

    http://www.pacbell.com

http://www.sbc.com

http://www.snet.com

Cable/Satellite Providers

http://www.rr.com

http://www.tci.net

http://www.direcpc.com

http://www.helius.com

CHAPTER 6

Internet Networking Operating Systems

NETWORK INTEGRATION

Choosing a network operating system used to be about deciding which platform fit your business needs and standardizing on it. Until recently, integration tools were nonexistent. Client platforms could often be configured to access multiple disparate network servers, but little or no effort was made to integrate the user and group administration among the network operating systems.

The focus of your accounting firm's network operating systems is now vastly different; no longer must you dream of the day when all your servers run on a single platform that fulfills all your needs. Today's typical accounting firm server has every network operating system (NOS) installed in it, and choosing one above the others is not an option. These NOSes justify their presence not because of their performance, directories, or ease of use, but because an accounting firm needs those applications and services that serve the greatest goal of all: the growth of the bottom line.

Many software wars have been fought over NOSes. Proponents of NetWare, Windows NT Server, or the slew of Unix variants feel the need to push their favorite NOS as the solution to all of an accounting firm's problems. But it is not all that simple. Each NOS has its strengths, and each has its weaknesses. Unix is renowned for its stability and scalability, making it perfect for mission-critical Web sites and applications. NetWare has long been the top choice for file-and-print sharing, and Windows NT is the leading platform for application services.

The big question: How can your accounting firm manage these different systems without spending a fortune hiring additional IT staff and training users? The key is in using a standards-based approach to make the NOSes work together and in utilizing third-party tools that ease the headaches of administration.

Accounting firms are faced with the issue of lowering the administrative and user training costs that have been growing steadily as each new server platform is added. Integrating the administrative tasks on these platforms is paramount. The better your servers work together, the less time your IT staff will have to spend massaging them into cooperating, and the more the users will be able to concentrate on doing their jobs.

The costs of adding a new system to any accounting firm's IT infrastructure can be high. However, with proper training of your staff, the right tools, and a standards-based approach, the bottom-line impact of this type of integration can be kept to a minimum. It is important to examine not only the tools and procedures for integrating a small network into a medium to larger-sized accounting firm, but also the costs involved. Are expensive third-party tools needed to make things work? Will the firm's staff need to make major changes to its infrastructure?

TALENT RETENTION

Retaining talent is everything to an accounting firm. In an Internet-obsessed world of start-ups gobbling up talented accounting professionals and competitive salaries rivaling those of professional sports stars, the managing partner must resort to innovative means to hire and retain. An open source, Internet-powered accounting firm can assure its partners and professional staff that they are on a career path that is relevant and leverages the same kind of tools they used when they were in college.

So how does open source appeal to your professional staff? Open source is current and cutting edge. Open source incorporates technologies that are mainstream, not proprietary to any single third-party ISV. For example, XML, Java, and Linux would never be accused of being proprietary. Open source incorporates standards. That means your staff knows its skills are always relevant. They are not painting their career in a corner with proprietary tool-kits and technologies. XML, WML (Wireless Markup Language), Java, Servlets, and EJBs (Enterprise Java Beans) are either standard or emerging standards.

CONSTANT STATE OF CHANGE

There is a comforting feeling that comes from recognizing that some things never change — like returning from a long vacation and seeing landmarks along a familiar drive.

The driving force behind the network server provider channel has always been the penetration of emerging technologies into broad market applications. Although the Internet has replaced the PC as the driving platform, the principles remain the same — or almost the same. Some things do change. Software has moved to the center, with hardware taking more of a supporting role. Service revenue has become paramount. What remains the same for vendors serving the accounting market is that solution providers become an even more critical part of the accounting industry equation as the market widens.

As the e-business continues to evolve into becoming everyone's business, leading providers of e-business technology are scrambling to figure out how to work with accountant partners in the new environment. The Big Five's integration units are focusing on services, not product sales. New solution providers that host applications require an entirely new type of partnering. The traditional systems integration partners are moving toward an e-business services model, creating a fluid situation where old partnerships are evaporating and new ones are being formed.

From the perspective of the accounting marketplace, the emergence of the Big Five integrators over the past few years is the tip of the iceberg. Today, accounting firms of every size, shape and form have added Web integration services to their offerings. If you have not yet climbed on board the e-business train, do not worry. The train has not yet left the station. In fact, it's only just arrived.

WEB-ENABLING SOFTWARE INTEGRATION

Oracle Corporation

Oracle Corporation, best known as a database software vendor, is quickly making a name for itself as an e-business enabler. Oracle got a jump-start on rivals a few years ago when it canceled client/server development in favor of network and Web-enabled software. Oracle has become a leader in Web-enabling software. Oracle's product offering includes the flagship database Oracle 9i, various back-office enterprise resource planning applications, and front office customer relationship management applications, as well as Internet and application development tools.

The Redwood Shores–based software giant has been reorganizing inside and out, from engineering, sales, and marketing, to its relationships with the accounting channel. It has successfully moved from its image as a maker of databases to that of an e-business software company. It recognized, early on, the need to redefine product lines, and internally run its own business like an e-business.

Sun Microsystems, Inc.

Sun expanded its sales channel organization to embrace accounting firms, Web integrators, ASPs, and other partners that do not necessarily sell hardware but do influence purchasing decisions. Sun derives the bulk of its revenue from hardware sales and Java licensing. Many integrators maintain that the largest part of their business is garnered from the services, the network architecture, and the design.

Several applications solutions providers with their own proprietary applications think of their relationship with Sun as symbiotic. They use Sun products to build their infrastructure and use Sun's partnership programs to network with other solution providers. In return, Sun increases hardware and software sales.

Not only has Sun's Solaris proved to be a great Internet server, but its capability at interoperating with other NOSes and servers is top-notch. The biggest migration cost is essentially limited to the method you employ to move users from an existing system to the new one. Solaris has always been based on protocols and open standards the rest of the industry is now adopting. It enjoys a singular advantage when it comes to interoperability. Introduction of or migration to systems using IP, POP, and LDAP, for example, should be painless.

Microsoft Corporation

While Microsoft has yet to unveil all the pieces to its e-business, its program includes tools, training, and support for solution providers, including the accountant segment. What is not missing is an enormous layer of glitz that may in part be designed to cover up the vaporware status of several critical components to the company's e-commerce platform.

Aggressive tactics are the one component that Microsoft's campaigns never seem to lack. Its marketing machine has forged an alliance with Big Five affiliate KPMG Consulting LLC as well as with smaller Web integrators. To give focus within the organization to its e-business initiatives, Microsoft created an eBusiness Solutions Group.

The Redmond giant also has deals with developers such as CommerceOne Corporation, Clarus Corporation, J.D. Edwards, and Great Plains Software to push its e-business platform. The platform includes Windows 2000, BizTalk Server 2000, Commerce Server 2000, Host Integration Server 2000, SQL Server 2000, and Exchange 2000.

Microsoft partnered with KPMG to form Microsoft Dot.com Practice. In the KPMG deal, Microsoft is helping staff a lab where KPMG clients can get assistance with development projects. This program is developing a very detailed, 40-hour course for e-strategists.

Cisco Systems, Inc.

Cisco is the leading supplier of the building blocks for the e-business infrastucture. In assembling its e-business offerings, Cisco started with the main functional areas and divided e-business solutions into four key segments, which include e-commerce, supply chain management, customer care, and e-learning.

As part of its e-initiative, Cisco has expanded its training and certification programs for e-business solution providers. Cisco partners can become certified specialists in areas such as security, voice access, network management, SNA/IP network management, LAN, ATM, and SNA/IP integration—all of which can be elements of a client's e-business infrastructure.

ACHIEVING END-TO-END MANAGEMENT

At one time the network world stood distinctly separate from software and computer system administration. E-commerce has changed that in one swift stroke, requiring a new breed of Internet-savvy professional accountants with responsibility for just about everything running end-to-end throughout an infrastructure.

Integration may be the single most overused and misunderstood word in the accounting/IT world. Integration should not be viewed as a technology problem; it's a process problem IT has to become intertwined with the accounting functions. Computer Associates, Inc., for example, is trying to make its software more attractive to the e-commerce enterprise by installing individual pieces of its flagship platform management product Unicenter TNG for customers. Management of new technology such as handheld and palm devices can be easily plugged into existing desktops as normal software distribution of the extended infrastructure.

Hewlett-Packard Corporation's HP OpenView — a favorite among network administrators because of its management platform "building block" attributes, including installation ease and extensibility — offers HP OpenView VantagePoint to address the enterprise dilemma. HP OpenView Vantage Point, which runs on Unix or Microsoft Windows NT/2000, is a suite of business-centric IT management products designed to translate business services through three models of intelligence:

- **Instant Intelligence**—Visibility
- **Active Intelligence**—Problem Notification
- **Business Driven Intelligence**—Business Rules

E-commerce is not showing any signs of slowing down. Accountants should not jeopardize the future success of their firms or of their clients' operations by succumbing to the pressures of current success. Keeping a watchful eye on the changes in the industry and possessing enough flexibility to implement new features or technologies should lead to a stable management system, both in and out of the digital landscape.

MIDDLEWARE DEMYSTIFIED

Middleware is a term that expands and contracts in meaning over time and is used differently by different people with varying agendas. Essentially, middleware is software that connects applications, allowing them to exchange data. It offers several key advantages over hardwiring applications together, which typically entails adding code to all of the applications involved, and instructing them on the particulars of talking to each other. Middleware adds an independent third party to that transaction: a translator.

Why Use It?

From a business standpoint, connectivity among applications is a given necessity. Inventory, accounts receivable, and advanced planning applications need to communicate so that clients can make accurate promises to customers, and executives can make educated decisions more quickly.

E-business in particular demands better integration by an order of magnitude. That's because Web customers commonly want to see several bits of up-to-the-minute information at the same time: product specifications, availability, shipping times, and account status. Call centers have reps logged on to multiple applications (to answer those kinds of questions). That's okay when the client is paying them to do it, but when the client's customers have access to that information themselves, the connectivity becomes too complicated. Enter middleware to tie together all those apps and connect them to a Web front end, hiding the complexity from the customer.

Middleware Benefits

From a technical standpoint, middleware offers several benefits, depending on the type you choose:

- **Simplicity.** In today's corporate computing environments, many applications must share data. Putting middleware in the middle can mean each application needs only one interface — to the middleware — instead of a separate interface to each application it needs to talk to. (However, if you're connecting just two applications to one another, it might be simpler just to code the two apps to talk to each other.)
- **Persistence.** Middleware can capture data and hold on to it until it has been recorded appropriately by all the applications or databases that need the information. In technical vernacular, this ability is referred to as "persistence."
- **Services.** If data must be checked for integrity, printed out, reconciled with data from other applications, merged, split, or reformatted, various kinds of middleware can handle those tasks

efficiently. This saves rewriting those services again and again to each application that uses them. As middleware products evolve, the breadth of services they can provide grows.

Basis of Middleware Confusion

- Technology space is fraught with incomprehensible jargon because there is a lot of legitimate technical detail. (This book doesn't aspire to cover everything, just the fundamentals.)
- Vendors regularly change their terminology and product names.
- Products grow in functionality, which makes it harder to delineate categories.

Types of Middleware

It isn't uncommon for clients to have several types of middleware at work in a single enterprise, with different kinds proving more appropriate for different integration chores. Larger installations, which usually have more complex integration requirements, tend to gravitate toward more sophisticated middleware products such as EAI (Enterprise Application Integration).

RPC—RPC stands for **remote procedure call,** which means a slice of code in a client application that invokes a procedure on the server application. RPCs aren't middleware proper by today's definition. Although still in use, they're the method that modern middleware often replaces because they require programmers to rewrite them over and over when wiring a group of applications together. Other middleware approaches are often more efficient as the number of applications grows.

Database Gateways—These fit the definition of middleware better than RPCs, since they are a third party facilitating access to data. Database gateways connect applications to a particular kind of database platform. For example, consider a client with legacy applications and data residing on an HP3000 server. Many new shrink-wrapped applications are designed for accessing common databases like Oracle or Sybase, but they may need a little help connecting to the 3000's older TurboImage DBMS. That's a typical use of a database gateway.

Message-Oriented Middleware (MOM)—Included in MOM are QSeries (IBM), MSMQ (Microsoft), and SmartSockets (Talarian). Message-oriented middleware takes charge of relaying data from one application to another by putting that data in a message format, akin to the way e-mail works. As with e-mail, a key advantage of MOM is that the data from application A goes into a queue (a waiting line or holding pen, if you will) and can be retrieved later, if necessary by application B. That protects the integrity of the data if, for example, app B happens to be down for a reboot at the moment app A is trying to pass along information. With this asynchronous approach, the middleware server waits for application B to get up and running again, then hands over the data in the queue in the right sequence. (This retention of the data-bearing messages is an example of persistence.)

MOM is commonly used for simple, one-way exchanges of data where relatively few operations are being performed on the data and where the timing of the data exchange is not critical.

Transaction Processing (TP) Monitors—TP monitors include CICS, Open CICS (IBM), and BEA Tuxedo (BEA Systems). Transaction processing monitors have been around for some time (longer than MOM), having been developed originally for mainframe environments. TP monitors sit between front-end applications and back-end databases to manage the writing and reading of transactional data.

TP monitors are much more application-intrusive than message-oriented middleware. That means they demand more modification of the applications themselves in order to take advantage of the monitor's specific services. They also provide extra security and data integrity protection. The typical usage is intended for heavy transaction load environments.

Object Monitors—Object monitors include IBM Component Broker, VisiBroker Integrated Transaction Server (Imprise), and Microsoft Transaction Server.

Object monitors, also called object TP monitors, are advanced versions of the TP monitors described above. An emerging product category, object monitors provide TP monitor functionality but are built according to object-oriented specifications like the object request broker models described immediately below. This increases businesses' ability to modify the services provided by the TP monitor, for example, without requiring changes to the applications. Typical usage includes electronic commerce applications such as online shopping carts and associated ordering applications.

Object Request Brokers (ORBs) and Their Architectures—ORBs include Common Object Request Broker Architecture (Corba), Enterprise JavaBeans (EJB) (Sun Microsystems), and Component Object Model (COM+) (Microsoft).

ORBs mediate between applications and network services (security, performance monitoring, and printing, for example). They are a key part of broader architectural standards for building services and interoperable applications.

The premise behind ORBs is this: Many applications need access to the same set of services as well as to other applications. The reality of computing today is heterogeneous computing hardware and operating system platforms, plus applications built with a wide variety of development tools and languages. To get all of those components talking to each other, the enterprise needs a consistent, object-oriented architecture.

Corba is historically focused on Unix environments, while Enterprise JavaBeans is an architecture best suited for clients developing in the Java programming language. The good news is that those two standards' efforts are meshing nicely.

Microsoft's middleware architecture and product plans have evolved, and so has its terminology, which is a source of some confusion for anyone who hasn't kept up carefully. The original designation was simply COM. Next came DCOM, for distributed common object model. Microsoft has now done away with DCOM and moved on to the current name (as of this writing), COM+. COM+ is also part of a greater Microsoft architectural plan called DNA, for distributed network architecture. DNA includes products and services well beyond the scope of middleware.

Enterprise Application Integration (EAI)—EAI includes Active-Enterprise (Tibco Software), NEON (New Era of Networks), e-Gate (Software Technologies Corp. [STC]), BusinessWare (Vitria Technology), and Geneva Enterprise Integrator (EI) (Level 8 Systems).

EAI tools typically use a message broker as their underlying mechanism for data transport. In addition, they can parse, duplicate, or transform the data into a palatable format for each idiosyncratic application that needs to receive the data. The next level of functionality for EAI tools, and probably the functionality that best distinguishes

EAI from other forms of middleware, is the support for business process rules. EAI allows the user to define proper business processes and make data integration subject to those rules; for example, the data moves automatically from the purchasing application to the accounts payable application, but not until it has been signed off by the appropriate authority.

Extensible markup language (XML) support is a key addition to EAI products. With most EAI products, users purchase a central module and the specific interfaces they need. Typical usage is for large clients that need to integrate many applications.

Prognosis

Which middleware is best for your firm or your clients? There's no single answer. Different kinds of applications and integration needs are best served by different kinds of middleware. On the other hand, using a single approach can offer great economies of scale and development effort.

Some of the biggest names in the computing industry are forming a consortium to set standards for Web applications that would supercede Java and other emerging Internet standards, including HTML, XML, and HTTP. IBM, Intel, Oracle, Hewlett-Packard, and Compaq have joined with several smaller companies to form OpenServer.org (http://www.openserver.org), which plans to create a "vendor-neutral environment" to ensure the compatibility of applications developed according to open Internet standards.

The group is concerned that the ongoing battle over Java between Sun and Microsoft and the proprietary mentality of both companies are hampering the development of Web applications. Oracle and IBM have so far refused to sign licenses for Sun's Java 2 Enterprise Edition, and IBM complains often about Sun's control over Java. Microsoft, meanwhile, is a problem for everybody.

OPEN SOURCE UNIX AND LINUX

Open source software is more than the Linux operating system and the Apache Web server. Open source software is a revolution in the software industry on the scale of the PC and Internet revolutions. It will have an impact as important to business as the impact of the Internet.

With access to the source code and a robust developer community, businesses are no longer beholden to any particular vendor to meet their software needs. Open source software offers flexibility and a level of control unavailable in a traditional "closed source" software product.

Businesses, by using in-house resources or outside consultants may modify software to meet any business need. Clients no longer need to fear that strategic investments will be made worthless by a software vendor discontinuing a product or going out of business.

Time-Tested Model

The business community has only recently become widely familiar with open source software, mainly due to the rise of Linux. Further, this visibility has been associated with a lot of anti-business, anti-Microsoft flavor. In fact, the concept and operational model of open source software has been around for more than 20 years. It has proven itself as a driver of innovation, beyond what can be accomplished within any single commercial enterprise.

The Internet itself is the result of a collaboration of developers around the world in an open source model. TCP/IP protocols, BIND (the naming service for the entire Internet), SendMail (the primary mail-forwarding engine), and scripting languages (such as Perl, Python, and HTTP) are all open source.

Apache, an open source Web server, serves nearly 60 percent of all Web sites. Linux is the operating system of choice for over 30 percent of all Internet servers. Internet connectivity has enabled the open source notion of cooperative, peer-reviewed software development to be deployed on a global scale.

Natural Progression

In the 1960s and 1970s the computer industry was all about proprietary hardware and software. DEC, IBM, Wang, HP, and Data General were all in the business of building closed, proprietary systems. They waged architecture wars, claiming to have better hardware, software, and networking protocols than their competition.

The IBM PC changed all that. Not because the PC was cheaper than the older platforms, but because IBM opened up and published the PC architecture. IBM let anyone build IBM-compatible systems, as well as plug-in cards and supporting peripherals. This openness launched a revolution.

Another parallel is the Internet itself. In the mid-1980s, proprietary networking protocols, such as DECnet and SNA, were dominant. Upstarts, like Novell and 3Com, were using XNS to network PCs. Heterogeneous networks were painful at best. Governments encouraged standards bodies to come up with a solution. OSI and the nearly forgotten OSI 7-layer reference model emerged to great fanfare (and government mandate), only to be eventually overtaken and overruled by the Internet's TCP/IP. The difference was that OSI was a lumbering mass of protocols created in committee rooms, while TCP/IP was built by a distributed community of researchers writing software, trying it out, keeping what worked, throwing out what didn't, sharing their results, and constantly improving their work and the state of the art.

Open source software is the natural progression of these two forces. Opening up the internal source code is akin to publishing the specs of the IBM PC. Distributing it on the net allows cooperative, real-time, real-worked development to take place on a global scale, 24 hours a day. Key software applications can now be truly thought of as open platforms, with constant, real-world, community innovation and improvement, and upon which new software applications can be built.

In the traditional "closed source" model, a software product is, in fact, a "right to use." You purchase a right to use object code and documentation, but have no rights to the software or documentation itself. You may not copy or modify the software or its documentation.

Within the open source model the software, both object and source code, as well as the documentation is free. You may download the free product from the Internet and do with it as you wish. You may also choose to purchase the product. In that case you will get the software on a CD, printed documentation, and, most importantly, the right to get support and service. The concept of "product" has changed from one of a "right to use" to a "right to get service and support." This new solutions and value-based model is a revolutionary development for the business community.

Viable Business Models

Open source also makes sense for accounting software developers, including product developers, IT developers, and professional accounting consultants. By helping to create a set of open software standards, we create a standard platform much like the IBM PC created a standard hardware platform. This platform allows us to continue to add value at higher levels, without having to worry about fighting underlying infrastructure battles.

It also allows us to earn a healthy revenue stream via support and service revenues. We create partnerships with our clients, build tailored solutions on top of standard platforms, and provide ongoing support. An open source basis allows these solutions to be both affordable and tailored.

Real revenue opportunities exist for open source sponsors and developers:

- **Packaging.** Download software for free or pay a small amount for the convenience of a CD, manuals, and the ability to get support
- **Support.** Traditional call-center client support
- **Service.** Deployment, customization, and application development
- **Training.** Train those who provide in-house support, as well as those who support their company's product, based on an open source technology

Open source makes sense for accounting firms attempting to minimize their dependency on third-party licensing of other technologies. For other e-commerce enterprises, an open source strategy means that they control more mission-critical Web-server computing.

Business Benefits

Components of a successful open source product are real-need, commercial-quality code and a strong, accessible community. As long as these criteria are met, open source has overwhelming business benefits:

- **Unmatched Flexibility.** Make the code do exactly what you want, fix bugs in real time (don't wait for a patch release), and add features in real time (don't wait for the next release).
- **Unmatched Control/"Future-Proofness."** Unlike traditional commercial products, open source products cannot be discontinued. As long as the product meets a real need, a developer

community will exist that will enhance, modify, service, and support the code. Reliance on any single vendor is a thing of the past.

- **Robust and Reliable Code.** Open source products are tested in real-world scenarios by a larger, more diverse group of developers than possible in a commercial product.
- **Rapid Deployment.** Functional code contributions are made by a larger, more diverse group of developers than possible in a commercial product. E-mail and newsgroup collaboration links in-house developers and the community at large.
- **Client-Focused Solutions.** The only people working on the code are those who are actually using it.
- **Comprehensive Support and Service.** Ranging from free, Internet-based user groups to commercial offerings, worldwide, 24x7 support is an e-mail or posting away.
- **Lower Cost.** Open source software is free and with a huge, easily accessible open source developer community, so is the support.

There is little doubt that Open Source UNIX (OSU) and Linux in particular have a bright future, yet the overwhelming hype surrounding this phenomenon makes it difficult to discern the true shape of things to come. OSU's simplicity, reliability, low cost, and widely distributed support make it ideal for accounting firms with limited IT resources.

Early adopters have used what can be called "first wave" applications—Web servers, file and print servers, and other network support applications—as proof-of-concept for Open Source UNIX. In these areas it has performed admirably and is poised for further growth. The question remains, will Linux and BSD remain mired in this networking "ghetto," or will they make the leap into the mainstream of corporate computing, running database servers, data marts, e-commerce applications, and other heavy-duty applications? Can Open Source UNIX be trusted with mission-critical applications? Responses to a study conducted by The Accounting Guild, Las Vegas, Nevada indicated that by January 1, 2002, the server share of OSU for eight major enterprise server applications will grow by over 100 percent—and in many cases, in excess of 200 percent.

Site	%
Software Supplier/ Developer	12
Education	11
Telecommunications/ISP	9
Manufacturing	9
Systems/Hardware Supplier	9
Accounting/Consulting	8
Engineering Services	7
Professional Services	5
Government	4
Finance	3
Media	3
Retail	3
Insurance	2
Health Care	2
Transportation	2
Banking	1
Other Industry	10

Source: The Accounting Guild, Las Vegas, Nevada, *Linux Server Study,* May 2000

Exhibit 6.1 U.S. Linux Server Sites by Industry, 2000

Exhibit 6.1 indicates the composition of U.S. Linux sites by industry. Exhibit 6.2 shows the applications at the sites. The top reasons reported in the enterprise study for not deploying Open Source UNIX in order of importance are shown in Exhibit 6.3.

Applications Adoption Preferences

The top ten applications that are being considered by enterprises for hosting on Open Source UNIX are as follows (in order of likelihood):

1. Web server
2. Database server
3. Firewall
4. Web application server
5. File and print server

Application	%
Web Server	42
File/Print Server	27
E-mail Server	22
Firewall/Proxy/Cache	18
Internet/Intranet Server	18
Database	10
Application Development	9
Application Server	6
Experimental/Testing	5
Router/Gateway	5
Networking	3
Systems Management	3
Backup	2
VPN	2
Accounting Applications	1

Percentages add to more than 100 due to multiple answers from some respondents.
Source: The Accounting Guild, Las Vegas, Nevada, *Linux Server Study,* May 2000

Exhibit 6.2 Linux Server Applications at U.S. Sites, 2000

- Lack of application support
- No perceived business benefit
- Lack of technical support
- No perceived technical benefit
- Lack of internal expertise

Source: The Accounting Guild, Las Vegas, Nevada, *Open Source UNIX Study,* May 2000

Exhibit 6.3 Reasons for Nondeployment of OSU

6. E-commerce
7. Data warehouse/data mart
8. Messaging (e-mail)
9. Network infrastructure
10. Software development

The most common hardware platform for Open Source UNIX is Intel. It is one of the ironies of the computing industry that Microsoft's monopoly of operating systems over the last few years, by helping to create the commodity Wintel platform, also created a nourishing ecological niche for its most credible challenger.

Next to Intel, Sun's 32-bit SPARC is the second most common platform. As the only major UNIX systems vendor that does not also offer Windows NT/2000 on its hardware, this puts Sun in an interesting and delicate position.

Disruptive Technology

Some of the more interesting data to result from The Accounting Guild's study came from examining the changing fortunes of various operating systems. This data confirms that OSU will enjoy robust growth over the next two years, while simultaneously debunking the hype concerning OSU's role as a "Windows killer."

Open Source Requires Community

All the benefits of open source are derived from the interplay of two forces:

1. Access to the source code
2. A community of interested developers

Both elements are required to have an effective open source product. Access to source code means than anybody can become an expert. Anybody can feel that they can answer questions of fellow developers. Experts become visible and well known on mailing lists, inspiring others to "rise through the ranks" to become fellow experts.

Conversely, beware of commercial products that are suddenly reborn as open source. No matter how popular the contributed technology, if there's no community, there's no vitality or "ecosystem" to support that

- Proprietary UNIX (any)
- NetWare
- Windows NT 4.0 Server
- Windows 2000 Server
- AS/400
- Mainframe
- Windows NT 3.5x Server

Source: The Accounting Guild, Las Vegas, Nevada, *Open Source UNIX Study,* May 2000

Exhibit 6.4 Network O/S Most Likely to Be Displaced by OSU

- Windows NT 3.5x Desktop
- Windows 95/98
- Windows NT 4.0 Desktop
- Windows 2000 Professional

Source: The Accounting Guild, Las Vegas, Nevada, *Open Source UNIX Study,* May 2000

Exhibit 6.5 Desktop O/S Most Likely to Be Replaced by OSU

technology. It is extremely difficult to build community. The process of natural selection is alive and well in the open source process. This is important and good news for you and your accounting profession's goals.

Exhibit 6.4 depicts the enterprise server operating systems most likely to be replaced by Open Source UNIX. Exhibit 6.5 lists the desktop operating systems most likely to be replaced by Open Source UNIX.

CHAPTER 7

Accounting Software Online and Off

ACCOUNTING: EVERY BUSINESS'S MISSION-CRITICAL APPLICATION

There aren't many applications more mission-critical than accounting. End users and accountants alike have to overcome the common misconception that there hasn't been much development or change to accounting applications. It simply isn't so. What is happening is a shift in the minds of business management, large and small, of accounting from merely reconciling the corporate checkbook to a more powerful business management tool. This shift places accounting applications in the same arena as other new technology tools such as data warehousing. This is accomplished by directly linking accounting systems to the business's e-commerce system to reduce the unnecessary expenses of rekeying inventory levels to account for Web-based transactions.

Even if the client isn't ready to make the jump to a fully integrated accounting solution, chances are they could get better mileage out of a Windows-based accounting system upgrade or transition to an online accounting solution. The newer programs are generally easier to learn and are more customizable than programs a few generations old. However, many accountants have refused to upgrade clients' systems out of fear of change and the notorious reputation Windows' applications previously had for crashing. In order to be successful, accounting professionals must alleviate any lingering doubts as to the stability of Windows' applications. An excellent approach would be to install the client's books on an online system and completely circumvent Windows' applications.

Before implementing a new accounting system or an upgrade, make certain the following is true:

- The software can be customized as the needs of the client change.
- The program offers a clear path toward e-commerce interoperability.
- The application offers multi-currency and multilingual capabilities.

Small business clients run their accounting applications for long stretches of time so it's critical for accountants to select their accounting software applications wisely and for the long term.

The accounting marketplace has grown substantially more comfortable with surfing the Internet. Less than 10 percent of small businesses—companies with under 100 employees—had a Web site in 1996. Now approximately 43 percent of the nation's small business marketplace have Web sites.

With the Web's ubiquity, more and more businesses are assuming that their trading partners will be online as well. Small businesses are using e-commerce as a major criteria when evaluating their accounting software options.

ACCOUNTING SOFTWARE CATEGORIES

Accounting software has been designated by the developers of the various commercial products as belonging to a particular category. The five accounting software categories are as follows:

- Enterprise Client/Server
- High-End Client/Server
- High-End
- Mid-Range
- Low-End

Example of Software Programs by Category and Costs

Enterprise Client/Server: $1 Million–$50 Million

SAP
Oracle Financials
J.D. Edwards

High-End Client/Server: $30,000–$100,000
> Dynamics C/S+
> Platinum SQL
> Acuity

High-End: $5,000–$35,000
> Dynamics
> MAS 90 Windows
> Platinum

Mid-Range: $2,000–$5,000
> Business Works
> Traverse

Low-End: $200
> NetLedger
> Peachtree
> QuickBooks

Typical Client Business Revenue

It is helpful to further identify the various software categories by the annual revenues of their typical business clients.

- Enterprise Client/Server — More than $100 Million
- High-End Client/Server — Less than $100 Million
- High-End — Less than $25 Million
- Mid-Range — Less than $10 Million
- Low-End — Less than $5 Million

Difference between Categories

The categories of accounting software differ with respect to criteria in terms relative to the following:

- Faster performance
- More features

- More expensive
- More difficult to deploy

Foundational Database Listed by Popularity

The foundational database that powers the software is listed in the order of popularity (sales).

1. MS SQL Server
2. Btrieve
3. Oracle
4. MS Access
5. Proprietary
6. Btrieve Scalable SQL
7. IBM DB2
8. Informix
9. Sybase SQL Server
10. OS/400
11. Scalable SQL
12. FoxBase
13. MS SQL Server Enterprise Edition
14. Centura SQLBase
15. dBase
16. Gupta SQLBase

Leading Client/Server Accounting Software Programs

The leading Client/Server accounting software programs in terms of sales are listed with their approximate suggested resale price at the time this book was written. The suggested resale prices are provided only for guidance purposes as software pricing fluctuates widely and is under intense competitive pressures.

- Navision Financials ($30,000)
- Great Plains Dynamics C/S+ ($50,000)
- State of the Art's Acuity ($30,000)
- Platinum SQL NT ($50,000)
- SBT Executive Series ($50,000)
- Solomon IV for Windows ($50,000)

High-End Accounting Software

High-End accounting software includes programs that are also the most likely candidates for online conversion. Within a relatively short period these programs will be offered by their developers, by ASPs, or by other financially stronger rivals, who will acquire and offer or consolidate the program. The following High-End accounting software programs are listed alphabetically and not in any particular order of rank or popularity.

- ACCPAC for Windows
- Great Plains Dynamics
- Macola Progression
- MAS 90 for Windows
- Navision Financials
- Platinum for Windows
- SBT ProSeries
- Solomon IV for Windows
- Traverse

Leading Mid-Range Accounting Software Programs

The leading Mid-Range accounting software programs are versions that have been primarily produced by the developers of the High-End for smaller business that would not readily purchase the higher-priced versions with more bells and whistles. Many of the developers and their value-added resellers use the Mid-Range software as a stepping-stone to a future High-End installation. The features of the various programs tend to be very similar and a level of commoditization has evolved. The intense competition in this sector has resulted in many takeovers and other forms of consolidation. The programs and their suggested resale pricing are listed in random order.

- Great Plains Dynamics ($6,000)
- MAS 90 for Windows ($5,500)
- Platinum for Windows ($6,800)
- SBT ProSeries ($5,300)
- Macola Progression ($7,300)
- Navision Financials ($6,000)
- Solomon IV for Windows ($6,000)

ACCOUNTING SOFTWARE PARTNERING

Application Hosting

Clients are having difficulty finding the information technology talent to run their own accounting departments. Many accounting services providers are concentrating on the application (accounting) solutions market. They are positioning their service offerings to exploit the situation of customers who are tired of shoveling money into new systems, software, and maintenance who will hand the keys to their accounting data to someone else to run at another site. The theory is that the vendor shoulders all the cost of keeping the system running, while the user can access the software from anywhere and doesn't have to worry about continually upgrading to the latest version.

Middle-market accounting software providers are also under pressure to formulate hosting strategies if only to combat high-end enterprise players attempting to move into their market space. Oracle, for example, is backing NetLedger, a San Mateo, California–based developer of online accounting software that has already drawn tens of thousands of users. J.D. Edwards recently entered a hosting partnership with MCI to deliver financial and other enterprise applications via the Internet.

BEYOND ACCOUNTING

It's not just accounting software providers who are exploring ASP. Tax software developers are also getting in on the action. RIA's GoSystem Tax RS (for Remote Server) is proving to be very successful.

Hosting offers the same attraction in the tax market: quick, easy accessibility from anywhere with an Internet connection. The appeal may be even greater for the tax business if firms can avoid the frequent software updates by accessing applications from the browser.

Practice Management

Elite Information Group in Los Angeles has formed an Internet subsidiary to provide online, hosted, time-and-billing services. The unit, Elite.com, will compete heads on with rival start-ups like Boston-based TimeBills.com.

Market Prognosis

Accounting services providers should welcome the trend. It represents increased income opportunities. Electronic business is always going to be business. All clients are going to have to perform some transactions electronically.

Accounting Software Vendor Resources

ACCPAC International
Pleasanton, CA
www.accpac.com

Bizfinity, Inc.
1601 South De Anza Boulevard, Suite 255
Cupertino, CA 95014
877-789-3464 (toll free)
www.Bizfinity.com

Creative Solutions, Inc.
7322 Newman Boulevard
Dexter, MI 48130
800-968-8900
www.creativesolutions.com

CYMA Systems, Inc.
2330 W. University Drive, Suite 7
Tempe, AZ 85281
800-292-2962
www.cyma.com

Cougar Mountain Software
7180 Potomac Drive
Boise, ID 83702
800-388-3038
www.cougarmtn.com

Great Plains Software
Fargo, ND
www.greatplains.com

Macola Software
Marion, OH
www.macola.com

Micronetics International
621 NW 53rd Street, Suite 240
Boca Raton, FL 33487
561-995-1477
www.axpert.com

Navision Software
500 Pinnacle Court, Suite 510
Norcross, GA 30071
800-552-8478
www.navision-us.com

NetLedger, Inc.
2955 Campus Drive, Suite 175
San Mateo, CA 94403
650-627-1000
www.netledger.com

Peachtree Software
1505 Pavilion Place
Norcross, GA 30093
770-724-4000
www.peachtree.com

Red Wing Software
Red Wing, MN
800-732-9464
www.redwingsoftware.com

RIA Group
345 Hudson Street
New York, NY 10014
800-431-9025
www.RIAhome.com

Sage Software Inc.
Irvine, CA
800-854-3415
www.sage.com

Solomon Software
Findlay, OH
www.solomon.com

Syspro Impact Software, Inc.
959 South Coast Drive, Suite 100
Costa Mesa, CA 92626
800-369-8649
www.sysprousa.com

Tax and Accounting Software
6914 S. Yorktown Avenue
Tulsa, OK 74136
800-998-9990
www.taascforce.com

The Versatile Group
4410 Spring Valley Road
Dallas, TX 75244
800-237-8435
www.tvginc.com

UniLink, Inc.
P.O. Box 1630
Jackson, WY 83001
800-456-8321
www.unilink-inc.com

Virtual Growth (Virtual Accountant)
118 West 22 Street, 11th Floor
New York, NY 10011
212-651-0241
www.virtualgrowth.com

Application Software Providers (ASPs)

Bizfinity, Inc.
1601 S. DeAnza Boulevard, Suite 255
Cupertino, CA 95014
877-789-3464
www.bizfinity.com

NetLedger, Inc.
2955 Campus Drive, Suite 175
San Mateo, CA 94403
650-627-1000
www.netledger.com

Virtual Growth (Virtual Accountant)
118 West 22nd Street, 11th Floor
New York, NY 10011
212-651-0241
www.virtualgrowth.com

Other Software Resources

Benefits

DATAIR Employee Benefit Systems, Inc.
735 N. Cass Avenue
Westmont, IL 60559
630-325-2600
www.datair.com

Checkwriters

Greatland Corporation
P. O. Box 1157
Grand Rapids, MI 49501
800-968-1099
www.micr1.com

Construction

American Contractor (The)
1500 41st Avenue, Suite 1-A
Capitola, CA 95010
800-333-8435
www.AmerCon.com

Industry Specific Software
1200 Woodruff Road, Suite B20
Greenville, SC 29607
800-877-2496
www.iss-software.com

Development Tools

Nelco
3130 S. Ridge Road
Green Bay, WI 54304
888-316-4340
www.wageforms.com

Direct Deposit

National Payment Corporation
100 W Kennedy Boulevard, Suite 260
Tampa, FL 33602
800-284-0113
www.directdeposit.com

Estate, Financial, and Retirement Planning

Cowan Financial Group
530 Fifth Avenue
New York, NY 10036
Richard Frazer (National Accountants' Specialist)
rfrazer@cowanfinancial.com

Financial Profiles, Inc.
5421 Avenida Encinas, Suite A
Carlsbad, CA 92008
800-237-6335
www.profiles.com

Financial

Financial Navigator International
254 Polaris Avenue
Mountain View, CA 94043
800-468-3636
www.finnav.com

Lumen Systems, Inc.
4300 Stevens Creek Blvd., Suite 270
San Jose, CA 95129
800-233-3461

usAdvisor, Inc.
1380 Lead Hill Road, Suite 145
Roseville, CA 95661
887-272-4636
www.usAdvisor.com

Fixed Assets

CCH Incorporated
21250 Hawthorne Blvd.
Torrance, CA 90503
800-739-9998
www.prosystemfx.com

Creative Solutions, Inc.
7322 Newman Boulevard
Dexter, MI 48130
800-968-8900
www.creativesolutions.com

Worth IT Software
2700 Matheson Boulevard, Suite 700 (W. Tower)
Mississauga, Ontario L4W 4V9
Canada

Internet Resources

Accounting Guild
8713 Short Putt Drive
Las Vegas, NV 89134
702-242-8725
www.accountingguild.com

Accounting Web
www.accountingweb.com

Electronic Accountant
www.electronicaccountant.com

Execusite
8001 Irvine Center Drive, 4th Floor
Irvine, CA 92618
877-393-2874
www.execusite.com

Greatland Corporation (Cytax)
2480 Walker Avenue NW
Grand Rapids, MI 49501
800-968-1099
www.cytax.com

Pro2Net.com (Formerly AccountingNet)
1730 Minor Avenue
Seattle, WA 98101
888-552-7762
www.Pro2Net.com

Inventory

Syspro Impact Software, Inc.
959 South Coast Drive, Suite 100
Costa Mesa, CA 92626
800-369-8649
www.sysprousa.com

Not-for-Profit

American Fundware
1385 S. Colorado Boulevard, Suite 400
Denver, CO 80222
800-551-4458
www.fundware.com

Blackbaud
4401 Belle Oaks Drive
Charleston, SC 29405
800-443-9441
www.blackbaud.com

Executive Data Systems
1640 Powers Ferry Road, Bldg. 27
Marietta, GA 30067
800-272-3374
www.execdata.com

FUND E-Z Development Corporation
106 Corporate Park Drive
White Plains, NY 10604
914-696-0900
www.fundez.com

Payroll

Advanced Micro Solutions
1709 S. State Street
Edmund, OK 73013
800-536-1099
www.1099-etc.com

Automatic Data Processing (ADP)
1 ADP Boulevard
Roseland, NJ 07068
www.adp.com

Paychex
Rochester, NY
www.paychex.com

Payroll Associates, Inc.
840 N. Lenola Road, Suite 6
Moorestown, NJ 08057
856-231-4667
www.paychoice.com

Phoenix Phive Software
7830 E. Gelding Drive, Suite 400
Scottsdale, AZ 85260
800-331-1811
www.phoenixphive.com

ProTym Systems
14023 N.E. 8th Street
Bellevue, WA 98007
800-451-4750
www.protym.com

UBCC
P.O. Box 768
Taos, NM 87571
800-827-8610
www.ubcc.com

UniLink, Inc.
P.O. Box 1630
Jackson, WY 83001
800-456-8321
www.unilink-inc.com

Point-of-Sale

CAP Automation
3500 Marquita Drive
Ft. Worth, TX 76116
800-826-5009
www.capautomation.com

Synchronics
1727 Kirby Parkway
Memphis, TN 38120
800-852-5852
www.sync-link.com

Practice Management/Time and Billing

BalaBoss
1 W. Pearce Street, Suite 405
Richmond Hill, Ontario L4B 3K3
Canada
888-635-1111
www.BalaBoss.com

CPASoftware
One Pensacola Plaza
Pensacola, FL 32501
800-272-7123
www.cpasoftware.com

CaseWare International, Inc.
2425B Channing Way, Suite 590
Berkeley, CA 94704
800-267-1317
www.caseware.com

Elite.com
5100 W. Goldleaf Circle, Suite 100
Los Angeles, CA 90056
323-642-5200
www.elite.com

ON-Q Software, Inc.
13764 SW 11th Street
Miami, FL 33184
800-553-2862
www.on-qsoftware.com

Time Matters Software
215 Commonwealth Court
Cary, NC 27511
800-328-2898
www.timematters.com

Timeslips
17950 Preston Road, Suite 800
Dallas, TX 75252
800-285-0999
www.timeslips.com

Property Management

Old Forest Software, Inc.
300 Petttigru Street
Greenville, SC 29601
800-562-0661
www.propertyboss.com

Promas/CMS, Inc.
311B Maple Avenue W.
Vienna, VA 22180
888-591-5179
www.promas.com

Property Automation Software Corporation
1100 Centennial Blvd., Suite 230
Richardson, TX 75081
800-964-2792
www.propertyautomation.com

Tax Forms

Nelco
3130 S. Ridge Road
Green Bay, WI 54304
888-316-4340
www.taxforms.com

STF Services Corporation
26 Corporate Circle
East Syracuse, NY 13057
800-541-7197
www.stfservices.com

Tax Preparation

Creative Solutions, Inc.
7322 Newman Boulevard
Dexter, MI 48130
800-968-8900
www.creativesolutions.com

Drake Enterprises, Ltd.
235 E. Palmer Street
Franklin, NC 28734
800-890-9500
www.drakesoftware.com

Lacerte Software
13155 Noel Road, Suite 2200
Dallas, TX 75240
800-445-1863
www.lscsoft.com

Orrtax Software, Inc.
13208 N.E. 20th Street
Bellevue, WA 98005
800-377-3337
www.intellitax.com

RIA
395 Hudson Street
New York, NY 10014
800-431-9025
www.RIAhome.com

TaascFORCE
6914 S. Yorktown Avenue
Tulsa, OK 74136
800-998-9990
www.taascforce.com

Tax Works by Laser Systems
350 N. 400 W.
Kaysville, UT 84037
800-230-2322
www.taxworks.com

Universal Tax Systems, Inc.
6 Mathis Drive NW
Rome, GA 30165
800-755-9473
www.taxwise.com

Trial Balance

ePace! Software
1400 N. Bristol, Suite 220
Newport Beach, CA 92660
877-693-7223
www.epacesoftware.com

Write-Up

Client Accounting Systems, Inc.
8616 La Tijera Blvd., Suite 408
Los Angeles, CA 90045
800-350-7696
www.clientaccounting.com

Howell Client Accounting Software/ABS Systems
605 Crescent Executive Court, Suite 300
Lake Mary, FL 32746
888-444-3564
www.mrasystems.com

Micronetics, International
One Park Place
621 NW 53rd Street, Suite 240
Boca Raton, FL 33487
561-995-1477
www.axpert.com

PC Software Accounting, Inc.
P.O. Box 4614
Sarasota, FL 34230
800-237-9234
www.pcsai.com

The Versatile Group
4410 Spring Valley Road
Dallas, TX 75244
800-237-8435
www.tvginc.com

CHAPTER 8

Application Software Providers

THE ASP MARKET

The ASP market evolved out of Internet service providers (ISPs) as a response to client demands for lower-cost application services. According to International Data Corporation (IDC), holder of one of the computer industry's largest crystal balls, worldwide spending on ASP services will be $2 billion by 2003. ASPs are an example of the old adage that the more things change, the more they stay the same.

What Is an ASP?

Broadly defined, the concept is the delivery of a software application over a network (such as the Internet) using pay-as-you-go pricing. Primarily targeted at small or midsize clients that cannot afford their own accounting, IT departments, or computing infrastructures, the ASP offering is compelling.

The client gets a fully functioning, big-time application (such as enterprise resource planning software) and accesses it through the Internet or a private network without having to pay for the installation, the hardware, or the software. A monthly fee that amortizes the ASP's costs of installing and maintaining the application over time, as well as a healthy little profit margin, is the client's fixed obligation.

Background

The ASP model of leasing applications (contracts generally run between one and three years) is having the same impact on small and mid-sized clients that the car leasing market is having on income-challenged car buyers: It lets them sign up for more powerful, sophisticated applications than they ever could have dreamed of owning outright. Of course, the same kinds of downsides apply: no equity, very little control over the applications, and some potentially harsh consequences for opting out before the contract expires.

At one level an ASP is nothing more than an Internet-enabled version of the old service bureau model. On another level, however, ASPs are a new and different way of delivering access to applications and related services. Service bureaus were popular in the 1970s and 1980s as a way to deliver applications to clients that couldn't afford computer centers. As computing power became cheaper, and more programmers entered the job market, many clients created their own data centers in the 1980s and 1990s.

In the mid 1990s there was a huge debate about whether clients should outsource computer center management. This movement was driven by corporate re-engineering initiatives popular during that period. Many outsourcers focused on managing a client's IT infrastructure as transparently as possible.

The outsourcers often hired the client's IT and accounting staff and managed its computer systems at the client's site. Most organizations that outsource applications, however, tended to limit them to accounting and finance applications or desktop deployment and helpdesk services.

Many client organizations retained control over business applications that represented a core business competency. The advent of packaged applications in the mid to late 1990s changed that dynamic and many clients decided to implement enterprise resource planning (ERP) software as a way of gaining competitive advantage. What they discovered is that the expertise required to effectively implement packaged applications is expensive and elusive.

Characteristics

The ASP represents the convergence of the service bureau, outsourcing, and packaged application business models. The ASP model is different from these other models in several ways:

1. The ASP hosts applications at a centralized data center belonging to the ASP, not the client.
2. ASPs tend to offer pre-configured packaged applications and typically don't manage customized applications written by, or for, the client.

3. ASPs usually support multiple clients in their data centers, enabling them to leverage and amortize their investment in equipment, infrastructure, and personnel.
4. ASPs deliver applications and services to the desktop using Internet technology. These services may be delivered using a private network, but increasingly ASPs are delivering software to end users over the public Internet. This is especially true for smaller clients that can't afford a virtual private network. This low-cost access is offset, however, by the unreliability, inconsistent throughput, and potential for security breaches on the Internet.

Advantages of Using an ASP

- The ASP model enables clients to reduce expenditures on hardware, applications, and staff.
- It allows clients to focus limited resources on core business functions.
- ASPs tend to have a professional staff that can afford to pay closer attention to availability, security, backup, disaster recovery, and customer support than internal IT organizations.
- The ASP model makes it easier to keep current with technology.

Exhibit 8.1 lists various Application Software Provider segments.

THE ASP MARKET HOLDS PLENTY OF PROMISE

Taking a close look at the application software provider (ASP) market is a bit like visiting Disneyland. You start off starry-eyed, but sooner or later you have to leave Fantasyland. At first, the ASP market appears to be a ripe opportunity for accounting professionals that are eager to serve small to mid-sized businesses. The sales pitch goes something like this: For a "nominal" monthly fee (usually about $20 per client desktop), an ASP can host mission-critical applications that a small business otherwise couldn't afford. The market researchers see plenty of dollar signs.

ASPs are doing for applications what the Internet did for data. They are making them universally available, affordable, and easier to deploy. The ASPs' reach into small and mid-sized clients is establishing a solid sales and referral foundation that will eventually spark an irrevocable

- Accounting Firms
- Accounting Software Providers
- Internet Service Firms
- Application Vendors
- Software Vendors
- Business Process Outsourcers
- Systems/Network Integrators
- IT/Business Consulting Firms
- Telecommunications/Network Providers
- Systems/Storage Vendors
- Value-Added Resellers
- Internet Portals
- Venture Capital/Investment Firms

Source: The Accounting Guild, Las Vegas, Nevada, *Accounting Solutions Provider Study,* May 2000

Exhibit 8.1 Application Software Provider Segments

change in the ways that all clients, regardless of size, buy professional accounting services.

Both established players and new entrants want a share of the market. Accounting firms, other professional services entities, ISVs, ISPs, hardware vendors, network and telecommunications providers, software developers, and ASPs are all jockeying for an inside position.

The ASP market holds plenty of promise for the accounting profession. Many in the accounting industry believe the ASP hype makes sense. The market certainly sounds right to those who worked in the service bureau and time-sharing markets.

The Promises

The allure of the ASP sales pitch is that it removes the two primary barriers that have kept clients from buying technology on their own. First to go is technology complexity. Buying software has always meant having to buy at once all the technology necessary to support it: networks, hardware and support software. The ASPs or accounting professionals remove that complexity from the equation—theoretically, at least—by providing all the supporting technology themselves. Clients buy a business service — customer service, accounting, human resources and benefits, logistics — rather than a software application and all that goes with it.

The second banished fear factor is risk. Pay-as-you-go pricing transfers much of the economic burden of buying software to the ASP. There are no big consulting fees or hardware purchases up front, just the monthly fee. ASP vendors make no bones about their target audience. They sell to the accounting function (CFO), and not to the IT department or CIO.

ASPs, and accountants with an ASP offering, target and have an advantage in the small and mid-sized client market because they have a skeletal (if any) IT department and, for the most part, they lack a CIO. The talent pool for qualified IT people — especially in hot areas like electronic commerce — is so tight that clients face a difficult choice: Either bring in outsiders like ASPs (with their attendant risks) or hold up the business while searching (often in vain) for qualified staff to do the needed work.

ADVISING A CLIENT ABOUT CHOOSING TO USE AN ASP

Consider these client factors when deciding whether to recommend or resell ASP services:

- Renting a packaged application is more advantageous than purchasing the package.
- Organization is large and distributed.
- Clients' desire to leverage Internet technology to deliver greater value to users.
- The business environment is dependent on keeping up with technological change.
- The control of data is not an issue.
- Customized applications are not necessary.

NEGOTIATING AN ASP DEAL

You need to do your homework and make sure the ASP you select has the ability to deliver the services you need. Be careful to negotiate good service level agreements, with appropriate penalties if the ASP doesn't deliver. Be sure your ASP has the staff to manage your systems, including developers, network administrators, and database administrators. Get to know these people and make sure the ones you met during the proposal stage will still be on the project once the contract is signed.

Questions to Be Asked and Answered

1. How dependable is the ASP?
2. What are the service level agreements (SLAs)?
3. What are the dimensions of the necessary support staff?
4. What are the clear and definable parameters of the infrastructure each party is to manage?
5. What are the security designs of the infrastructure?
6. Who owns the data generated by the application?
7. Is there an extra fee charged for accessing or extracting the data?
8. What happens if the ASP is acquired or goes out of business?
9. Would you rather rent an application than buy one?

ASPs' CONTRACT CHECKLIST

The same things that make ASPs so tempting — no network or application license fees to pay, no servers to upgrade, no support or implementation staff to carry — also make them considerably risky. The newness of the market and the labyrinth of intertwined vendors that lurk beneath the shells of most ASP offerings add fragility to even the best-written ASP contracts.

1. *Keep the contract term as short as possible.*
   No one knows what Web hosting will look like in six years. Mainframe outsourcing contracts used to be 10 years. Writing a contract for excessive periods will only lock you into an argument with a vendor.

2. *Benchmark through vendor competition.*
   Pricing for ASP services is still in the "Well, it depends" phase. Most accountants and clients benchmark ASP prices by trying to estimate what it would cost to provide those services themselves. But how can you reliably build in all the cost compo-

nents if you've never done them before? Instead, have three or four ASPs submit detailed bids for your work.

3. *Establish a metric — any metric — that tracks usage growth.*
   If you don't agree on a metric to measure growth against the price of the service, when the contract renews you could find yourself at the mercy of a vendor that exploits the lack of data to justify a surreal cost increase. Use one or two simple metrics (for example, the number of users of the ASP application, the number of transactions processed through the e-commerce Web site, or the number of business documents developed using the application) in order to track the growth in usage. Agree on a firm price for how much more the service will cost as usage grows.

4. *Create performance penalties that truly motivate.*
   ASPs make more money by serving as many clients as possible. If stretched, as most inevitably are, they will respond first to the contract that screams the loudest. Make the penalties escalate each time a problem recurs. Extend the interval for counting recurrences over as long a period as possible — at least a few months.

5. *Have an out that won't cost you anything.*
   In case of chronic underperformance, you'll need to be able to get out of the contract and find a new ASP. Expensive exit fees and troublesome software ownership clauses can get in the way. You need to be able to get out clean and take whatever you need — data, customized applications — with you. If this means having to buy licenses for your customized software up front, it could well be worth the extra money. Otherwise, the ASP owns your software, and you may be stuck if you want to make a switch.

6. *Don't expect to cut costs unless you want lower levels of service too.*
   The chances are your ASP contract will be for niche services rather than massive outsourcing. Don't expect to save money on a niche offering. The scale isn't there for the vendor to customize it to your needs and run it cheaply too. Most outsourcers try to keep profit margins above 25 percent, which means that the vendor has to run the application at 65 percent of your cost

of running it to make the margin back and lower your costs by 10 percent. That's not easy to do. The outsourcer has to drastically cut its own costs to get a profit and cut the client's costs. And then they are being asked to improve service levels. This is a major reason that SLAs fail. The client is expecting both, and that equation just doesn't balance.

ASPs FROM A TO Z

Application software provider (ASP) is a service that hosts and manages software for a client, especially applications used for the internal operations of the client.

Bandwidth that is cheap, plentiful, and reliable is a necessary prerequisite to Web delivery of critical applications.

Colocation is the hosting of the hoster, wherein an ASP sets up its servers at the heavy-duty data center of an Exodus Communications (www.exodus.com), UUnet (www.uu.net), et al. Some ASPs have their own facilities. As infrastructure players, the colocation companies have one of the most attractive business models in the ASP industry.

Dot.coms are a natural constituency for the ASPs, which can scale down to meet the needs of a start-up and then scale up to meet rapid growth, all the while off-loading the expense of an information technology staff.

Estimates of the ASP market range from huge to enormous, depending on the definition of terms. To ask if it's really going to be a $20 billion market by 2003 misses the point: If the market behaves like it's supposed to, a great deal of businesses will be using it before long.

Funding from venture capitalists is available for young ASPs, provided a market correction doesn't melt down the entire stock market.

Guarantees from ASPs makes customers feel better about locating critical applications outside their direct control—but could hurt the service providers' bottom lines if they don't live up to their promises.

Hype is in plentiful supply in this sector, percolating at roughly the level that surrounded the introduction of the PC.

Integration of several applications from different vendors is a selling point for many ASPs, while another ASP called CSPSource (www. cspsource.com) promises the next logical phase: integrating hosted services.

Jargon is as plentiful as hype, from the category-defining acronym to colocation services with clustered servers hosting your app-on-tap.

Killing off conventional methods of delivering software, such as the CD-ROM, is what its more aggressive proponents say the ASP model will do.

Large companies such as dot.coms as well as smaller to mid-sized clients have become an increasingly important target market for ASPs.

Managing applications is an expensive business, so figuring out how to grow while controlling personnel costs will be a key to success for hosters.

Nothing is what some ASPs charge for their services, but they all expect something in return.

Online or Internet-based accounting offers custom applets appended to users' Web browsers, permitting use of core accounting software from remote locations.

Profits are a distant rumor for most ASPs, but the pressure to explain where they'll come from will increase as time goes on.

Quick implementation, even of intricate systems such as Enterprise Resource Planning (ERP), is a promise that ASPs are keeping.

Rental income is how most ASPs plan to make money, though many sell big packages such as ERP on a lease-to-own deal, and some don't charge users at all.

Staff, or lack thereof, is one of the charms of an ASP from the client point of view, as the client doesn't need to hire expensive staff to implement and maintain its software.

Time is not on the side of many "ASPiring" providers as their venture capital is not replenished by operating profits.

Usinternetworking (www.usinternetworking.com), a leading ASP, booked $75 million in new business during its first quarter, with 42 new service contracts.

Vertical service provider is an industry portal on steroids. The VSP is an ASP that rents applications to a particular industry, also providing access to other business services and relevant content.

Web-enabled software is a must for ASPs, giving start-ups that have developed their applications specifically for ASP delivery an edge over their more established competitors.

XML and XBRL are the new Internet designed languages that accelerate ASP offerings.

Years of predictable earnings from renting applications, rather than fat and lean quarters from selling them, are the reason software companies like the ASP business.

Zero is the number of large, established clients yet to convert to hosted applications for their core business systems.

AGGREGATORS, BSPs, MSPs: THE NEXT GENERATION SERVICE PROVIDERS

One presenter at a recent accounting society meeting joked that the job of an analyst is to invent new acronyms—the more numerous and confusing the better. In the hosting field, she may be right.

Enter the BSPs—Business Solution Providers—a term coined by one of the early players in the space, eConvergent. eLoyalty is another entrant in this nascent market. BSPs not only offer hosted solutions, they also provide integration and consulting services. BSPs represent the new way business solutions will be delivered. In the older model the client had to go around and select products and then arrange to integrate them or find an integrator. The BSP model provides one point of contact for managing the many vendors in a complex business solution.

Management service providers, or MSPs, represent another viable alternative to internally hosted management applications. Because hosting client applications is their primary business, MSPs can offer a scalable, rentable infrastructure that most clients, especially smaller to mid-sized businesses, simply cannot build from scratch for lack of time and money. Management platform vendor Hewlett-Packard estimates that deploying its internally hosted software and similar products costs three to nine times the price of the software itself, plus staff costs.

The key question that must be asked is whether there's strategic benefit in owning management technology. Clients and accounting firms that turn important business applications over to outsiders relinquish control when they outsource an important IT function. It's impossible to keep the same real-time tabs on performance of Web sites, applications, and networks when this information is in the hands of an outsider. So it's critical to spell out contractually with whatever ASP, BSP, or MSP your firm selects, what level of responsiveness, access to data, and oversight your practice requires.

ASP aggregators have entered the fray and offer one-stop shopping for hosted application services. Aggregators such as Agiliti Inc., Jamcracker Inc., and ePanacea.com Inc. help clients by bringing together services offered by multiple ASPs. They provide the client with a single point of contact for contracting ASP services; accessing those services over the Web; tracking performance; and if necessary, finding new ASP providers should service levels fall short of expectations. Moreover, these aggregators claim to be able to do this at little or no premium over what the individual ASPs would charge.

Sometimes selling through partners, such as system integrators, accounting firms, consultants or ISPs, these ASP aggregators are initially targeting small and mid-sized clients. The aggregators say they can match ASP pricing because they are able to negotiate wholesale rates from ASPs, which then no longer have to spend money to market to and sign up new clients.

Some clients are resisting a relationship with an aggregator and say they would rather work directly with the ASPs that are hosting the applications than through another party that is yet another step removed from the data center. The more fingers one has in the pie, the more complex projects tend to get.

Aggregators counter that, rather than adding an unnecessary administrative layer between clients and ASPs, they offer extra protection for clients. Along with tying disparate hosted applications into a single platform, aggregators say they can help distinguish trustworthy ASPs from fly-by-night operators. Jamcracker, for example, views itself as an aggregator of best-of-breed ASPs that have been tested by its team of engineers. Aggregators also develop and track the service-level agreements among application providers.

Prognosis and Accounting Profession Implications

Ultimately, many aggregators plan to be more than just middlemen coordinating relationships between ASPs and clients. Many say they intend to develop a range of value-added services. They are moving toward selling access to hosted applications on demand so that, for example, a client could pick a project management application to match a single project. They also plan to provide tight data and transaction-level integration between hosted applications.

Inevitably, aggregators may end providing the most value to clients by aligning themselves around specific industries and markets where they can begin to understand and implement end-to-end business processes to meet clients' needs.

The aggregator model is one that accounting firms should consider as a targeted market niche to incorporate into an online practice. Such a market specialty would become more focused and able to provide the practice with a deep integration between applications. When the dust has cleared, those left standing will have wrapped themselves around vertical professions such as accounting or specific industries. This appears to be the natural endgame of the entire ASP revolution. Exhibit 8.2 lists aggregator pros and cons.

PROS

- Single provider
- Centralized access and management
- More flexibility in pricing and switching applications
- Potential for application integration
- Ability to work through trusted resellers such as systems integrators and ISPs

CONS

- Aggregators are new and untested.
- Number of participating ASPs is limited for now.
- Clients have no direct relationship with application provider.
- Less customization of applications.
- Pricing models are not fully developed.

Exhibit 8.2 Aggregators: Pro and Con Checklist

CHAPTER 9

Information Technology

The Currency of Online Practice Development

STRATEGY

It took 38 years for 50 million American users to get radio. It's taken 4 years for 50 million American users to get on the Web.

As much as the Internet has revolutionized our personal lives, it has transformed the world of accounting even more. E-business and accounting are moving at the speed of light. Accounting firms revise their business plans seemingly every month to stay on the cutting edge of e@ccounting. And as we head into what some analysts are terming the second wave of e-business, the pace of change is accelerating. In the first wave, those appointed to the e-business team had to convince the rest of the firm that their vision was true. This was not always easy. Many managing partners primarily thought of e-business in terms of online versus offline. Whatever billings they gained from the Internet, they figured they would lose with the brick-and-mortar clients.

Some e-business issues have been e-solved; others are still being ironed out. But no one is disputing the value of Web-enabling business processes anymore. Now the question is, how to hone an e@ccounting business strategy to gain the maximum competitive edge.

In the past two years, most firms, no matter what size, have started overhauling their traditional management strategies in a mad dash for on and offline market share. They know they need to move quickly, for in the fast-moving world of accounting, the first firm to seize mindshare is hard to overtake (e.g. Amazon.com). Once an accounting firm falls behind, it may never get a chance to catch up.

Dichotomy of Strategy

There is a dichotomy in e@ccounting between the sense of rushing blindly into something, and the sense of pausing and focusing on sustained value. Accounting firms must face the challenge of recognizing the difference between wildly scrambling to get things done (doing something short term) and taking a deep breath, thinking it through, and developing a better underpinning to sustain growth.

Internet Time

E-business and accounting operate at a frenetic pace. It no longer matters whether you're a dot.com, a not.com, a client.com, or something in between. Everyone seems to be operating on Internet time. The result is that all clients demand that their projects be done faster than ever before — particularly if they are e-business projects. Accounting professionals are being given mandates to complete involved e-business undertakings and have them online in months.

Accounting firms are finding comfort and assistance from partners with project management software to reflect the concerns of the e-business client world. The accounting firm's mission with the assistance of allies' software is to bring some order into the potential chaos. Enterprise management tools and services help accountants to map out current commitments, future requirements, and the available resources in order to meet their objectives on schedule.

The fast-moving nature of an e-business project is a major cause of stress. Accountants realize that they can't do this by the seat of their pants and at the same time can't go with a slow-boat process either. The dramatic increase in the pace has prodded the industry to figure out how to develop new business processes.

In this new setting, accounting professionals will be able to collaborate and share information. Newly developed portals will be accessible by anyone in the project management community. Moving at Internet speed is a problem, but it's even tougher when the firm is short-handed,

and right now, many accounting firms are facing severe resource shortages. For an accounting firm to succeed, skilled people are a must.
Staffing and knowledge are both required in the Internet accounting
business world. How strong is your accounting business? To find out,
answer the questions in Exhibit 9.1.

---

1. What share of your firm's gross annual sales will come from professional services in 200X?

   a. Less than 25%   0 points
   b. 25% to 49%   1 point
   c. 50% to 74%   2 points
   d. 5% or more   3 points

The more your business model is focused toward Internet professional services, the more ready you are for the e-business accounting revolution.

2. What do you estimate your firm's gross profit margin to be in 200X?

   a. Less than 25%   0 points
   b. 25% to 34%   1 point
   c. 35% to 50%   2 points
   d. More than 50%   3 points

Professional services are generating the kinds of profit margins that make
for a healthy bottom line.

3. What share of your firm's gross annual billings will be derived from
   e-business in 200X?

   a. Less than 25%   0 points
   b. 25% to 49%   1 point
   c. 50% to 74%   2 points
   d. 75% or more   3 points

E-business is still a small percentage of annual billings for most accounting
firms. If you specialize in e-business market niches, you're ahead of your
competition.

(Continues)

Exhibit 9.1 How Strong Is Your Accounting Business?

4. What share of your gross annual billings will be derived from e-business in 200X+1?

    a. Less than 25%   0 points
    b. 25% to 49%   1 point
    c. 50% to 74%   2 points
    d. 75% or more   3 points

The faster you move toward providing e-business accounting solutions, the greater your edge over the competition.

5. With e-business accounting solutions, which of the following components does your firm provide?

    a. Strategic formulation
    b. Creative design/branding
    c. Solution development
    d. Enterprise deployment integration
    e. Staff training
    f. Post-installation support
    g. Applications hosting

(Award yourself one point for each item checked—maximum of five points.)

The more your firm can become a one-stop shop, the greater your competitive advantage.

6. Which part of your firm's e-business accounting solutions menu of services is growing the fastest?

    a. Strategic formulation
    b. Creative design/branding
    c. Solution development
    d. Enterprise deployment/integration
    e. Staff training
    f. Post-installation support
    g. Applications hosting

(Award yourself three points for item "c," two points for item "d," and one point for any other item checked.)

Symposium participants report solutions development and enterprise deployment as the most profitable offerings.

(Continues)

Exhibit 9.1 *(Continued)*

7. How long does your firm's typical engagement or project last?

    a. Less than 6 months   3 points
    b. 6 to 11 Months   2 points
    c. Approximately a year   1 point
    d. More than a year   0 points

If engagements or projects take too long to finish, your firm will be installing yesterday's technology in tomorrow's businesses.

8. To fuel the growth of your e-business portfolio, which of the following will your firm consider?

    a. Reducing write-up engagements
    b. Selling assets or increasing debt
    c. Discontinuing non-e-business operations
    d. Pursuing a merger, affiliation, or acquisition
    e. Establish Application Solutions, ERP, or EDI niches

    (Award yourself one point for each item checked.)

If you're making plans to fuel e-business growth, you're serious about this exploding market.

9. How many accounting market niches do you target?

    a. Four or more   2 points
    b. Two or three   1 point
    c. One   0 points

If your firm targets several accounting market niches, you're protecting yourself against financial disaster if one dries up.

SCORING

26 points or more: Congratulations. You've joined the e-business revolution.

21 – 25 points: You're becoming e-savvy, but aren't quite there.

16 – 20 points: Do you really want to stay in the e@ccounting business?

15 points or less: You aren't close to being in the e-business accounting market.

Source: The Accounting Guild, Las Vegas, Nevada, e@ccounting Strategy Symposium, June 2000

Exhibit 9.1 (*Continued*)

WHAT DO PROSPECTIVE CLIENTS WANT FROM AN ACCOUNTING FIRM?

When you know what your prospective clients want from an e-business accounting relationship, then morphing your practice to meet their needs is easier. Some require value skill and expertise above all else. Others want quick response and certain technique in their project management. Still others value a relationship the most.

1. *Size doesn't matter.*
   The size of an accounting practice is insignificant on most small to mid-sized prospective clients' radar screens. When asked to name the most important characteristic in selecting an accounting firm, none of the prospective clients with an e-business plan identified their provider's total staff as a number one criteria. From the perspective of the small to medium-sized market, at least, heavyweights like the Big Five and IBM Global Services do not have an advantage.

2. *Expertise does count.*
   Prospective clients of all sizes overwhelmingly said that expertise of a specialized kind is most important. Topping the list is the accounting firm's technical expertise, while strategic expertise followed, and creative expertise trailed the list.
   Compared with their small-business counterparts, enterprise clients gave disproportionate weight to the partner's technical expertise and placed less emphasis on strategic and creative capabilities. The reason may be that smaller clients are more dependent on third-party consultants for strategic advice. That is good news for accounting professionals, who should aim to become enduring partners to their clients' business plans.

3. *Don't sacrifice price.*
   Do not think that the price tag for your e@ccounting implementation is of paramount importance to the prospective client in an outsourcing decision. The clients realize that the potential long-term return on e-business investments dwarfs the immediate cost. Value-add and ROI, not cost, are what your clients want to see. About 20 percent of accounting services providers use

fixed-price/fixed time as their primary billing method. Nearly half bill for time and materials, and one-third typically have a service-level agreement (value billing) with clients.

4. *Objectives vary by size.*
   What is the typical client's primary e-business accounting services objective? How do your clients evaluate the success of an e-business initiative? Overall, more than one-third seek to increase sales. But smaller clients are more likely to focus on sales than their enterprise counterparts (43 percent, compared with 27 percent of enterprises) and less likely to target improved efficiency (23 percent, four points less than for large respondents).

5. *Clients are ready and willing.*
   Although the e-business objectives of clients can vary widely, they rely on accounting providers for all the major components of an implementation. Asked which components they outsource or plan to outsource, more than half named creative design/branding, systems development, or enterprise deployment/integration. Staff training trailed closely behind. Twenty percent are willing to entrust the strategic formulation of e-business projects to their accounting providers, and an equal share hire out post-implementation support.

6. *Focus your service area.*
   Accounting providers' service offerings map well to what prospective clients outsource: Two-thirds of accounting professionals develop e-business solutions and 54 percent provide enterprise deployment integration. One warning sign: 20 percent of all accounting providers are not involved with e-business at all. The savvy accounting providers are targeting market niches and picking up the work overlooked or ignored by others.

7. *There's still room for improvement.*
   Clients are outsourcing all components of e-business projects, and accounting providers are reaping the benefits. Clients expressed varying degrees of satisfaction with the work performed by their outside partners. Satisfaction was highest among smaller clients.

E-BUSINESS GOALS OF MOST CLIENTS

It's called e-business. Clients that want to participate over the next few years in the estimated $5 trillion in transactions up for grabs must not only build an IT infrastructure that supports e-business, but also dramatically change their management philosophies and business cultures.

A Delphi Group survey of 600 IT and business managers points out that most clients fall short: Although 90 percent of those polled had some e-business initiative in place, only 31 percent had successfully made the transition to e-business or had put the necessary management components in place.

E-business is defined as the comprehensive automation of a client's collection of relationships — business partners, competitors, customers, employees, and suppliers — into a unified value chain, all based on IP and Web applications.

"E-active" Clients

- **Recognize the power of strategic partnerships with their business constituencies.** The alliances foster the complete transaction loop — from product search to shipping confirmation with inventory updates. Few have arrived, but all grasp the importance.
- **Implement a flat management structure.** This permits better response to changing market conditions. The fewer layers of management, the better.
- **Form partnerships with competitors if the business case can be made.**
- **Actively pursue change management.** These clients are willing to reorganize internally if necessary to respond to new business environment realities brought on by the Internet and new business models.

Clients' Differing Perceptions of the Internet

One of the subtlest but most important distinctions between clients who are e-active and those who aren't is how they view the Web. Clients that fall into the e-active category realize not only that the Web changes realities in irreversible and virtually uncontrollable ways, but that the Web enables that change.

In response to the new markets spawned by the Web, the number of marketing employees has grown by a factor of 14. The firms that have recognized and implemented this phenomenon are now 14 times more likely to develop opportunities with newly discovered potential customers.

The movement of information is going to be a major strategic advantage for accounting services provider organizations. The accounting firm that makes e-business a pillar of its strategy will have a definitive marketplace advantage. That strategy is definitely e-active.

ELECTRONIC DATA INTERCHANGE (EDI)

History

During the Berlin Airlift in 1948 and 1949, the United States Air Force was faced with the need to unload and turn aircraft around on the ground at unprecedented rates. They solved this problem partly with the help of a new system, invented on the spot, for using Morse code to radio the freight manifest of each flight to the ground teams responsible for unloading that plane in advance of the actual landing. Legend has it that when the personnel behind this effort returned to civilian life, they realized that their codes could be used in another application: teaching computers to understand business.

The idea was to assign standard names to classes of business data, specify standard relations among those classes, and design standard representations for those data and relations. Once these standards were coded into programs and distributed, machines would know which data served inventory and which served personnel. Automation would be simpler to design, business interactions would turn over more quickly, paper-handling costs would be reduced, and data entry errors could be minimized. Companies were formed and by the late 1960s and early 1970s articles began to appear about the concept we now know as EDI, for electronic data interchange. The first applications were in transportation.

EDI Evolution

In the 1970s EDI was developed almost entirely inside large companies as a way of making the data and operations maintained on an enterprise's mainframe mutually comprehensible to all departments. Many of those enterprises developed their own EDI language, but during the 1980s common standards were agreed upon in several industries. EDI users were soon eager to start using these industrywide standards to support buyer-seller transactions: purchase orders, inventory, invoices, remittances, and the like.

Unfortunately, most of these value chains had a mix of company size, and the smaller firms, those without mainframes, were nowhere near as ready. Remember, even in the 1980s most businesses used computers only for payroll. From their point of view EDI came with serious extra costs, including hardware, software and software management, access to a value-added network (VAN), and data entry costs.

The Internet has initiated the imminent adoption of XML as a standard way of coding EDI standards. XML is an object representation language that is designed to include a flexible and dynamic range of information about the object it represents. XML (Extensive Markup Language) is a way to add tags to text files to create self-describing, cross-platform, machine-readable files that offer new searching and computing capabilities. However, it may be overcome by future developments. (See the section about XML later in this chapter for additional information.) This makes it ideal as an EDI template. XML will allow standards bodies to concentrate on business models without worrying about technical or syntactical details, which will make it easier to move EDI into new sectors and extend its range in old.

EDI Prognosis

EDI has always worked best among partners that need to exchange stable and well-defined data sets. Where you have innovation, competition, rapidly changing business models, EDI can be a drag.

Global business seems to be moving toward the end of the spectrum that makes EDI less useful rather than more. The technology might still fulfill the needs of its adherents, but EDI is still going to take patience, dollars, and time.

ENTERPRISE RESOURCE PLANNING (ERP)

What Is ERP?

Enterprise Resource Planning is:

1. Software
2. A conceptual strategy
3. A confusing buzzcronym

Tech and accounting industry insiders use the ERP term to describe the digital automation of any, and sometimes every, task a business might do every day. Using a comprehensive set of software and a good bit of IT ingenuity, an ERP system can tie processes such as purchasing, inventory maintenance, customer service, marketing, sales, and accounting into one cohesive system that works across an enterprise of any size.

Deploying ERP involves a substantial investment, of both money and personnel-hours. The Internet has enabled affordable installation, and maintenance costs — while still expensive and complicated — are now at least possible for most businesses. At this time, implementing ERP is a decision. Soon enough, it will be a necessity.

How Does ERP Work?

The theory of ERP can be explained using an illustration of the bouncing check. Let's say a client orders a software program and pays for it via snail mail with a check. In the paper-based world, that process would take that check through a number of different departments and desks — sales, accounting, inventory — before the check would be found to be in default. With ERP, once that check is entered into the system, every department has access to it at the same time. Assuming the system is tied into the bank, the check might even be accrued in real time. The same process that might have taken days to transact can happen in hours, if not minutes.

Why Do I Want ERP?

Everyone having access to the same data at the same time can have an enormous effect on a client's efficiency and productivity. Data are entered only once which reduces the likelihood of mistakes. Everyone's "in box" receives the data at the same time, which eliminates the time lags of the linear paper world. Work gets cycled more quickly, which means capacity can increase. Management can track the workflow in real time, which means smarter decision making when it comes to things like creating work schedules or ordering supplies. Having all this information at a CEO's or CPA's virtual fingertips also means more assured strategic planning at the top.

Where Do I Get ERP?

Here's where the software comes in. ERP systems come in all shapes and sizes. The most popular right now are all-in-one, top-down solutions. You can self-assemble your own ERP using a variety of different applications. Either way, have a consulting operation capable and ready to provide the client with the best solution for its needs. The major consulting firms in the corporate market that have turned their sights towards smaller businesses include SAP (www.SAP.com), Peoplesoft (www.peoplesoft.com), and J.D. Edwards (www.jd-edwards.com). Since no ERP system will work without a bulletproof database management system, Oracle is also a good place to start. Also search out smaller software developers that might provide an ERP-type solution in your firm's particular vertical market niches.

ERP Vendors

J.D. Edwards launched a site of business-to-business solutions dubbed "ActiveEra" and has entered into a strategic relationship with business-to-business pioneer Ariba Inc.

Industry leader SAP has also grown aggressive in the e-commerce space, with its mySAP.com initiative and mySAP.com Marketplaces. SAP is offering its customers three ways to implement its integrated business-to-business architecture:

1. An application that the customer purchases and installs itself
2. A dedicated "instance" of the application run and hosted by SAP
3. A shared business-to-business portal co-developed by SAP and any number of partners in a given industry or market niche

The mySAP.com architecture makes extensive use of XML, widely seen as an excellent way to share data across the Web among multiple trading partners. Many clients already have successful EDI implementations in place. The most successful ERP/business-to-business solutions providers will be those who offer clients a transition strategy. Applications providers will have to give their clients the option of talking to some of their partners via EDI and some via XML.

Other Significant ERP Vendors

Hundreds of independent, industry-specific Web markets have opened including Chemconnect.com and Metalsite.net. Business-to-business software specialists, such as CommerceOne, Ariba, and i2, have set up operations in the e-marketplace arena, as has manufacturing supply-chain specialist Manugistics.

Oracle Corporation unveiled its trading hub strategy in 1999. In e-commerce time, mid-1999 classifies as a prior paleontological era. Part of what is driving the market is a strong belief in first-mover advantage: If one can be first, one can basically freeze out the competition. In 1999, Oracle, unlike many of its competitors, had demonstrated a thorough understanding of what Internet-exploiting enterprise applications are all about. Of all the ERP vendors, Oracle is the one who has had its act together the most. The company's ERP and newer applications have been infused with Larry Ellison's (Oracle's founder and chairman) big-server, small-client zeal.

The flagship example of this is Oracle 11i. It culminates the company's efforts since 1996 to make a completely Internet-based suite of applications. The software provides a global view of data from a centralized store accessible from anywhere.

ERP Prognosis

An increasing number of clients are looking beyond the giant ERP vendors for their new breed of enterprise applications. Every month another upstart blazes more trails in the enterprise application marketplace.

The evolving needs of the clients are compelling them to take closer looks at their trusted accounting providers to provide for their ERP needs. The glory is past for many of the giant ERP vendors even as they try to recapture their former empires. If accounting firms do their jobs really well, then the clients will ultimately find them again.

EXTENSIBLE MARKUP LANGUAGE (XML)

XML reflects and extends whatever it touches. Because of its extensibility, and a human tendency to make simple concepts more complex than necessary, XML has been surrounded by misconceptions, making it difficult to get an accurate view of the technology.

XML Is Not a Glorified HTML

Both XML and Hypertext Markup Language (HTML) are descendants of Standard Generalized Markup Language (SGML). Like HTML, XML is a markup language with tags and attributes. With XML, however, you define your own tags, or use agreed-upon vocabularies shared by business partners or a user community.

HTML enables you to publish content in a particular structure, but the data are inextricably intertwined with their displays (an <H1> tag or image-size attribute). Elements have no relationship with one another or even with cascading style sheets (CSS), and an HTML file has no internal order. XML files contain the information and describe its semantics, instead of its presentation: a chunk of data is identified as a unit price, not "<H1>$5.00</H1>".

XML is really a family of technologies, some of which are still in draft form (i.e., not yet a final standard), and these can work in concert to provide Web pages. The optional, but usually present, document type definition (DTD) spells out the schema of an XML file. The DTD defines the content's acceptability, such as establishing that, in this kind of file, a unit price must be accompanied by a part number.

One related misconception, repeated way too often in documentation and XML books, is that XML files need a DTD, or they're incorrect. Although it is a good idea to have one, a DTD is necessary only if you plan to exchange your XML data with others.

CSS can work with XML-enabled browsers and tools, but the Extensible Stylesheet Language (XSL) standard defines how XML data is presented. XSL defines fonts, bolding, and other display considerations. Its scripting language lets you conditionally execute instructions based on the document's data or structure. The XSL standard is in two halves: XSLT (the transformation language) and XSL FO (the formatting language).

XML is also a very powerful tool for anyone doing database projects, especially when you need to exchange database information with other providers. Because XML data conform to a grammar and each element is defined, a shared vocabulary within a community (such as accounting providers) can be defined. Once agreed upon, swapping data can cease to be a problem that has to be solved anew for every new client that joins the firm.

Structured documents have benefits besides the ability to parse and display database information. They make it easier to build and use search engines and other data-management tools. XML also makes it significantly easier to cause the same data to appear on a Web site, in a database transaction, on a wireless device, and in a printed manual. Nearly every database vendor has XML support, and most applications that mas-sage data (from Web content management to directory services to middleware servers) promise some level of XML interoperability. Exhibit 9.2 shows the XML family of standards.

EXTENSIBLE BUSINESS REPORTING LANGUAGE (XBRL)

The AICPA has joined accounting software vendors and other entities in developing and launching the Internet-standard XBRL. XBRL for Financial Statements is an XML-based specification that uses accepted financial reporting standards and practices to exchange financial statements across all software and technologies, including the Internet.

Developed as the first product in a future family of products, the new language streamlines the financial information chain that connects public and private companies, the accounting profession, data aggregators, the investment community, and all other users of financial statements. It offers such benefits as technology independence, interoperability, efficient preparation of financial statements, and reliable extraction of financial information.

Information is entered only once, allowing that same information to be rendered in any form, such as a printed financial statement, an HTML document for the company's Web site, an EDGAR filing document with the SEC, a raw XML file, or other specialized reporting formats.

Technology	Purpose
XML	Basic document structure and syntax
DTD	Grammar definitions for XML documents
XSL	Transform and formatting
DOM	API to create and manipulate XML
Xlink/Xpointer	Richer links
RDF	Metadata and semantic networks
XML Schemas	Replacement for DTDs
Namespaces	Multiple vocabularies in same document

Exhibit 9.2 XML Family of Standards

CHAPTER 10

Databases, Data Warehouses, and Data Marts

DATABASES

Background

The ancient alchemists' quest to turn base metals into gold has its modern-day counterpart in accountants who turn client data into knowledge and transform that into gold for each to share. Hidden deep in the gigabytes of data that clients have been generating — and paying dearly to store and backup — are nuggets of informational gold just waiting to be panned. Detailed data about customers, products, potential markets, and other key performance indicators are waiting to be exploited.

These assets have gone mostly untapped because of the high cost of the hardware and software needed to effectively sort and analyze the large volume of data. Now, accounting professionals, with the aid of affordable computer hardware, combined with new data analysis techniques, make data mining a viable service for even the smallest businesses.

The science for this has been around for about 40 years, but traditionally has been the domain of Ph.D.s and mathematicians who would spend months, often even years, writing custom algorithms for specific projects or tasks. Today, accounting professionals are answering the clamor to bring this technology to the masses. With the improvement in available tools, a new definition of data management is emerging.

Data management and data mining make possible the semi-automated knowledge discovery process of extracting previously unknown, actionable information from very large databases. Accounting professionals utilize data mining to automatically find previously hidden patterns, trends, and correlations in data. Some are obvious and others very subtle. These findings enable the client to make more informed decisions and more accurate predictions about the future.

The key concept is semi-automated or automated. New data manipulation software uses a combination of statistical analysis, modeling, improved database technologies, and something called artificial intelligence, or AI, to reveal those hidden relationships. Typical applications include market-basket analysis, market segmentation, forecasting, and fraud detection. As important as knowing what data mining is, is knowing what it isn't. It is often confused with data reporting, but reporting can only tell you what happened. Data mining can tell you why it happened, enabling you and your client to make changes that will affect future outcome. Reporting gives you lagging indicators, while mining gives you leading indicators.

Database Definitions and Jargon Clarification

Algorithm: A rules-based formula or a step-by-step procedure for solving a problem or finding relationships in data. All data mining techniques employ algorithms, either established ones or new ones created by the user. A recipe for baking a cake is an example of a simple algorithm.

Data mart: Also refers to a collection of databases, but one that is focused on a single subject or department. A data mart can be a subset of a data warehouse created for a specific project or to provide quick access to targeted data for a specific department like sales or marketing.

Data visualization: A method of data reporting that visually represents information that traditionally was displayed in complex tables and mathematical terms. The human brain can discern patterns and relationships faster when they are visually represented.

Data warehouse: Jargon from the late 1990s that refers to combining databases from across an enterprise in one location, and/or with a common access if not a common format, to support strategic business decisions. It can include disparate types of information that together give a comprehensive picture of a client's current condition.

Dimensions: Attributes or variables in the data being mined. Dimensions are equivalent to an individual field in a flat file record or a column of a relational database table.

Domain: The set of a field's valid values. For instance, a date field can't contain the word "terrier."

Field: A group of associated characters stored in a table's column. Fields are usually classified by data type — character, numeric, date, currency.

Foreign key: A column or combination of table columns whose values match those in the domain of another table's primary key. Foreign key values need not be, and usually are not, unique.

Join: The resulting rows showing columns of information from all tables that are selected by matching the values of related columns in two or more tables.

Normalization: The separation of data elements into naturally associated groups and defining the correct or right relationship among them: one of the first and most crucial steps in the design of an effective relational base.

Null value: A missing or inapplicable data value as opposed to a blank string or zero numeric value.

OLAP or Online Analytical Processing: is a popular reporting tool that can provide useful analysis of historical data. Since it is multidimensional reporting using data from multidimensional or relational databases, users can drill down or examine data from different views.

Outer join: A join of information from tables that includes information from rows where a null value in the specified common column of one table does not match any value in the common column of the other table.

Query: A string of statements that when executed returns a data set from one or more tables.

Record: A group of related fields (all the columns) stored in a row of a database table.

Referential integrity: A database characteristic that assures that no entry in a child table can exist if its foreign key does not match a value in the domain of a parent's primary key.

Relation: A database table where each row is different from all other rows; all rows are distinct. Relations have primary keys.

SQL: Structured Query Language (pronounced "sequel"). A language for expressing and presenting information requests, for updating contents, and for creating/altering the structure of relational databases. ANSI/ISO SQL standards have been published, and SQL is considered the language of choice for relational databases. The SQL SELECT command is universally used to query relational databases.

Table: A row-and-column structure or arrangement of data values, typically composed of fields (columns) and records (rows). The central organizing element in a relational database. Rows may be and usually are unordered.

Validity checking: The process of assuring that all values entered for a field fall within an allowable domain of values. For instance, a typical validity check would make sure that only numerical digits are entered in a social security field.

View: Literally, a view to table information returned by a query. A view can include data from multiple tables.

"Relational" Defined

Every database is just a model for structuring, updating, and retrieving information. Unlike many models, a relational database doesn't use addresses, links, or pointers to establish relationships between data sets; instead, it relies on the values in the data. Data is stored in spreadsheet-like tables with rows for each record and columns for each field. All tables have unique names and any table in which all of the rows (records) are different is mathematically known as a "relation."

By organizing data in tables that have values in common, relationships can be established without caring about the order in which the data is stored or where it is located. The data entries can be in any order and any set position.

Relational databases should also include system tables that define the database structure and provide a systematic method for dealing with missing information (known as null values). There should be support for a well-defined language that allows table definition, data manipulation, integrity checking, access authorization, and transaction processing. SQL is widely recognized as the relational database language of choice. The extent to which a database management system includes these features and supports the ANSI/ISO SQL standards is a measure of how relational it is.

Database Knowledge

Once you become adept at using databases, you'll discover that the projects that were so complex and arduous on a spreadsheet are much easier to handle on a database. Following are some of the key reasons databases are very useful:

- **Data Independence.** Once data is entered into a relational database grouped in tables, it can be combined in myriad ways. The software takes data in one table and relates that information to data in another table: hence the name relational database.

  If a database contains information on a client's customers in one table, its products in a second table, and the history of what each customer buys in a third table, their interrelationships can be used to produce a wide range of relational information. Each data table is complete in itself and reports produced by the software will not affect the tables' makeup. Therefore, data can be combined for totally different purposes without copying or otherwise disturbing the underlying information.

- **Data Sharing.** Related databases can easily generate ad hoc reports that enable information to be shared among many users. This feature ensures data integrity and eliminates data redundancy. In addition, users can customize the screen displaying a report so only selected data appear. Also, those selections can be customized for different viewers. Each view can be password-protected for security.

- **Data Accuracy.** Input data screens can be designed to accept information only if the data are formatted in a particular way — a technique called validation checks. If a user tries to enter any other information in any other format, the information is rejected.

- **Ad Hoc Queries.** Another feature that makes a database powerful and convenient is its ability to accept ad hoc queries. For example, it is impossible for the developer and designer of a database application to know ahead of time exactly how the information will be used or what questions the database will be asked. Database applications allow users to set up an infinite number of queries. As long as the underlying data exists and relationships can be ascertained, the software can report those relationships.

- **Report Generation.** Most databases come with predesigned templates for commonly used reports, but it's easy to create new ones.

- **User-Friendly Development Tools.** Although the newer database programs are designed for ease of use, you'll need some training for nearly all database applications—even the ones that promise you can start using them the moment you get them out of the box. Most come with handy one-on-one teaching programs (assistants or wizards) that walk you through a series of steps (and provide a range of design options) for creating customized queries, forms, and reports. These intuitive development tools make it relatively easy for you to handle sophisticated projects.

- **Database Size.** Spreadsheets can manage 5,000 records, but databases can effectively handle up to a million.

- **Importing.** Most database applications allow you to open, use, and store files in many formats. Thus, databases can handle pictures, graphs, audio, video, spreadsheets, and word processing documents—all of which can be incorporated into reports.

Choice of Database

As accounting professionals recognize the need to add a database application to their cache of professional software, they increasingly ask which is the best package. The answer is that there is no best package; there is no one product that meets everyone's needs. There is only the product that best suits you. This is determined by multiple factors:

- Frequency you plan to use it
- Time you're willing to invest in learning how to use it

- Complexity of the databases you plan to create
- Links to other software applications

Using Databases

Just as a modern miner of precious metals uses an array of tools for different parts of the extraction process, an accounting professional must often use various algorithms or techniques for any one extraction. There are a number of techniques employed by the professionals, but in this guide, we'll concentrate on the most popular and accessible to accountants.

Association and Market-Basket Analysis

Association is the technique used to discover the fact that beer buyers usually also buy baby diapers and not peanuts, as widely assumed. Association algorithms identify events that occur together and then enumerate their frequency. For example, when miners buy new, longer drilling bits, 14 percent of the time they also buy dynamite for blasting. Association analysis takes lots of transaction data as input. Market-basket analysis is an association technique used by large retailers to determine how best to lay out stores. This is also one of the techniques used to uncover the buying patterns of Web site visitors.

Segmentation and Classification

Segmentation and classification are tools used extensively in the analytical research departments of advertising agencies and forensic accountants. The process groups segments together according to selected characteristics. Clustering, a type of classification that looks for groups within groups that aren't labeled in any way, uses much less data and tries to find automatic groups that stand out. Fast food chains use clustering to identify the best locations for new stores.

Caveat

It is important for the accounting professional to convince the client that he or she really has an understanding of the client's business and markets. That is the accountant's foot in the door.

Decision Trees

Decision trees are a type of classification analysis that distinguishes between different classes of data. Using a tree metaphor, one makes decisions at each branch of the tree. "If this happens at the same time this happens, then this will happen." Tax forms are an example of a decision tree because you're instructed to do one thing if your answer to a question is "yes" and another if your answer is"'no." Decision trees are good for identifying cross-selling opportunities, analyzing credit risk, detecting fraud, and analyzing the effectiveness of promotions or mailings.

Neural Networks

Neural networks, along with decision trees, are popular for forecasting and fraud detection. A neural network is AI based: you present it with a large number of observed cases or behaviors, one at a time, and then allow it to update itself repeatedly until it learns the task. The program can teach itself to retrieve such information through the use of mathematical algorithms. A neural network can then apply mathematical models for predicting and classifying the data. This tool is not good for qualitative or quantitative pattern recognition, the backbones of data mining. Neural networks are primarily used for tracking stocks or predicting future stock performance.

Drill Down or Blast?

When deciding which of the data mining techniques will apply to your client's projects, remember that your results will be only as good as the data you're using. Garbage in/garbage out really has the same impact in data mining as it does in client write-up.

Databases are rarely collected for the purpose of data mining, and therefore must be cleaned or brought to a state where all the data are consistent. Pay attention to the data being collected, making certain there's a consistent method of data entry. Most importantly, make sure that data are collected as events take place. Data enhancement, using services that can supply demographic, financial, or other data you're lacking, can go a long way to improving the state of your clients' data, as well as the outcome of your extraction.

Once the data is clean, determine the focus of the information you're seeking and what data you have to support that kind of extraction. Many projects fail because they don't have a defined objective, or the accounting professional lacked the domain or business-specific knowledge to take advantage of the questions the data suggested.

Privacy Issues

Keep in mind, too, that any time you're working with information about people, whether it's buying habits, income, age, or any type of personal information, privacy can be a major issue. Make sure you know how and who is going to use the resulting information, and whether it's legal and ethical. The more general your statements drawn from the results, the better.

DATA WAREHOUSES

Your client calls for assistance with a request that has produced a paroxysm of file-searching, late-night spreadsheet entry, and MIS overtime at the client with no solutions in sight. Unfortunately, in many cases, the answer would be "the data's there, but we can't get to it."

That's because data is usually spread in incompatible formats across multiple databases, locked in operational transactions, or simply unavailable for analysis. As a result, data warehousing, which allows easy access to analysis of data across an enterprise, is growing rapidly in corporate, client America. Data warehousing can produce annual gains of 20 to 50 times the initial investment, and is often bonded with a client's reengineering efforts.

Tour through a Data Warehouse

A data warehouse comprises data from a variety of sources. These could include everything from mainframe databases and encapsulated business rules to video clips and desktop spreadsheets. Users can easily access this information with a variety of ad hoc queries, eliminating the need for their accounting consultant to write custom reports. Data from a data warehouse are up to date, optimized for access and analysis, and consistent across an organization. Data coexist peacefully with existing information systems, although much of the data might be shared.

A common misconception is that data warehouses merely give users access to data copied from operational systems. That is data access, not data warehousing. Data warehousing supports borderless information analysis across organizational boundaries. This gives management and knowledge workers operational and historic data that can be viewed from a variety of angles to illuminate the patterns in a mass of business details.

Popular applications for data warehousing include customer profiling, product or segment profitability, database marketing, and risk analysis. Data warehousing solutions often require top-level strategic decisions on the appropriate data model: how to populate that model with the right data and how users can access the data. Solutions typically include tools to get data into and out of the warehouse, to clean and manage data within the warehouse, and to assist with multidimensional queries.

Because of this complexity, data warehouses are built, not bought. They touch on complex issues involving client/server computing, legacy integration, business modeling, security, external data linkages, and decision support. Because warehouses typically incorporate data from dozens of databases, they will scale to hundreds of gigabytes or even terabytes, affecting storage management, disaster recovery, and other concerns.

Accounting Professionals in High Demand

Data warehousing can encompass everything from client/server applications to middleware and various query tools. Accounting professionals who master the necessary skills can expect to be in high demand. There is a tremendous need for clients to have access to information for decision making. This opportunity can be very profitable to accounting consulting firms.

Producing the long-term payoff demands short-term intensity. The project you're working on is intensely important to the client and receives a great deal of high-level scrutiny. If the project is successful, it becomes a huge opportunity for the accounting consultant firm. If it fails, you will probably never get another chance.

Partnering with Database Vendors

Accounting firms are typically seen as nonthreatening by the clients' IS organization, which needs all the value-added horsepower it can get. There's rarely any embedded expertise, so clients are eager to partner with those who can help meet their strategic objectives.

Accounting consultants can't expect to solve all the problems alone. Data warehouses are very difficult for one organization to put together, so you need to partner with database and tool affiliates. These should not be casual relationships, but a true partnership that produces the best possible solution for your client.

Accounting firms with data warehousing experience are received well among clients, but this knowledge must be more than skin-deep. Clients are very savvy about what they need. They recognize that data warehousing requires the same integration between business and technology as client/server computing. You need to know what the technology can do and how to implement it within the client's environment.

Database vendors are eager to work closely with you and have a variety of formal and informal programs to help you get up to speed on their technologies and secure engagements. The support includes product discounts, early product access, extensive training, joint client visits, seminar programs, and specialized product support. Database vendors also often have relationships with tools vendors that complement their own products and can help enable data warehouse implementations.

Data Modeling

About 70 percent of the time involved in data warehousing is spent in data modeling. Some of this is because current systems lack documentation, but mostly it's because how data are modeled is determined by the client's proposed use of the data. Data modeling is a great specialty area for accounting professionals. Otherwise, they risk always competing against the Big Five and large consulting organizations.

Data Warehouse Solutions and Prognosis

No one accounting firm or database vendor has a complete warehouse solution; therefore, they often make alliances to fill in the gaps. Press-release partnerships need to be taken with a grain of salt, since many provide no technology integration and are merely marketing agreements.

Almost no data warehousing project fails because of a technical breakdown. It fails because it was built based on technical — not business — requirements. One of the most important factors is interlinking the data warehouse with management processes and the strategic information systems plan.

Be prepared to deal with the obstacles that go into building a data warehouse. There are about 30 technological components that go into the building of a data warehouse, and you have to understand, implement, and integrate them all. You also have to build the business case and be able to put together a demonstrable return on investment.

Accountants' Opportunities

The fast-growing data warehousing market offers opportunities for accountants, but they must understand the complex, unique needs of clients, integrate tools and databases from multiple vendors and affiliates into a customized solution, and be prepared for changing business requirements. It's also a market where small to medium-sized accounting firms can wind up competing with the Big Five or other large organizations, unless they specialize in a piece of the data warehousing puzzle.

Data warehousing has the potential to bring tidy profits and high margins. But not every accounting consultant has the skill set needed for these projects. Some data warehousing projects last three years. In addition, they use every ounce of energy you can muster.

DATA MARTS

Smaller data warehousing projects — commonly called data marts — require at least two special skill sets, while full-sized projects require at least three. For any data warehousing projects, accounting professionals need to have database administration skills because data warehouses are essentially enormous databases. The second critical requirement is industry-specific knowledge, which gives you a turbo boost in your sales presentation. You need not only to be able to put the data together, but also to tell the client which data to select in the first place. For the more traditional super-sized undertakings, a third skill is required. You must have tremendous connectivity skills because what you're likely to be building is a platform that integrates data from lots of different sources.

Target Your Database Market

If your firm lacks the resources to organize and implement large projects, focus on the growing number of prospective clients looking for data marts. Small to medium-sized clients often need the same access to information that their larger competitors enjoy, so they make prime candidates for smaller data warehousing projects. Other targets you can hone in on are departments within large organizations that want their own data marts separate from the larger corporate databases.

The theory behind data marts is relatively simple. Data warehouses are on too large a scale for the average business client. One of the reasons data marts and data warehouses in general are becoming more attractive to clients is the lower costs of all of the pieces involved in data warehousing solutions and the increased returns they generate.

The migration to the data mart method bodes well for the mid-sized accounting consultant firm, which has historically represented less than 20 percent of all data warehousing engagements. Rather than having to partner with multiple vendors, an accounting solutions provider can offer the client an end-to-end solution targeting a specific task.

Smaller accounting systems integrators have the ability to take more of the market. It's a profitable market, since data marts are a high-service business. Of the total number of dollars spent on building a data mart, half is spent on services. Data marts are opening doors to a wider range of clients.

Data Mart Tools' Necessities

Each attribute a data mart product lacks makes selling an engagement more difficult:

1. Low cost
2. Easy to use
3. Heterogeneous platform support
4. Seamless integration with existing infrastructure
5. Ongoing technical support

Clients' Hopes and Fears

The value proposition for marketing data mart engagements usually focuses on strategic business decision support, enhanced customer service, and cost savings through consolidated purchasing. Data marts stand a better chance of success because the technology is more manageable. Re-adjustments can be made as necessary.

One of the hurdles in selling a data mart is allaying clients' fear of noninteroperability. This relatively complex service requires a big educational process. The more the accountants can shield their clients from the technology's complexities, the better.

YOUR BEST SHOT

The notion that data warehouses are not an ongoing process tends to trip up some accounting firms. Don't expect to go in, set up the data warehouse or data mart, and get out. Once the installation is up and running, then the real work begins.

You shouldn't go in with the idea that you're going to get it 99.9 percent right because that's not possible. Take your best shot. Build in the expectation that it's going to change and the flexibility to allow that change to happen.

CHAPTER 11

Data Mining, Document Management, and Storage

DATA MINING

Data mining — the use of mathematical algorithms to seek hidden patterns or associations in data — is now widely accepted as an affordable way to sharpen a client's competitive edge. No longer the exclusive domain of million-dollar enterprise-class software like SAS, data-mining features have become integrated into a broad range of packaged application tools, helping businesses of all sizes sift data in search of patterns that reveal hidden insights. Tools that used to range in cost from the hundreds of thousands of dollars to millions of dollars and required specialized expertise can now, for a fraction of the cost, automatically select which ads or promotions to present Web site visitors and help decipher what performance improvements are needed to boost sales.

Data mining is increasingly being seen as a competitive weapon by many types of business clients. Until recently, software developers had found it difficult to sell generic data-mining tools to general business users. A few years ago, it appeared that data mining would never penetrate the business world, as several providers failed at selling data mining to business users. However, the situation has changed dramatically with more and more clients using the database algorithms built into the latest customer relationship management (CRM), customer tracking, and performance-monitoring tools to analyze customer behavior. Data mining is there, but the users never see it. Customer analysis is becoming the application of choice of data mining.

One of the fastest growing classes of suppliers now offering data-mining features wrapped in e-business applications are ASPs. Applications are designed to unobtrusively capture visitor information on a Web site and aggregate it into an online customer profile. This helps take the guesswork out of site design and recommend performance improvements to clients.

Data mining has become more widely accepted as it's integrated into other business applications. Being able to do that effectively will accelerate separating the business winners from the losers, which is why more clients are using data-mining tools to sharpen up.

Definition

Data mining is the process of discovering ideas in data. Other business intelligence methodologies, such as standard reports, ad hoc queries, and online analytical processing (OLAP), move in the opposite direction. They begin with an idea and then gather data to support it.

Data-Mining Algorithms

The definition of data mining becomes clearer when you look at the four most popular data mining algorithms:

1. **Associating.** Identifies patterns or groups of items. You might find that men who buy red ties also often buy symphony tickets.
2. **Sequencing.** Identifies the order of items or events. You might find that men tend to buy red ties before lunch and symphony tickets after lunch.
3. **Segmenting.** Identifies clusters of items with common attributes. You might find that men who buy red ties and symphony tickets also usually have wine at lunch and pay by credit card.
4. **Predictive Modeling.** Identifies a likely outcome from item clusters. You might find that men who buy red ties and symphony tickets and have wine at lunch are very likely to buy a midnight blue Mercedes within two years and finance their purchase with stock market investment profits.

All of these algorithms may be used in other business intelligence methodologies. However, in data mining, facts are used to discover patterns with a greater degree of complexity than is possible with other methods.

Procedure

Although the procedure for setting up a data-mining project is similar to one for setting up a data warehouse, two factors differ:

- The scope of a data-mining project is generally more strictly defined than the scope of a data warehouse project.
- Data-mining projects usually require special expertise in data-mining techniques and a clear understanding of the kind of data involved.

Data-Mining Project

A data-mining project has five basic steps:

1. **Determine the scope.** Includes deciding if the correct data is available, quantifying the data elements (for example, defining a "good customer" as one who makes purchases of more than $500 per month), and defining the goals of the project.
2. **Build the data-mining database.** Includes locating the data, extracting and selecting it, preparing the data by cleaning it and making it conform to a model, sorting, and loading it. Aggregation may be used, but generally data are mined on an elemental level.
3. **Explore the data.** Includes deciding which data-mining algorithms are appropriate and exactly how they are to be applied to explore the data. For example, if you want to segment data to search for a particular cluster of attributes, you must decide which attributes are to be used at this stage.
4. **Analyze results.** Includes deciding if the results are too general or too specific and whether further mining is required to yield useful results.
5. **Present results.** Includes presenting the meaningful relationships that have been uncovered and making recommendations for further study.

Mining Your Accounting Firm's and Your Clients' Web Statistics

Accounting firms are setting up data-mining projects to analyze their Web site statistics as well as those of their clients to study the behavior of Web site visitors. All figures from an e-commerce site are normally included in a data warehouse, but the special nature of other Web statistics makes them more suitable for storage in a separate database.

Generally, a Web statistical record is generated each time a visitor accesses a new page or, in some cases, a page element such as a graphic. For this reason, not all of the statistical records are useful, and you can often eliminate huge quantities of records before any other processing takes place. In addition, Web statistical records are usually stored in files on a daily basis, and you will need to merge the records in these files to study patterns over time.

What kinds of patterns can be studied in Web site statistics? It's easy to find out what services or niches are to be questioned on an e-commerce site through query and information request records, but only a data-mining analysis can shed light on which services were considered and rejected and in what order. You can also discover important patterns in search engine usage data and in the way visitors access white papers and online brochures.

Such studies can deliver extremely valuable business intelligence. A company that sells hobby kits and supplies on its Web site discovered that visitors who put comments in its guest book generally didn't buy anything, but people who bought expensive R/C (radio-controlled) models almost always clicked on the customer service area before ordering. This knowledge led the company to enhance it customer service pages and limit development of its guest book.

DOCUMENT MANAGEMENT AND BUSINESS INTELLIGENCE

Consider the possibilities of consolidating the vast resources associated with paper-based document management and redirecting those resources toward enhancing corporate productivity and business intelligence. It's happening, and it's changing the face of business and accounting services.

What Does Document Management Do?

- Reduces cost in the business
- Eases paper flow
- Allows documents to flow in a way not possible with paper
- Enables multiple sites and workers to work with the same items at, or nearly at, the same time
- Stores images for the following purposes:
  - Retrieval
  - Retention
  - Documentation
- Requires a change in basic methodology

Document Management Is More than Simply Imaging!

Document management entails much more than the simple imaging that is most commonly associated with this activity. Among its various components are the following:

- Tracking documents and revisions
- Imaging (Text and Graphic Images)
- Optical Character Recognition (OCR)
- E-mail workflow tools
- Productivity software
- Intranets

What Document Management Relies On

- Source must be reliable (accurate representation).
- Retrieval must be easy (little or no training of user).
- Data must be available in the future (retention).
- Document must be nonmodifiable (security).
- Storage costs are reduced (overall less than paper).
- Long-term availability is possible (10, 20, 30+ years away).
- Data may be transported to others who may need the information (sharable).
- Installation, operation, and maintenance must be easy.

Managing Information as a Corporate Asset

The adage about what you can measure, you can manage is just as appropriate for data as for any other facet of business. Data can be segmented according to structure. Examples of structured and unstructured data are as follows:

Structured Data (10%)

Structured data is well understood and under control:

- Customer ID
- Company
- Address
- Phone, fax, e-mail

Unstructured Data (90%)

- Faxes
- Paper documents
- Computer reports
- Electronic documents
- Folders

Document Managing Requirements

Whether you offer document management as a client service or use it for internally managing your documents, the following is required:

- Powerful hardware
- Powerful software
  - Vendor software must be Windows-compatible.
  - Instructions must not only be well documented, but intuitive to follow.
  - Software must stay with standard conventions.

Planning Is Critical to Success

- Who will use the system and how?
- Who will scan images?
- Where will they be stored?
- How will they be retrieved?
- What about electronic documents?

Define the Economic Life

- How long does the document have value?
- What are the stages of a documents' life?

- When should the document be moved during its life?
- Is moving it a manual operation?

Who Is Responsible?

- Who is responsible?
- What are the various levels of responsibility?
- Is Document Management a responsibility of MIS?
- What happens in the file room?
- Validation is part of the process.

Once a System Is Selected

- Don't jump for joy ... yet!
- Changing vendors down the road could be a difficult task.
- Plan to maintain hardware compatibility for the long term.
- Update software versions when new releases come out.

ENTERPRISE REPORTING AND DATA MINING

It all starts with a remarkably simple idea — capturing print data and storing it for secure, reliable, online access throughout the enterprise by anyone with a Web browser, email client, desktop application, or even fax machine. Electronic report distribution, or enterprise reporting, represents a new way of thinking about managing, manipulating, and distributing reports — a way of thinking that can benefit clients of all sizes, regardless of their existing reporting infrastructure.

Clients new to enterprise reporting will benefit from significant savings of time, money, and effort over conventional printing, storage, and distribution methods. Other key benefits include markedly enhanced availability of online reports, better security for sensitive information, and optimal use of corporate intranets and the Web for customer service, business-to-business, and human resources operations.

For clients with existing electronic reporting or archiving systems, such as magnetic or optical disc storage capability, the solutions enable online distribution options for on-demand viewing, sorting, indexing, and filtering of reports, document-level or page-level security, and other powerful and convenient services.

Overlay features enable display of live data on existing report templates and development of custom reports that accept data from multiple sources. Clients preparing to exploit the vast resources of information contained in a spectrum of current and historical reports benefit from advanced reporting and data-mining solutions. These products consolidate business intelligence efforts and enable sophisticated analysis of trends for applications in marketing, customer service, enterprise resource planning, and other data-intensive needs.

END-TO-END REPORT MANAGEMENT

Building a successful reporting strategy requires taking stock of the client's existing printing infrastructure. Print and report management systems have to be designed to work together to produce an optimal result. Above all, that means getting print data off the host in a format the reporting software can accept.

Because reporting and data-mining systems vary widely in terms of the formats they accept, the more flexible and powerful the print management solution is, the better. Critical print data in the enterprise originate from a spectrum of platforms, including mainframes, AS/400s, UNIX systems, Windows NT/2000 machines, and many others. These systems, in turn, host applications that produce print streams in a variety of data formats, ranging from line data and escape sequence-based printer languages to full-blown compositional formats and page definition languages. These considerations present significant networking, hardware, and data transformation challenges for a print management solution that must support end-to-end report management.

Report management and data mining will quickly become the gold standard for print distribution in the enterprise. Accounting system providers are now capable of giving clients the opportunity to get ahead of the game by maximizing investments in current technology and obviating the need for modification of host applications.

STORAGE

Once data is captured it must be stored properly for reliable, secure, online access throughout the enterprise. Decisions must be made concerning the use of magnetic or optical disc storage capability and which of many techniques to utilize.

Beyond Terabytes

The following are the seldom-used terms that designate the units of storage when dealing with numbers of hardly imaginable orders of magnitude.

$$1000 \text{ Terabytes } = \text{ Petabyte } (1,000,000,000,000,000)$$

$$1000 \text{ Petabytes } = \text{ Exabyte } (1,000,000,000,000,000,000)$$

$$1000 \text{ Exabytes } = \text{ Zettabyte } (1,000,000,000,000,000,000,000)$$

$$1000 \text{ Zettabytes } = \text{ Yottbyte } (1,000,000,000,000,000,000,000,000)$$

Storage Trends

Storage is provided through three primary channels:

- Fibre Channel: A storage network topology allowing very high bandwidth between storage devices.
- Storage Area Networks (SAN)
- Network-Attached Storage (NAS)

The SAN is the twenty-first-century solution to storage for the enterprise. This Local Area Network dedicated to storage is supposed to solve all problems. All that is required is a proper configuration of the fabric, interconnects, and zones. Everything should then be available all the time to every user. It sounds good, yet tools are still needed to determine the initial configuration, as well as to monitor and manage all those different elements and their relationships over time.

A SAN will have performance advantages for the enterprise as a whole because it will isolate one of the critical but resource-intensive storage management processes, namely back-up. Also, it provides users with multiple paths to the data of interest if the network is configured properly and can transfer large blocks of data at high speed to wherever it is needed.

SANs are isolated networks dedicated to storage. They require high-speed network technology to attach storage directly to the network.

Consolidate and Manage Data

SANs help consolidate and manage data. SANs offload the storage devices from the main corporate network to a specialized back-end network. The SAN is essentially a dedicated link between multiple servers and storage devices that have been moved into their own mini-network.

Most SANs consist of servers, storage devices that could include RAID or even SCSI-based boxes, networking devices such as hubs and switches, and software to manage it all. All the devices are then connected with a high-performance network of some sort. In most middle-sized to larger installations, the network of choice is Fibre Channel, a high-bandwidth transmission technology that supports speeds up to 1 gigabit/second with some 2 gigabit/second products entering the market.

Fibre Channel, a standard being shepherded by the Fibre Channel Industry Association (www.fibrechannel.org), also allows storage devices to be scattered across an area up to 10 kilometers (6.2 miles) wide. That distance can be tripled by the use of extenders. SANs allow easier and more cost-efficient data management, and the time to access data is decreased. Data can be consolidated either logically or physically, and then managed as one central pool.

The SAN offloads data traffic from the main network, so it's fairly common to see boosts in the performance of most of the major corporate applications as well. SANs also provide high scalability and better availability of data.

Fibre Channel is supposed to eliminate all performance problems that result from the finite capacity of the network bandwidth. From a storage perspective, the rule of thumb has always been that space usage will increase to fill whatever capacity is made available to it. So far, the same has been proven true for network capacity.

Even with warp drives, basic storage resource management is essential. Otherwise, the system will crash harder and burn brighter. Where key files are located, who is using which devices, what are the possible access patterns, where is the real workload, and where should new files be allocated are still vital questions. A SAN doesn't eliminate any of those, but adds new ones (e.g., zoning).

Explosive Data and SAN Benefits

A SAN will expand the ability of users to create more data. With more people having more access to more data along with the ability to do more with it, storage resource availability requirements will change. As a result, there will be an increasing need to monitor and deliver service from application-related perspectives. Business-relevant groupings will become increasingly important. Effective management of storage costs is but one reason. Ensuring availability is the critical requirement in determining the real costs and benefits associated with a SAN.

In an environment that fosters data growth, recovery will become even more difficult. The point is that the mass backup of files is still just that. With enough bandwidth or enough mirrored capacity, you can get it all backed up. Recovery is another story.

In addition to continuing to manage storage resources, SANs are going to drive the demand for intelligent backup. This means that the backup process includes only necessary data, and the restoration is guided and synchronized to account for the distributed nature of data and applications. The process is also highly automated and self-monitoring. Once the automated restoration is complete, even manual clean-up that is still required is guided for administrators. This ensures that applications can be restored to service efficiently.

Reality Check

The ultimate promise of SANs involves true file sharing across platforms and real any-to-any connectivity (i.e., hooking all vendor's hardware together). All the hardware vendors speak as if this will all be available tomorrow and they were leading the charge for the development of open systems standards, but no one has committed to a month, day, and year. In the meantime, activity and competition continue among manu-facturers, as well as among software vendors, to deliver first. In addition, the promise of openness just may force all the players to become as open as their marketing literature claims. Given the sheer number of different technologies and vendors required to field a SAN, the estab-lishment of standards might not be the result of one competitor van-quishing all the rest. That alone would be a good thing for the user community.

RULES FOR DEALING WITH VENDOR PROPAGANDA

- If a press release is not announcing the delivery of a product or function, ignore it.
- Architecture over Marketecture. Translation: White papers are nice, but technical specifications are a lot better.

- Selecting hardware is not like getting married. You are not looking for monogamy.
- If a product offers promises of "futures," get them in writing, or don't get the product.
- Invest in professional expertise for staff services to help you define your needs. Have the same people implement them, train your people, and come back in a year for a review. This professional talent is an essential component of your firm's staff for in-house and client assignments.
- Everything has to be managed effectively or it will cost you.
- Automate everything that you can or you will never have time to do anything else.
- Hardware (microcode) is only so smart. Even hardware vendors are adding software for dynamic, flexible management, as well as to replace revenue lost from falling hardware prices.
- First isn't always the best. While being on the leading edge has its rewards, remember you are only a nanosecond away from the "bleeding edge."

Network-Attached Storage (NAS)

NAS, wherein storage devices are connected to a LAN for access by servers and workstations over the Ethernet, is best suited to the quick addition of storage devices for file sharing. SANs, which put primary and secondary storage on a separate network, are best for dynamic disk allocations, storage connectivity at longer distances, and backup pooling.

Network Appliance, Inc. and Auspex Systems, Inc., two leading NAS vendors, have realized that they need the disk capacity of SANs and that they can use the disk pooling of a SAN. NAS is a much more developed technology at this time and SAN is less developed.

The next step — integrating SAN with NAS — will take time and over time will make a great deal of sense. But given what the best use of a NAS is and the areas it is best suited for, it will be a long time before it is pulled into the SAN. However, there is no reason the storage tied to the NAS should not be integrated into the SAN. Storage eventually will evolve into one of two formats: traditional SAN and IP via NAS devices.

NAS will be available on the Ethernet connected to storage devices on the SAN instead of inside the NAS box, making storage simple to use, fast, and inexpensive. This evolution is resulting in the connection of

NAS boxes to the LAN via an Ethernet connector and to hard drives or tape drives on the SAN via SCSI or Fibre Channel.

Connex Inc., a San Jose, California–based NAS vendor, introduced storage management software aimed at managing both SAN and NAS devices, and is concentrating on SAN/NAS convergence.

Regardless of what happens in terms of the convergence of SAN and NAS, there should always be a place for traditional NAS products because of their customized operating systems. The value proposition of NAS is in its approach to fast I/O, and in the operating system, not the disks. All disks spin at the same speed.

Fibre Channel Overview

- Fibre Channel is the storage interconnect technology of choice.
- Major storage vendors are bringing Fibre Channel products to market now.
- Major networking companies will bring Fibre Channel products to market beginning in 2000.
- Knowing high-end storage will mean knowing Fibre Channel.

Fibre Channel

- Removes a traditional system bottleneck
- High bandwidth I/O for rapid data access
- Networking capabilities to tap into data stored on local or remote servers
- Highly scalable
- Highly manageable
- A critical link in building SANs

Fibre Channel—How it Works

- It's a little bit SCSI and a little bit Ethernet.
- 1 Gigabit I/O speed.
- Plans for 2 Gigabit speed.
- Can use copper (coaxial, twisted pair) or fiber optic cable.
- Nearly instant access storage up to 6 miles away with fiber.

Storage Area Networks

- Embraces the legacy network devices already successfully implemented:
  - Fibre Channel to SCSI bridge
  - Fibre Channel to Ethernet bridge

- Includes the standards for the latest storage solutions
- Prepares an enterprise for future storage solutions

What Will You Store

- Firm/Client policy and standards documents
- Catalogs
- Correspondence
- Legal announcements
- Legal documents
- Brochures
- Anything in print worth saving

Other Types of Imaging

Computer On-Line Document Storage (COLD)

- Deals primarily with electronic reports that would normally have been printed
- Accessible from user stations
- Saves cost on printing
- Archival purposes

Other Tools

- OCR software
  - Textbridge
  - Xerox
  - OmniPage Pro
  - Caere
- Images
  - Corel Photo-Paint
  - Photoshop
  - Other image capture and touch-up software

Total Cost of Ownership

Management is the largest contributor to the total cost of ownership of even the most-expensive mass-storage devices. With the decline in fully configured prices per MB, non-declining costs assume a bigger slice of the cost pie. Management costs are climbing along with the capacity.

With mass storage devices and even SANs, there has been an assumption that just installing more and smarter hardware was the most efficient solution for business availability. Many times, this has not proven to be the case, yet the myth is perpetuated. The bottom line is that availability is not dependent upon the total size of the storage device or how "smart" it may be, but on how well the device is managed: space, performance, and events from the various logical and physical perspectives.

Get It on Tape for Business Preservation

Magnetic tape has been meeting computing's storage needs since the earliest commercial computers were introduced in 1950. As tape and other storage technologies evolved, a "storage blueprint" emerged. Offering high capacity and an exceptionally low storage cost, tape became the traditional backup and offline storage medium. The steady and sometimes breakthrough advancements in performance and capacity have helped tape maintain its leadership in the backup arena for decades.

With the coatings that are now a part of tape manufacturing, even the longevity issue has been resolved. In earlier times, it was a common practice to refresh reel tape because the magnetically encoded information would "print through" to adjacent wraps of tape. This argument is still sometimes used against tape technology by those promoting other alternatives; however, with the newer coatings, it is considered a nonissue, so information can basically be stored indefinitely on magnetic tape.

The demand for low-cost tape solutions with higher capacities and faster transfer rates is being driven by the fact that organizational storage requirements are growing exponentially while the window available for backup is shrinking. With the 24×7 availability of the Internet, an increasing number of corporate databases must be available around the clock and the cost of downtime has gone up.

Targeted Applications

Both the established and the new tape technologies are delivering solutions targeted at specific desktop, server, and enterprise applications. The most important factors to consider when selecting a tape backup option are the drive and its underlying technology. The most important drive characteristics to consider are listed below. It's a combination of factors that impact performance.

- Tape capacity
- Transfer speed
- Seek speed
- Reliability

Outsourced Storage

As e-business demands widen and the talent pool narrows, more clients are expected to outsource their storage systems. We can expect more managed storage offerings to emerge, according to vendors and industry analysts. Many clients will turn their data management over to what is being termed storage service providers, or SSPs, to manage data either on site or at a vendor hosting facility.

Like other outsourced IT services, hosted storage lets client organizations offload a cumbersome but critical function. When a client needs more capacity, it doesn't need to add disk drives or arrays. Administrators just alert the provider.

A key adaptation driver will be mounting capacity requirements. In addition, the difficulty and cost of hiring qualified people to manage storage systems will persuade many clients to outsource that function. Storage demand is doubling every year. While the cost of storage hardware is decreasing 25 percent to 30 percent annually, the cost of managing it is five to seven times the hardware costs.

Growing volumes of e-mail, which in many cases must be archived, are the number one storage hog, according to a Dataquest survey of IT organizations. Acutely affected are accounting firms and financial services firms that are required by law to archive all communications with customers.

Many dot.coms are farming out their storage because they don't want the headache of managing storage hardware. Accounting services providers may look upon adding an outsourced storage service to meet the growing storage needs of clients and gain an excellent profit center.

CHAPTER 12

Business Intelligence and Knowledge Management

BUSINESS INTELLIGENCE

Until recently, this market belonged to the Big Five consultants, large integrators and high-end specialty research boutiques, which served up complex — and expensive — solutions to Fortune 500 clients. Workaday accounting services providers needed not apply.

But now, business intelligence is permeating into the mainstream. A new generation of software tools puts business-intelligence solutions — systems that analyze business data to help clients make better decisions — within reach of a broader range of organizations. Accounting solution providers now have an opportunity to promote business-intelligence solutions, as the technology hits middle-market customers and dotcom startups.

Mid-tier and smaller clients are starting to embrace business-intelligence consulting services. Wider client adoption is fueling explosive growth. Gartner Group Inc.'s Dataquest unit predicts a fivefold growth in the business-intelligence applications market over a five-year span, from $602.3 million in 1998 to $3.2 billion in 2003.

Beyond the promising market data, business intelligence can serve as a logical follow-on sale to electronic commerce, customer relationship management (CRM) or enterprise resource planning systems, all of which generate teems of data that require analysis. Although business intelligence is finding a wider audience, it is still far from becoming a commodity. Business-intelligence solutions must be tailored to individual clients or specific vertical markets, so there's plenty of opportunity for an accountant's value-added services.

Customization

Accountants need a thorough knowledge of a client's operations to succeed in a business-intelligence niche market. For accounting firms stronger in business processes than technology, strategic hires with specific knowledge of business intelligence or alliances with business consultants would be necessary.

An accounting professional focused on database applications would be well served by looking long and hard at the business-intelligence marketplace. Vendor executives expect business-intelligence consulting revenues to take off over the next few years, as declining price tags and easier-to-use technology draw more clients into the market. In the past, a business-intelligence solution often required a half-million dollar or more investment in software and implementation services. The technology appealed mainly to large companies with great pain or lots of money to spend.

Aligning with Your Client's Information Technology Functions

Although more accounting professionals are devoting resources and effort to capturing and analyzing the client's intellectual capital, they often overlook a vital aspect of the client's knowledge management: the critical need for a client/accountant's IT knowledge consulting responsibility brokerage. Most clients' Chief Information Officers (CIOs) will admit they do not have a complete view of their global IT universe, including hardware, software, and services (such as training and consulting expenditures). The more complex and global the client's operations, the tougher it is to stay on top of information technology:

- Which plants and offices are using which brand of personal computers?
- With which microprocessors?
- Which software applications?
- Who has Internet access?
- How much are they paying for it?

- Which customized applications are running at which locations?
- Who's purchasing maintenance services and on what terms?

Clients' CIOs are refocusing their duties. Rather than being the direct providers of IT services, they now engage accounting professionals to broker IT resources for their companies' various business units and facilitate business-driven demands. Under this new structure, the CIO's direct control over IT budgets and governance will decrease. But he or she still will be expected to hold the accounting firm responsible for obtaining the right services at the right prices for the business units as well as for corporate operations.

The scope of IT decision implications will continue to grow, too. CIOs and their accounting firm will remain responsible for application deployment to support e-business, integrate mergers and acquisitions, and empower other enterprise initiatives—even as these implications grow more complex.

The accounting firm will be accountable to the client for results even though the firm won't have complete control over how things get done or who does them. At the same time, with less direct responsibility for selecting and procuring hardware and software, management will concentrate on becoming a core business engine, or change agent, driving innovation and creating new value propositions in e-commerce, supply-chain management, and other areas. These opportunities will help shape and achieve the strategic goals of the company—and make the client and accountant full business partners, not just technology experts that support other business people.

Client/Accountant IT Consulting Brokerage

An IT brokerage may be particularly helpful for clients in rapidly transforming industries such as telecommunications and financial services. It would also be advantageous for clients that are active in mergers and acquisitions, fast-growing enterprises that can barely keep up with business, and early adopters of new technology. These clients don't have the time or inclination to create and follow cumbersome asset-tracking methods. However, they do need to show results from IT investments, which an accounting-driven IT knowledge brokerage could put at the CIO's fingertips. In addition, an IT brokerage could help some clients that are playing catch-up with technology confidently assess their situations and map out workable strategies to move forward.

To provide maximum value, an IT brokerage should include several critical components:

- Worldwide inventory of all technology equipment
- Software
- Services
- Continuous update of information as new items are added or subtracted
- Market information of client versus competition
- Comparisons with best practices in the field (regardless of industry)
- Comprehensive, independent assessment of available technology options and the strengths and weaknesses of providers, plus details on the associated costs

Prognosis

As technology becomes increasingly ingrained in the fabric of the accounting profession, the importance and usefulness of an IT Client/ Accounting Brokerage relationship becomes increasingly compelling. Without it, clients will be forced to continue estimating and even guessing too much of the time about such fundamental matters as what locations have what technology, what technology those locations actually need, and in general, what to buy, when to buy, and what price to pay.

As clients lose more direct control over the delivery of IT services, their grasp of their company's IT environment will become less accurate. Worse, without this basic knowledge, they will be at sea in determining how — or if — all these IT investments will pay off in strategic value for their companies.

It's not a situation that clients can afford to continue. Too much, including survival itself, is riding on the outcome of critical IT-driven initiatives. But an accounting provider with superior technology capabilities could go a long way to helping clients truly understand their IT universe and make the most of it.

Online Analytical Processing (OLAP)

The latest generation of business-intelligence software has reached a much lower price point. The declining price of online analytical processing (OLAP) — the heart of a business intelligence solution — has made the technology more accessible. OLAP provides users with a multi-dimensional view of data, permitting trend analysis, what-if modeling, and other forms of data manipulation.

Vendors such as Brio, Business Objects, and Cognos have harnessed the power of OLAP in a lower-cost, desktop form. Oracle Corporation has branched into business intelligence with its Oracle Discoverer query tool, Oracle Reports reporting software, and Oracle Express OLAP platform. The company also markets a Business Intelligence System as part of Oracle Applications Release 11.

The OLAP Market

The author of The OLAP Report (www.olapreport.com) recently released the preliminary results of his annual OLAP market share report for 1999, which includes a review of the market size in recent years. Once again, Hyperion Solutions Corporation (www.hyperion.com) maintained its lead in the OLAP market space. Cognos Inc. (www.cognos.com) crept closer to Oracle Corporation (www.oracle.com) and is challenging for the second-place position.

The OLAP sector has grown considerably in the past few years. In 1996 the market was estimated at about $1 billion; it increased about 40 percent in 1997. In 1998 the market ended the year at about $2 billion, at which point many analysts expected the growth of OLAP would slow. They were correct: 1999 figures hit about $2.5 billion, an increase of about 20 percent. The market is expected to reach $4 billion in 2001.

The fast-growing business-intelligence sector has given rise to numerous solutions covering data warehouses, data marts, and analytical tools. With an eye to this market, SAS Institute (www.sas.com) and IBM Corporation (www.ibm.com) announced the formation of a joint consulting practice, and the eventual offering of bundled solutions that incorporate SAS software with IBM's DB2 Universal Database and server platforms. The three-year agreement between IBM and SAS Institute, and the joint development efforts will result in the creation of a consulting practice in IBM Global Services specializing in SAS solutions. SAS solutions will also be more tightly integrated with IBM's DB2 Universal Database, which runs on all IBM server platforms, including Netfinity, AS/400, RS/6000, NUMAQ, and S/390.

SAS Institute's software solutions cover customer relationship management, enterprise resource planning, data warehousing, supplier relationship, and procurement management. The agreement exceeds typical marketing agreements in that it tightly integrates the two vendors' solutions. IBM's relationship is another of its strategic alliances designed to move it out of the direct applications business and to more heavily rely on business partners that dominate specific sectors. IBM has also entered into relationships with Siebel Systems (www.siebel.com) to sell into the CRM space and with SAP AG (www.sap.com) for the ERP space.

Business Intelligence as a Market Niche

Every one of an accountant's business clients—no matter what their industry or size—need business intelligence tools and applications developed. They may also need your professional expertise to retrieve information, analyze it, and assist them in making timely decisions.

You may say, "Our clients (and we) do that with databases, report writers, and spreadsheets." Yes, and before that you did it with file folders, calculators, and columnar tablets. As the PC spreadsheet was to the paper spreadsheet so BI tools are to the PC spreadsheet. Business-intelligence tools sprang from the intersection of spreadsheets and databases. If it's too tedious to get the reports you want in all their near-infinite variety from a database and you need legions of spreadsheets to present your data in all the various ways that might be needed, you and your clients are prime candidates for business-intelligence tools.

The term "business intelligence" was coined by Howard Dresner, vice president and research director at Gartner Group Inc., to describe the multi-dimensional software. Although history may view them as an evolution of the two-dimensional spreadsheet, business-intelligence tools will prove to be one of the most important developments in the history of business computing. These tools give the accountant a paradigm in which they can make sense of the complex data strictures that are required to understand and measure their multidimensional business world.

Vendors Seek Your Expertise

Accountants with expertise in database technology and vertical markets are being courted by business-intelligence software vendors. They need accountants to penetrate what they perceive to be a growing middle market for their software and customize solutions to fit given vertical markets.

Vendors are rolling out programs to help cultivate the accountant channel and get accounting professionals and integrators up to speed on business-intelligence technology. Business Objects' Alliance Partner Program covers accountants, integrators, and consultants, among others (www.businessobjects.com/partners/index.htm). Hyperion Solutions Corporation (www.hyperion.com/alliance.cfm) has more than 300 alliance partners. In addition, IBM Corporation (www.4ibm.com/software/data/busn-intel/initiative.html) is courting accountants with a specialized business-intelligence program. IBM reported that more than 350 partners have joined the company's Business Intelligence Partnership Initiative, which has more than doubled in size since its launch in 1998.

Most of the vendors' partner programs feature accountant and software consultant segments. Accountants typically team with partners who sell, install, and customize the vendors' products, while the accounting professionals embed the vendors' products in their own software solutions.

KNOWLEDGE MANAGEMENT (KM)

Knowledge Management (KM) is more than another accounting practice niche. It should also be used by clients for managing their intellectual resources, transferring knowledge within their organization, and making optimal professional judgments in a timely manner.

For an accounting firm with a good strategy and a few new tools, it can mean explosive growth. For smaller and mid-sized businesses, knowledge management is making its way down from the corporate heights of General Motors and General Electric to the level of Yorky's Heating and Air Conditioning. What it is and how it will affect your practice depend a lot on the degree to which you embrace this market niche.

Some businesses work on managing their business knowledge by controlling its source (e-mail, Web sites, documents) and find ways to preserve the information and archive it. Other efforts begin at the functional level with attempts to improve the knowledge and culture of sharing information.

Tacit Knowledge

The accounting professional's tacit knowledge or expertise of knowledge management develops from repetitive professional experiences. Essentially, each professional audit judgment provides the practitioner with an opportunity to gain new insights about a task or audit situation.

It is the collection of these insights, accumulated and stored in memory over time, that best describes tacit knowledge.

KM provides firms with a formal process for capturing, cataloging, and incorporating tacit knowledge in decision making. The success of a knowledge management program hinges on the ability of the organization to capture the tacit knowledge of its senior people in a manner that facilitates efficient retrieval by professional staff. If an accounting firm is to leverage its intellectual resources, it must bridge the tacit with the explicit.

The best teacher is experience, your own or someone else's. KM is the perfect way for senior staff to impart their special knowledge to others in the accounting firm and maintain a competitive advantage over other firms. If knowledge management can be implemented internally, there should be little problem developing it as a practice niche and persuading clients of its benefits.

Peter Drucker, the father of modern management and the guru of knowledge work, had said, "Don't talk about 'knowledge management.' There is no such thing. There are only knowledge people." Systems meant to capture knowledge actually contain only information. Drucker said, "Information becomes knowledge only if someone knows what to do with it — and that's between our ears."

Intangible Assets

Many clients still think of knowledge management as an IT solution to moving information around, which is a huge mistake. Others think of it as just sharing knowledge, and the more they share, the better. That is also wrong. You can share a lot of mediocre knowledge and get nowhere, just as you can spend an enormous amount of money to build an IT system and not get a benefit equal to the investment.

Knowledge management is the leveraging of expertise from one area of the business to another to achieve better performance. Classical finance includes such intangibles as brands, patents, and licenses, research and development among knowledge assets, of course, but ignores basic operating expertise and team member skills that reside in the business.

Combining knowledge and management in one term can create a false sense of control, comprehensiveness, and accuracy in the minds of executives. There is also a nagging sense that what some call knowledge management is just a fancy name for commonsense problem solving.

Two Faces of Knowledge Management

Codification

- People-to-documents-to-people
- IT-intensive
- Focused on explicit knowledge (facts, statistics, processes)
- Easy, instantaneous access
- Model of information "reuse" drives revenues

Personalization

- People-to-people
- Seldom IT-intensive
- Focused on tacit knowledge (understanding, insight)
- Often conducted ad hoc as personal schedules permit
- Customization model drives profit margins

Insight

In today's new business era, customer intelligence is the most sustainable competitive advantage. Businesses are immensely rewarded because they are competing for a business-to-business relationship that lasts for the lifetime of that customer or client. In essence, e-businesses are competing for the long-term loyalty and repeat patronage of their most valuable customers.

A major challenge is identifying these best clients and satisfying them with the goods and services they want by better understanding their desires and interests. Traditional business-customer relationships have shifted. To succeed, businesses must combine traditional selling methods with new technologies that provide personalization, improved one-to-one marketing relationships, and customer (business) intelligence.

Recently, the rise of the Internet has opened up incredible opportunities for businesses and accounting firms of all sizes. Nearly every business can now afford to utilize technology as a potent weapon for reaching customers. Start-ups leveraging the Internet are challenging established players in all industries. This new competition has rewritten the rules for marketers. Now, there's little — if any — margin for error. By the time you notice a problem, it can be too late to fix it.

Combining these conditions has created an atmosphere of constant change. Organizations can either thrive or perish in this environment, depending on how well they respond to market requirements. Changing market dynamics present enormous opportunities for all organizations — even small businesses that can react to shorter windows of opportunity quicker than their large competitors. Fortunately, rapid technology advances have allowed businesses to adapt and even thrive in this atmosphere of constant change.

KNOWLEDGE MANAGEMENT MARKET

Knowledge management investment converges around customer relationship management (CRM), workflow tracking, and search and document management platforms. The CRM software products market had reached $1.7 billion by year-end 1999. The market is predicted to grow at an average rate of 60 percent per year, to a total market value of $10.7 billion by the year 2003.

The market for workflow tracking products had reached approximately $269 million for the year ended 1999. This market should grow at an average rate of 35 percent over the next three years to a total of approximately $887 million by 2003. Key issues regarding the workflow tracking products are whether it will continue as a separate segment or if it will be absorbed into the CRM or platform market, as both of these segments continue to add functionality.

The estimated market for unbundled search and document management products (not a part of Lotus Notes, Exchange, Oracle Office, or any other system that provides more extensive functionality than just search and retrieval) is $468 million by year-end 1999. The market is expected to reach approximately $2.3 billion by 2003.

Growth in this market will be fueled by the need for organizations to adopt better tools for searching and managing large amounts of information. The platform product market recorded $1.7 billion in sales for the year ended 1999. The demand in this market will continue to grow at an average rate of 35 percent over the next three years, to a total estimated market value of $5.6 billion by 2003.

Considerable market turnover will take place as smaller players are acquired by larger rivals while other new vendors enter the market. Knowledge management is an area where there will continue to be great experimentation, which will serve to foster continual innovation in a number of existing technologies such as Web mark-up languages, databases, security systems, networking, and operating system design in general.

ACCOUNTING: ACQUIRING AND ANALYZING CLIENT INFORMATION

Basic customer relationship principles require that a client establish a line of communication with its customers based on knowledge of their preferences, behaviors, and purchases. However, the customer information required for such relationships is often fragmented and buried in silos of operational systems. Customer data can come from custom applications, legacy systems, the Web, ERP applications, and purchased demographic data, to name a few sources. This also means the data can have different formats and semantics. These technological obstacles make the integration process protracted. E-business urgency mandates fast and adaptive implementations — taking a complicated situation and turning it into something useful.

Even when you have reconciled and integrated your client's customer information, analysis can still be protracted. This dilemma arises from the limited scope and the lack of integration between business intelligence and knowledge management tools. You are also challenged with issues of performance and data volume.

To attack and solve this dilemma for your client, you need efficient and effective data integration, a high-performance database designed for data warehousing, and a full spectrum of functionally rich analysis tools. Oracle Intelligent WebHouse is one of the most comprehensive and integrated solutions in the marketplace. It creates an infrastructure for data analysis and feedback. This allows the accounting professional to reap profitable revenues through providing the client insight gained from customer analysis.

SELECTING A ROBUST INTERNET PLATFORM

Building an e@ccounting practice puts new demands on the information technology that runs your firm. You need a software foundation that delivers full-featured applications and the scalability to handle fluctuating demand and rapid growth. Ideally, such a platform should also be based on open industry standards to protect your investments and make integration with other systems easier.

Oracle is one of the leaders in Internet computing, offering a comprehensive set of products that eliminate implementation chaos and simplify the development and management of sophisticated Web sites and e-business applications. Oracle's Internet database and application server, directory services, development tools, content management capabilities, and system administration products can provide you with a comprehensive foundation for e-business applications.

START WITH DATA INTEGRATION

Your practice and your clients have data, some of which has been accumulating over long periods of time. Some of it is purchased customer demographics, and a high volume of it is streaming in from the Web sites. How can you design and deploy an Intelligent WebHouse of actionable information from so many fragments of client and customer data?

The answer is a product such as Oracle Warehouse Builder (OWB). OWB enables the design and deployment of enterprise data warehouses, data marts, and e-business intelligence applications. It does this by providing an integration framework for all the components of Oracle Intelligent WebHouse. OWB allows the integration of traditional data warehousing sources with new e-commerce-based sources. Oracle CWM — a common warehouse metadata mode — is used to professionally manage the consolidation and sharing of metadata across the enterprise. This is accomplished through the use of bridges for metadata sharing. OWB also tightly integrates with Oracle 9i and Oracle Business Intelligence tools for acceleration of design and deployment of Intelligent WebHouses.

SCALABLE STORAGE, HIGH PERFORMANCE, AND DATA MINING

Relational Database

Necessary capabilities of the relational database should include the following:

1. Optimal scalability
2. Timely analysis
3. Support for future growth
4. Support for large volumes of data through data management systems

5. Enhanced capabilities for managing growing numbers of users
6. Appropriate resource allocation for each query
7. Maximized throughput
8. Summary management to allow administrators to quickly create summary tables within the database to accelerate performance
9. Built-in analytic functions, which enable calculations on data within the database to minimize movement of large volumes of detail data to applications

Multidimensional Database

The database server must provide powerful online analytical processing (OLAP) capabilities that include forecasting, "what-if" scenarios, and financial modeling. Select a server that is optimized for the query and analysis of client data such as sales, marketing, financial, manufacturing, or human resources data, without requiring special programs or reports from Information Systems (IS) personnel.

Data Mining

It is very important to implement server-centric architecture to provide technology to mine data within the server. This will enable the transformation of data warehouses into intelligent warehouses with highly productive client and customer information repositories. Such software, available from several vendors, puts powerful data-mining techniques in the hands of accounting professionals and consultants alike. With easy-to-use wizards that automate data mining, programs provide advanced users with full control over all options and parameters.

SUMMARY

To exploit the challenges of this new Internet business era, utilize the business-driven leverage of technology. Complete your due diligence and select a software and hardware partner that powers all of the components on an end-to-end solution.

Competitive vendors offer a range of choices in products that start from the limited end of the spectrum to full offerings of warehouse generation, data storage, and integrated business-intelligence capability. Your partner must be one who provides an architecture based on open standards, scalability, availability, and shared metadata.

Your professional goals should include knowing your clients and their customers better than your nimble, market-savvy competitors.

SUGGESTED FURTHER READING

Working Knowledge — How Organizations Manage What They Know by Thomas H. Davenport and Laurence Prusak, published in May 2000, by the Harvard Business School Press

Intellectual Capital: The New Wealth of Organizations by Thomas Stewart, published in December 1998, by Bantam Books

Excellence By Design: Transforming Workplace and Work Practice by Turid Horgen, Donald A. Schon, William L. Porter, and Michael L. Juroff, published in November 1998, by John Wiley & Sons

Assessing the Possibilities and Planning for a Successful Online Accounting Practice

BASIC PREPARATION

In a world of disposable employees, the ranks of consultants are mushrooming. There is a world of consulting other than that inhabited by those who toil for consulting giants like Arthur Andersen. A growing army of solo practitioners has been created by company cutbacks or the need for autonomy. However, flying without a Big Five or other corporate safety net can be daunting. How many consultants can the economy reasonably absorb? How much money can they make? How many consultants can dance on the head of a pin?

Who knows?

Right now is the best consulting market that has ever been seen. You can make huge profits, which is great news for all accountants interested in growing a consulting practice. There are some pitfalls.

As obvious as it sounds, CPA consultants have to make certain that their clients see them as consultants or accountants and not as vendors. Clients may perceive vendors primarily as shamelessly self-promoting salespeople whose primary goal is, naturally, to sell their products. Once CPAs fall into the trap of being viewed as vendors, the harder it may be for their clients to see them as consultants or accountants. The avoidance of such fuzzy perceptions is why the author encourages separating compilation and reliance services into separate professional entities.

The answer for the revenues question is that a successful accounting professional can expect to earn $300,000 yearly by the end of three years of practice. The customary billing is $200 per hour, but with the recommended value billing concept, the rate depends on the market.

One lesson in entrepreneurial survival: It's not for everyone. If you don't like slaving over petty details, recoil from computers, are not Internet literate, and can't stand risk, stay ensconced in the corporate suite or polish up that resume.

Invest sufficient time to research the market before quitting your job. Who are your potential clients? What do these potential clients need? Where do you want to be in three and five years? How could you win your market? Write a detailed business plan that projects revenues and budget for taxes, savings, health care — even home rent and a salary. Be brutally honest with yourself.

BALANCING OUR PROFESSIONAL AND PERSONAL LIVES

Most of us seek a balance in our lives, peer recognition, some time to ourselves, and monetary compensation. While most seek such balance, fewer find it — and usually only when they have begun to build their own practice.

The traditional route seldom works anymore, if indeed it ever did. Long before becoming eligible for a company watch, most entrepreneurial accounting professionals find themselves having a hard time adapting to the way corporate accounting operates.

The belief in loyalty has vanished. It isn't wise to be loyal to an accounting firm that lays off the accountant's supervisor and a few people in tax preparation while the professional was on a plane headed for a consulting engagement in another city. Loyalty is a two-way street. It has nothing to do with leaving the office at exactly 5 P.M., which by some in management is seen as a lack of dedication.

E-ENTREPRENEURSHIP

The concept of e-entrepreneurship allows accounting professionals to work however is best for them — setting one's own hours and juggling a work schedule around doctors' appointments, holiday shopping, and health club exercise. An entrepreneurial accountant is valued primarily for professional contributions, not for what's printed on the business card or the size of the expense account. Time is available to attend a child's Little League game or vacation with a spouse. Financial rewards are related to the amount of effort that is put into work and the revenues the professional brings into the firm.

CONSIDER A PART-TIME CONSULTING FORAY

An off-the-job interest can pay dividends on the job. The right kind of activity enhances the person, broadens experience, and lends prestige and visibility. It certainly worked that way for Hewlett and Packard. Part-time consulting just might do that for you. It could also give you another source of income. But much depends on your field of expertise and on how receptive your current employer might be to the idea.

If you've been thinking about the possibilities, you're certainly not alone. A recent survey by the accounting portal www.pro2net.com reported that approximately 67 percent of professionals at conventional accounting firms are considering leaving for an Internet-related enterprise.

Sage advice is to secure your employer's blessing before starting a part-time practice. Smaller firms are more sensitive to the matter and larger firms more permissive. Unless you're looking to be fired, don't hide your interest, intention, or plans. Map out those plans and make it very clear that there's no appearance of competition in letter or spirit.

In selling the idea to your employer, stress the following:

1. This will be a weekend or evening activity, requiring no more time and energy than if you worked with a community group as a volunteer.
2. The knowledge you gain will help you on the job. You may learn more from part-time consulting than from taking an MBA, simply because it's a way to gain practical, not theoretical, experience.

LAUNCHING THE PART-TIME CONSULTING VENTURE

- **Market yourself discreetly.** Start preparing the ground before going into the business by joining professional societies and trade associations, becoming as visible as possible. Writing articles on your specialty and giving speeches to groups among which there are potential clients are other useful tactics.

- **Look for the first client.** Draw up a list of all your professional contacts. Send an e-mail to everyone on the list, announcing your new venture as well as describing your background. In addition, to the ten or fifteen most likely prospective clients, draft a special letter (conventional snail-mail), along these lines: "I'm entering the consulting field and would very much appreciate your advice. Would you have lunch/dinner with me some time later this month?" Seeking advice is a highly effective way of securing clients.

- **Sell your services correctly.** Use a consultative approach by concentrating on results and benefits when discussing your services with a client. Avoid getting into procedural and technical details. Be careful not to give away too much at the diagnostic stage. When you're trying to figure out the problem with the client, don't throw in any free consulting. Information is a valuable power for you to use in building client dependency.

- **Practice a "go-away-bring-back" arrangement.** This means you discuss with the client what is to be done, then go away, do it, and bring back your finished product to the client. The advantage to you, if your services are adaptable to such an arrangement: minimum time spent in meetings and in the client's workplace, maximum time available to do the work in your off-hours.

- **Always get it in writing.** Make sure the agreement makes two things clear: what you will do for your client and what your client will do for you. The letter of agreement should specify how much, when, and how you are to be paid. The agreement should be for a fixed price rather than for time. The results must be measurable. Be sure the method of measurement is to your satisfaction and reasonably within your control.

- **Caveat.** A reputation for high ethical standards is an irreplaceable asset as a consultant. Being totally aboveboard about your plans with your present employer will help enhance that. However, be totally realistic about your situation and any probability that a disclosure to your employer may result in detriment to your career or continued employment.

COVERING YOUR PROFESSIONAL ASSETS

If changes within your organization pose a threat to your job, and you want to keep it, the following measures may improve your odds of survival:

- Don't be an ostrich. Keep your eyes and ears open. Pay attention to rumors; they're usually true.
- If a merger or consolidation is pending, research the new firm and its culture. The more you know, the better you can market yourself to the new regime.
- Don't be antagonistic. Present yourself as a team player, ready to adapt to organizational changes.
- Make sure your job skills (especially Internet-related) are fine-tuned, not just for your own firm, but for the marketplace in general.
- Broaden your skills to include related fields such as dot.com companies, software and hardware vendors, or marketing. And make sure the managing partner knows about your range of expertise.

MAKE LEMONADE WHEN DEALT A LEMON

The end of a job doesn't mean the end of a career if you've made sure your parachute is in working order.

- Always have a game plan, even if you think a layoff will never happen to you.
- Keep a record of your achievements, and build a portfolio that illustrates what you can do. Include practice brochures, letters of commendation, client kudos, and profiles of clients.

- When interviewing with a prospective firm or associates, research their financial stability.
- Get involved in an industry association. A network of colleagues can provide moral and practical support in the event of a layoff or the launch of your own practice.

PERSONAL FINANCES

Get your financial house in order before you start a business. Set aside savings for taxes, Social Security contributions, and a cushion against financial reversals. Discipline is probably the most important word an independent consultant must constantly keep in mind. It takes discipline to work when no one is looking over your shoulder and it takes considerable discipline to maintain a household and to save enough to cover your tax bill at the end of the year. If you are not a self-starter and you are not a self-saver, you will not survive in your own practice.

Even with an accounting background, the hardest area for any independent consultant to maintain discipline is with money. When you have an independent practice, you have to look at your income in an entirely different way than you viewed a paycheck. Salaries flow in at regular intervals, while practice owners usually get paid on a very irregular basis. Learning to budget until the next projected check arrives is essential.

Although accountants should know better, withholding taxes are many a fledgling practice's stumbling block—especially in the beginning when everyone is accustomed to having an employer deduct the taxes from their paychecks. Another item to deal with is health care. If you leave a job to begin an independent practice, you should continue under your prior health plan. Continued coverage must be made available by law in most states, and it is infinitely less expensive than purchasing new coverage.

PAY ATTENTION TO DETAILS

In solo or smaller practices, everything counts. Expenses must be meticulously tracked—from car mileage logs to home-office square-footage to supplies—to be used as tax deductions.

VIRTUAL OPPORTUNITIES

CPA firms and accounting professionals of many designations are discovering new opportunities related to the Internet. Many are building practices that include Internet consulting, electronic mail communication with clients and a network of informal partners that make up what can be called a "virtual practice."

Primarily these e-entrepreneurs work out of their own homes or small offices, where they communicate by e-mail, telephone, and fax. They provide management advisory services, tax preparation, long-range strategic planning, and information technology consulting to nonprofit organizations, trade associations, physicians, dentists, lawyers, and a wide range of small to medium-sized businesses.

The Internet has leveled the playing field. Nobody knows how big you are when you're on the Web.

OVERCOMING OBSTACLES

Develop your team. A successful online accounting consulting practice requires both technically competent accounting professionals and sales and marketing talent. From day one, you need to create a business and marketing plan that lists services to be provided. Keep in mind that most successful consulting practices limit the services offered. Less is often more.

FAILURE FACTORS IN STARTING AN ONLINE ACCOUNTING CONSULTING PRACTICE

1. *No support among partners for the start-up.*
   This is first and foremost, because partners are often stuck in the mindset that a typical staff accountant has to produce a certain number of billable hours per year. In consulting, billable hours can average from 1,000 to 1,200 hours, or could go as low as 750 hours. With a start-up, consulting is extremely difficult to schedule, as it occurs at different, unpredictable times (not like the recurring annual work to which accounting firms are accustomed). Gaining partner consensus leads to referrals from within your own client base.

2. *Unrealistic expectations.*
   During the first few years, expectations of how large profits will be can be a problem. It is a very capital-intensive business and can take a year or longer for efforts to pay off. Firms that make the most money are the ones that use a good mix of marketing activities and keep at it.

3. *Offering too much in too many markets.*
   By offering too wide a variety of services, you can't staff effectively or perform enough work in any one area to generate significant experience or revenues. Clients are willing to pay premium dollars for professionals they perceive as experts.

4. *A lack of a full-time approach and professional/staff support.*
   The team requires continuous training. Too many firms lack a full-time approach and field a part-time team (both professional and staff support). Firm-wide support and understanding are required, especially during the first year or two of the formation and growth process.

5. *Inconsistent marketing and promotional activities.*
   The highest-value marketing activities are fee-based seminars, consistent electronic newsletters, and e-mail campaigns coupled with telemarketing. The lowest-value marketing activities include direct mail, yellow page advertising, and print advertising. Sound advice with regard to any marketing activities is to do it regularly and consistently. Only novices fall into the trap of doing something once and expecting it to produce a huge amount of revenue, or abandoning each attempt and looking for the next home run. The most successful consultants are those who are willing to choose, then use their marketing activities and patiently wait for them to work and yield profitable results.

Consulting practices that fail tend to do so because they haven't put forth enough effort, funds, and expertise in the marketing area and they haven't gained partner support by managing expectations. To succeed you need to invest in technical consulting people and in sales and marketing professionals. One consulting staff person with no backup marketing support is a recipe for failure.

SUCCESS FACTORS IN STARTING AN ONLINE ACCOUNTING CONSULTING PRACTICE

Focus

Consulting firms that succeed in building substantial practices are focused on delivering one or two consulting services to their clients. For most firms, this means selecting one or two niche service offerings, becoming expert in them, and focusing their efforts around these services. There is a saying that if all you have is a hammer, then everything begins to look like a nail.

Many accounting firms that are just starting an ancillary consulting practice tend to provide smaller services such as disaster recovery planning or system selection. Firms that are serious about consulting should avoid offering too many services.

How would a prospective client perceive your practice if it thought you provided a service just once a year? "How good can you be?" they might ask. And if you have just one person providing a specific service, and that person unexpectedly leaves—surprise, you are no longer in that business.

Marketing and Selling

Marketing ranks as one of the most misunderstood functions involved with growing any kind of practice. The word selling appears in hardly any CPA text. It is no mystery, therefore, that a great many CPAs and CPA firms feel very uncomfortable with the term and the concept. Selling is a fact of economic life. The truth is that if a practice didn't do it they would be out of business or never even start in business. Nothing happens until somebody sells something.

If your practice has chosen to offer business intelligence and knowledge management consulting services, which are among some of the largest opportunities in technology consulting, then commit to selling. And nowhere is this more important than in the midrange business market. Many of your competitors, who also provide excellent professional services to their clients, also have people without enough to do because they are unwilling or unable to sell the engagements you are offering and selling.

If you are going to compete in this market, hire a competent marketing person who can sell. Although, technically, selling is function of marketing, there is a chasm between the two functions. You don't have to deal in semantics. You want engagements. Your salesperson must be technically conversant in the consulting services that you offer. This person must be able to engage in consultative sales so that the needs of the client are determined and a follow-up visit with a technical specialist is scheduled followed by completion of an engagement agreement. You don't send a technical person on a sales mission. The marketing person must function as a communications medium between the client and the firm. An excellent resource for further information is the Association for Accounting Marketing, www.accountingmarketing.org.

Success Building Blocks

1. Build brand awareness around your firm.
2. Do regular, planned, and budgeted marketing activities that entice prospective clients into your sales funnel.
3. Know your service offerings and where they fit.
4. Sell the services only where they fit.
5. Provide excellent service.
6. Cultivate patience.
7. Invest for the long-term.

Success Indicators

Success in any business requires more than entering a field and declaring your business's establishment. It's not just about technical skill, intelligence, or an aptitude with technology. It's not about following the path various seminars and vendors say ought to be taken to maximize profits. Enjoying what you are doing, achieving satisfaction from providing a needed service, makes success far easier because it clarifies goals and provides the emotional spark to propel a practice along the road.

So, if you're not in the business, how do you suddenly develop this intense desire and liking for the business? How do you transform a traditional accounting firm into the sleek, battle-ready consulting organization that's adept at technology? Wanting to make more money is always a good incentive for entering a new field. But it is also clear that business can't take old attitudes into new ventures and expect that business as usual in the old field will be business as usual in the new field.

Recognizing market opportunity is a pre-condition. If you don't see an opportunity, there probably isn't one there for you. Embarking on any new venture requires being able to break away from preconceived notions. It requires a tolerance for taking chances.

The next step is to join people who know the business and care about it. Everyone does not need to be a consulting enthusiast, but there must be someone who can work up some excitement, and who can market and communicate that excitement to both the clients, prospective clients, and partners.

Finally, develop a plan. Know what you're trying to accomplish. Know how you are going to measure success. If you don't know where you are going, how will you know when you get there?

The secret to consulting is evaluating the market, developing a plan, and teaming the right people.

YOUR BUSINESS PLAN

Things change very quickly in this market. To achieve and maintain profitability, your business plan should change too. Forget about long-range goals and focus on your ability to identify and react to technology and market trends.

Most professionals with an accounting or finance background understand the importance of having a solid business plan. Yet, many don't think that their practice's very survival might depend on skills as technology prognosticators.

At one time, writing your business plan was a bit of a struggle, requiring a few late nights and a founder's vision. The process was straightforward, and an abundance of guides, rulebooks, and rudimentary shrink-wrapped software were available for assistance.

Today, market niche life cycles are much shorter. New technologies are emerging almost as fast as the vendors can announce them. Many accounting and consulting firms are undergoing massive consolidations that threaten the very existence of some practitioners. You need a good business plan more than ever, because the questions are tougher than ever:

- Which technologies should you adopt?
- What facets of the Internet present the best opportunities?
- Which market niches should you target?

Adapting to Change

The paradox of business planning is that the same dynamic environment that necessitates a solid, thorough business plan is also what makes the process so difficult. The following tactics can help buffer your business against the perils of an unpredictable environment:

1. *Focus on your marketplace.*
   The most important safety net for planning in this maelstrom of change is staying attuned to your clients. You must understand your clients' applications, preferences, needs, and technical directions. You must also learn what changes are occurring in their industries and plan accordingly. Consolidations and down-sizing are two changes that are occurring in industries other than accounting services.

2. *Form close alliances.*
   Use two or three of your clients as touchstones for evaluating services, products, pricing, and market trends.

3. *Emphasize short-term goals.*
   Even the strongest proponents of business planning have de-emphasized the long-range portion of their plans. In the consulting business, the five-year plan has been reduced to little more than a mission statement. Medium-term (two- to three-year) plans are, however, a must for every accounting consultant.

4. *Anticipate changing market conditions.*
   Coping with a changing business environment requires a dynamic living plan that blends focus with realistic elasticity.

5. *Reevaluate your growth strategy.*
   Planning for revenue growth rather than profit growth is risky business. Rapid revenue growth places a strain on cash flow and also places invested capital at risk.

6. *Perform worst-case analyses of cash flow to account for unfavorable turns in your practice.*
   Today's pro forma financial statements should be more conservative (higher liquidity and stronger cash flow) than those of recent past years.

7. *Consider where you'll be in two or three years with your current business model.*

Even if you follow all of the above points, your business plan can still fail if you're using the wrong business model.

Planning Pitfalls to Avoid

- **Doing it alone.** You may be the smartest accounting professional in the business, but don't underestimate the power of collective thinking. Involve all partners and consultants in the planning process. If you don't have a board of directors, form an advisory group that meets quarterly.
- **Quixotic goal setting.** Each goal should be based on a solid understanding of how it will be achieved.
- **Putting all your eggs in one basket.** Try to plan for diverse, but compatible, sources of revenue. Build in annuity sources (service revenue and recurring engagements, for example).
- **Rigid technology directions.** Sinking capital into technology that won't be here next year can sink your practice. Study technologies that add flexibilities.
- **Ill-considered revenue goals.** Be cautious of revenue goals that threaten cash flow. Consider sacrificing some projected revenue in the interest of short-term profit and cash reserve.
- **Turning your focus away from clients.** Don't make a common mistake of thinking your clients will always bend to technological pressure. Clients are the best source of planning information.

A MODEL ONLINE ACCOUNTING PRACTICE BUSINESS PLAN

Navigating the Minefield

An effective business plan will help you delineate objectives, directions, and strategies. It will be useful for you and your associates to reach a consensus about your practice's future. The business plan will contribute to bolstering the confidence of existing and potential clients. Industry partners, lenders, investors, and creditors will be influenced by the plan's demonstration of your practice's ability to repay debt. Your business plan takes the unexpected into consideration, directs your business in good times, and stabilizes it during the bad. That is why a business plan is one of your most important tools: it guides business growth by providing a map to navigate the minefield toward a successful future.

A well-crafted business plan should be used as a living document to assist you in managing your business. Your business plan is the representation of all of the components of your practice — the services you offer, the clients you target, and the ways you deliver one to the other. Your plan will facilitate your reasoning in determining how you will build and maintain the ability to meet your clients' needs. This ability to meet your clients' needs represents the underlying value of your business. *There is no substitute for thinking your accounting practice through and taking the time to put it down on paper.*

A well-written business plan tells the reader what your practice is, where it's going, and how it will get there. It contains the information a potential partner, investor, or affiliate would want to see, without being verbose.

The preparation of your business plan presents you with a unique opportunity to consider all phases of existing or new ventures. A business plan gives you the space to refine differing strategies before testing them in the real marketplace. Remember, though, to assess your business's actual performance against the plan. Then revise your business plan accordingly. Consider the alternative consequences of marketing service offerings and targeted market niche strategies. Determine the human and financial resources required to launch, develop, and prosper the business. All of this simulation comes without the cost and heartbreak of trial-and-error operation.

Your plan should be as long as is needed to tell your practice's value proposition. An ideal length is 25 pages: a start-up plan should not exceed 50 pages. A good plan should take at least six months to write. *Developing a business plan is widely considered to be the most important thing you do before going into business.*

The process of putting a business plan together forces you to take an objective, critical, unemotional look at your entire business proposal. For a start-up, the business plan is an assessment tool. As you work your way through the plan, you will have to continually reaffirm the viability of your business rationale.

Here are the minimum requirements for a comprehensive business plan. Your plan will also address issues specific for your practice (any contingency plans, for example).

1. **Cover Page.** Include your firm's name, address, telephone number, URL, and the contact person's name.
2. **Executive Summary.** This part of the plan, appearing first but written last, is a concise selection of highlights from the areas

listed below and is designed to entice the reader to start and continue to read the plan. Summarize key points for each section. Write in a narrative fashion with no sub-headings. Use plain English. Avoid the jargon of the industry.

3. **The Mission Statement.** A high-level word-picture of what your practice intends to be. Generally contains goals, objectives, and strategies along with the corresponding professional vision.

4. **The Practice Profile and Strengths.** Describes your practice's business structure, history, partners, staffing, demographics, and so forth. A summary of past performance (or a start-up plan for a new practice), types of service offerings, resource dependencies (e.g. legal), and availability is also included.

5. **Services/Products Strategy.** Covers services and products both current and planned, R&D, and milestones. Key technologies, expertise, service differentiation and positioning, facilities, and sourcing considerations should also be included.

6. **Market Analysis.** Discusses in detail market definition, needs analysis, client profiles, market share, and competition. This section should support the above-mentioned strategy for service differentiation.

7. **Sales/Marketing Plan.** Reviews sales strategies, promotions, advertising, and publicity plans. You should list and explain approaches to targeted market niches and possible complexities.

8. **Financial Plan.** Contains current and projected income statement, planned and available sources of funding, balance sheet, and cash-flow, break-even, and ratio analyses. Financial data and calculations are the make-or-break component of any business plan. Your goal is to show that the business will be profitable. If your plan is to raise capital, take a conservative approach to enhance credibility with investors and lenders.

9. **Appendices.** Include resumes, references, market studies, patents, intellectual property rights, authorizations, certifications, agreements, and the like.

FINDING YOUR OPTIMUM FIT

The more you work with your business plan, the more you'll realize how useful it is. An important factor to recognize is you do not have to prepare an intricate plan to have an effective management tool. You can pick and choose from among the parts of the formal business plan that are the most relevant at any given time.

The traditional professional accounting services model has vanished and is morphing into new and unpredictable forms. The business models that provide the most buffering from external forces are those that stress high-margin, service-based revenue sources, such as consulting, training, and systems integration.

However successful your business is today is no guarantee that it will be as successful tomorrow. New technologies, more available knowledge, changing client profiles, new or additional competition, and a host of other external factors may arise. To prepare for tomorrow you should know your business and your client's business as well as, or better, than they do. Then you can anticipate what they're going to need and reengineer your practice to deliver these needs in a profitable way. Internally developed software and training programs will continue to return higher margins, but even here, rapid change has dulled the luster once associated with these revenue sources.

PROTECTING YOUR FUTURE INVESTMENT

- Consider using Application Software Providers (ASPs).
- Balance your development with services.
- Partner wisely with appropriate vendors.
- Investigate buyouts or joint efforts with other firms whose services and expertise complement your own.
- Know your clients' needs better than any of your competitors.
- Know what value must be provided to satisfy those needs.
- Know what component of that value you will provide and who will provide the remainder.

Thorough planning puts you in control of the process and will help ease the practice's way through the difficult transitions every accounting practice faces sooner or later.

SOFTWARE TOOLS

A number of shrink-wrapped, inexpensive business-planning software packages are available. These programs are not recommended for start-up or seasoned practices. All the available planning packages have been designed generically for common denominator businesses and for neophyte entrepreneurs. The software itself provides little more than the ability to link financial statements (spreadsheets), associated graphics, and written text, a common feature of every word processing program.

Although these planning software packages arm a general user with useful checklists, outlines, and time-saving templates for selected businesses, they address only traditional businesses and traditional situations. The materials contained in this text are ample to see you through the entire planning process.

It's your job to include contingency planning. You must ensure that strategic plans are viable, that you've considered technology and vendor-related changes, and you have addressed client and marketplace directions and conditions. By accomplishing these moves, you'll build more than just a solid, dynamic practice business plan. You'll create a navigational system that can safely guide your business to its chosen destination.

RESOURCES

Small Business Administration (SBA)

The SBA provides useful, free information about business plans, as well as other business assistance. The SBA, Small Business Development Center, and relevant state agencies provide information on starting, financing, or growing a business. Many agencies also provide no-cost individual counseling. There are also special programs for women, minorities, and veterans.

The SBA's Web site (http://www.sbaonline.sba.gov) allows you to download useful publications. However, be advised that most of the counselors, with the exception of SCORE volunteers (Service Corps of Retired Executives), have never started or managed a private sector business. Many of them have never even worked in a for-profit business. Their experience is generally centered around working for the government and receiving a steady paycheck on a regular basis. Consulting with the SBA can be like seeking good tax advice from the Internal Revenue Service (IRS).

The Accounting Guild

A comprehensive review and evaluation of your business plan is available on a confidential and timely basis from the author, through the facilities of The Accounting Guild. For more information consult the Guild's Web site (www.accountingguild.com) or e-mail the author at jackfox@accountingguild.com.

CHAPTER 14

Identifying Goals
Laying the Practice Foundation

PROSPECTUS

Prospectus, according to the *American Heritage Dictionary of the English Language,* is a formal summary of a proposed commercial, literary, or other venture; it is Latin for prospect.

Describe your proposed online accounting/consulting business in detail. State the services you plan to offer and the niche markets you propose to market your services to. Emphasize any unique appeal or value propositions of your services. Carve out in one sentence the theme of what your business plan is selling.

Mission Statement of the Practice

A practice's mission statement provides a specific direction for all members of the practice to follow. Some management consultants advise practitioners to articulate their purpose in a single sentence or phrase. If one can do this, one should probably seek a career in advertising rather than accounting, consulting, and the online permutations. The firm's mission statement should define its primary goals. For illustration, Exhibit 14.1 states the mission statement of The Accounting Guild, Inc.

STRATEGIC GOALS

An expert is one who knows more and more about less and less.
Nicholas Murray Butler,
commencement address, Columbia University

The mission of The Accounting Guild is to serve as the catalyst for effectively meeting the practice development needs of the online accounting services provider community. Forming a consortium of practitioners, software developers, application software providers, and other vendor members of the accounting industry will bridge the chasm of traditional and technologically, state of the art accounting and consulting services.

Source: The Accounting Guild, Las Vegas, Nevada © 2000. All rights reserved. Used with permission.

Exhibit 14.1 The Accounting Guild Mission Statement

The specific identification of your firm's target market niches is your foundation for creating strategic goals to build an organization that will allow you to accomplish your mission.

Steps to Identifying Goals

- **Define and refine the practice's direction.** Each team member's goals should support and further the mission and direction of the firm.
- **Members of the team set their individual goals.** The participants or potential team players candidly disclose the professional goals they established and how those goals will support the mission and direction of the venture. Hidden agendas will damage a firm more than any competitor.
- **Consider the history and experience of the firm.** Past performance and perception have a significant impact on clarifying and publishing the firm's goals. The firm that is an off-shoot of a traditional accounting firm will have differing goals than a firm that has just been created without any baggage.
- **Determine each participant's role.** Goals can be realistically achieved only when correlated with the expertise and effort available to meet them.
- **Goals should not contribute to limitations.** Goals should enable opportunities and be near enough to achieve but far enough to require stretching.

- **What you can measure, you can manage.** Establish goals and milestones as targets to reach. Measure your distance from them.
- **Set short-term goals.** Short time-frames (six months) facilitate focus. Also set mid-term and longer-term goals.

Formulate Specific Goals

- Areas of specialization
- Target market niches
- Revenue potential
- Market size and share goal
- Competitive landscape
- Services
- Quality/client satisfaction
- Capitalization
- Cash flow
- Strengths and weakness of management and team members
- Equipment, software, and facilities

BUSINESS STRUCTURE

Strength is not the absence of weakness
but how we wrestle with our weaknesses.
Noah ben Shea

On the upside, incentives abound for entering the online consulting market. Consulting offers the higher margins and upmarket positioning for which many traditional accounting firms have been searching. The ability to provide consulting services is particularly important for resellers considering the transition from scorekeeper to solutions provider.

On the downside, building an online consulting business is not a simple task. A significant investment must be made in hiring personnel, adopting a consulting engagement methodology, aligning with the optimum industry vendor partners, and most fundamentally, radically rethinking how to approach clients.

Accountants have traditionally been too timid about presenting their value and charging enough for planning and implementation services. They beat themselves up about giving away compliance services in order to get the consulting engagements and then are too busy during tax season to do the consulting work.

Online Accounting Consulting Market Demographics

The IT consulting services pie is sliced into 11 categories:

1. Business process re-engineering
2. Change management
3. Business strategy
4. Process improvement
5. IT strategy
6. IT design
7. Operational assessment
8. Needs assessment
9. Benchmarking
10. Capacity planning
11. Maintenance planning

Who Do the Clients Call?

Consensus among clients is that if you need to fix one thing (such as design and manage the construction of some system) the independent consultant is the best fit. If the client needs an army to come in and hit everything, the Big Five might be best. The top consulting firms also have the capability to apply their large staffs and storehouse of knowledge to a range of projects. With deep bench strength, they can send 10 people to a site, but have thousands more in backup. If one person isn't a right fit, they can replace that consultant quickly.

On the downside, clients and analysts say that larger consultancies can have inexperienced (if quick-learning) people and Byzantine reporting channels; show a lack of interest in small, annoying jobs; and cost a great deal.

With a tight job market, there are not a lot of skilled people out there who have much to offer. They leave a job on Friday, go online over the weekend, and become a consultant on Monday.

Small consulting shops can often provide specific technical and business knowledge and may be more accessible than their behemoth brethren. Technical specialty is part of the allure of smaller consultancies. On the other side of the ledger, smaller shops can potentially be less stable than the larger firms — and sometimes just as expensive.

Why Make the Move?

Pressure on auditing and tax work is a key factor driving accounting practitioners to provide services such as online consulting. The Big Five have gone after services in a big way and now rank consulting, integration, and online-related engagements among their most significant and profitable activities.

Classic Consulting Model

The classic consulting model is a pyramid organization with the most billable resources at the bottom and the least billable at the top. The pyramid structure is prevalent among consultancies and consists of a practice leader at the top and staff consultants — the foot soldiers of the consulting scheme — at the base.

Elevating the Position

Another benefit of consulting is that it elevates the position of the accounting practitioner at the client site. Consulting engagements typically arise from the highest levels of the client's organization. Getting involved with the corporate decision makers means getting in at the ground floor of emerging systems and e-commerce opportunities. It also means preventing competitors from eating your gourmet lunch while you are occupied with the compilation, review, or audit.

What many accountants don't understand sometimes is that the consulting specification they are bidding is a specification they could have been writing. Somebody else got a lot of high-margin dollars for doing that.

Accountant's Consulting 101

What does it take to transform an accounting practitioner into a consultant? The list of particulars is long and varied, but there are a few fundamentals.

- **First on the list is a professional to lead the consulting effort.** Some industry executives suggest that an accounting firm recruit their consulting practice leader from a top-tier consulting firm. You've got to have someone with a tried-and-true career in a consulting environment.

- **Smaller firms should turn to the middle tier of the consulting pyramid.** They should offer a rich vein of talent that small to mid-sized clients can afford to tap. Senior-manager-level personnel at the Big Five and similar consultancies typically offer 10 to 12 years of experience. Annual salaries for these consultants range from $170,000 to $200,000, and such talent have joined online accounting consulting firms with annual revenues as low as $6 million.

- **The practice leader brings to the accounting consulting firm a knowledge of project management and an understanding of the consulting process:** data gathering and analysis, report writing, recommendation development, and implementation planning.

- **The managing partner of the existing accounting firm takes on the role of consulting partner and takes the lead in dealing with clients.** A peer-to-peer relationship is critical when calling on a client's executive suite. In consulting, most executives believe it is a bad idea to have an accounting firm's regular staff make the high-level contacts. The accountants of the past are not going to be as successful in solutions selling.

- **Fleshing out the remainder of the consulting practice, combine the training of incumbent staff and external hiring.** New hires and transfers lacking consulting experience are taught consulting craft skills, such as business-process analysis, activity-based costing, and change management.

Practice Lifeblood

Having the right people is not enough. New consultancies also need to have a formal process in place for engaging clients and managing projects — in other words, a consulting methodology. Methodologies have been the lifeblood of consulting firms for years. The all-important methodology governs the entire spectrum of consulting activities, from

- Plan
- Order
- Gather Data
- Set Up and Install
- Group Training
- Data Input
- One-on-One Training
- Enter Balances
- Enter Transactions
- Produce Reports
- Accounting Procedures
- Back Up Procedures
- Test and Finalize
- Conclusion
- Follow Up

Exhibit 14.2 Basic E-commerce Accounting Process Methodology

marketing the service, to winning the client's business, to determining when and how to charge the client. The methodology also covers managing the consulting project, setting milestones, and reporting back results.

Accounting firms often stumble when they try to offer consulting services because they don't have the fundamental methodologies in place by which to engage in that kind of work. In contrast, accounting professionals that maintain a methodology are marketing a repeatable process. The methodology—the consultant's services encapsulated in tangible form—is what gains clients' confidence. Accountants don't need to develop methodologies afresh. Hiring a practice leader from a leading consultancy will solve that problem. Exhibit 14.2 is a checklist of a basic e-commerce accounting process methodology.

THE PARTNERING OPTION

It may be too difficult and expensive to build an online accounting organization from the ground up. Two good ways of moving into consulting are through an alliance with a consulting firm or an outright acquisition. Even so, the synergies between the consulting and accounting businesses may not outweigh the major differences between the two. Differences in value propositions, business and professional cultures, and services can result in conflict.

Look at joint ventures as a wedge into consulting. In this scenario, an accounting firm enters a two-year venture, as a prelude to a merger, to see if the accounting business and the consulting and implementation business align. Do this with firms of small, manageable size, and manage the two businesses separately. Allow the integration of the accounting, and consulting firms to occur gradually over time, instead of trying to force it.

One temptation for an accounting firm-turned-consultant is to go too far, too fast. The accounting firm that seeks to pursue high-end, e-business-strategy consulting from the beginning has a huge credibility gap to close. Accounting professionals should make a stepwise progression into consulting services, starting with what they know best.

Soul Searching Question—What is the firm good at?

After Answering Question—Focus on what the firm is good at. Identify and pursue a niche in which the firm can really excel.

TRANSITION

Accounting professionals considering the field of online accounting consultation must be willing to turn their business model on its ear. They have never had a method or process by which to market and perform something that had previously not been a component of their practice. In the haste and pressure of the compliance business, shielded by years of licensed monopoly, they are now entering the gladiatorial arena without the armor of a CPA certificate. With the proper investment and a true commitment from management, an accounting firm-turned-consultancy can evolve into a very profitable organization.

Run your consulting practice as a stand-alone Profit & Loss. Set up a "Chinese Wall" between your compliance activities and your reliance services. The two businesses operate on different financial models. Consulting tends to run on a rainmaker basis and high fees while the compliance business involves large number of implementers and low per-person billables. Combining $650-an-hour consultants and $85-an-hour auditors under one roof is a recipe for cultural catastrophe, given the wide disparity in their respective billing rates.

USE TAX SEASON TO PROBE CLIENTS' TECHNOLOGY PLANS

If your firm is considering an online accounting consulting practice, tax season presents an opportunity to get some important preliminary work completed. Many accounting firms reduce their marketing efforts during the tax season. However, tax season presents an opportunity to meet face-to-face with clients and prospective clients and ask some revealing, leading questions about their e-commerce needs.

PROBING QUESTIONS

The following is a list of questions you should ask your clients and your competitors' clients to determine their needs for your services:

- How is e-commerce affecting your business?
- What are the top three e-commerce technology issues you must address this year?
- Do you have the right personnel to implement, operate, and maintain your current systems?
- Are your personnel adequately trained? If not, what are your top priorities in training?
- Do you know how much you are currently spending on technology?
- Does your financial reporting system properly account for your technology investment?
- Do you have a written technology plan and budget?
- Would you be interested in executive e-commerce technology education?
- Whom else do you know that could use our consulting services?

With a large enough proportion of your client base and some of your competitors' clients answering these questions, you should have a better understanding of their technology needs. Tax season is an excellent time to sow marketing seeds and uncover opportunities your firm may have in e-commerce consulting within your own and your competition's fields.

TAKING THE NEXT STEP

Firms that are serious about e-commerce consulting efforts must commit resources to the programs and change the way they do business. If your firm is serious about technology consulting, the following steps are necessary to get there:

1. *Write the business plan to outline how your firm will be involved in technology consulting.*
   All other steps flow from this plan. You must decide the business you will be in and how you will get there. Unless you can verbalize your concepts, you cannot execute your ideas.

2. *Assess the skills of your staff.*
   Do they have the skills to implement the program you've outlined? Can you hire additional staff or train existing staff for a new role?

3. *Inventory your firm's technology infrastructure.*
   Do you have the hardware and software to embark on a new business? You're not going to impress anyone who visits if you have outmoded equipment and you're probably not going to be able to do the job.

4. *Develop a technology budgeting plan.*
   How much will equipping your firm cost and how and when will you buy it?

5. *Survey and resurvey your markets.*
   Who are your potential clients? Will they want the services you want to provide? Who are your competitors and how formidable are they?

6. *Develop a marketing plan.*
   How will you reach prospects?

7. *Create a disaster plan.*
   You should have one of these no matter what business you're in. But if technology is the foundation of your operations, you

must protect your data and be ready to operate in case disaster destroys your facility.

It's time to get moving. This book, the AICPA, your state society, and your firm's associations are not going to do it for you. They cannot determine your goals. Going to 20 seminars and training programs and boot camps will not help unless you have a plan.

CONSULTANT OR CONTRACTOR?

In general, it's agreed that if a client is going to require critical, strategic thinking on a project, it is looking for a consultant. If the client just needs to supplement its workforce, it could be looking to hire a contractor, independently or through an employment agency.

In the real world the distinction between a contractor and a consultant can be a subtle point, with the word consultant being used by those hoping to confer a higher status on themselves. Many of the most able accounting professionals sometimes work as contractors. They are usually people with years of experience in a variety of roles in the development process including management. And there are many self-dubbed "consultants" who would not be all that comfortable going into detail on what they were doing for a living one or two years ago. Whatever's on their business card, the persons or company that a client outsources to could themselves be working with additional partners.

COMMUNICATION

Although technical facility and expertise are crucial to the success of a project, equally important — and too often overlooked, according to clients and consultants alike — is communication. Clear messages need to be sent prior to and during specification, as well as through execution of your consulting projects.

The consultant that is too lazy to do preliminary problem analysis is most likely to end up with problems throughout the project and wind up with fee write-downs. If the client's problem and the consultant's vision are clear, the capable consultant will help the client develop the best technology solution.

Internal communication is just as important as realistic expectations and ongoing communication with your client. If political issues on both sides of the agreement are not worked out and buy-in is not achieved locally, the result will be an inadequate consulting solution.

▶ Demand brutal honesty, including honest assessment of any problems, organizational and technological. If consultants aren't telling the client something they don't want to hear, they're probably not doing their job.

CHAPTER 15

Practice Strategies and Structure

INTRODUCTION TO STRATEGIC PLANNING FOR AN ONLINE PRACTICE

In order to arrive at a strategy for an online accounting practice, the owner or partners must establish goals. Some may plan to build a profitable practice by expanding the client base through aggressive marketing efforts. If successful, the result will be ample business and many revenue opportunities.

Other smaller to medium-sized accounting firms, as a result of years of experience, have developed niches or specialties. This acquired expertise can be invaluable in many ways. The CPAs can command higher rates for their work. The specialized work can be spread over the nontax season. This type of practice can focus on a particular type of clientele and potentially eliminate the sub-standard or undesirable clients.

Yet another group may elect practice priorities that combine a good income balanced with a high quality of life.

Each instance will differ, but the process, if it is to be successful, will be similar.

Questions Concerning Future Plans

1. Where are you now?
2. Where do you want to go?
3. How will you get there?

Client Demographic Study

Most firms concentrate their efforts on the existing client base, develop additional expertise in existing skill sets, and seek new clients that fit their refined firm model. In order to do this effectively and to determine your present position, study your clients' demographics. The study should answer some important questions:

- Why are clients attracted to the firm?
- What is the profile of the typical client?
- Which market segments are served by the firm?
- What are your firm's most desired services?
- In which areas is the firm noncompetitive or out of place?

As the accounting profession continues to evolve, so too must practitioners respond by altering their service offerings. The findings of your demographic study will reveal the firm's strengths and identify the potential areas for additional or different service offerings. Without taking on a single new client, the firm may discover enormous new service opportunities within this existing client roster. Although this is by no means a new concept, only those firms who identify the opportunities and exploit the new services will likely achieve a significant level of success in the future.

Pruning Clients That No Longer Fit

Not enough can be said about the need to prune clients that no longer fit into your firm. The periodic elimination of clients yields several benefits, not the least being stress reduction. Dismiss clients who are uncooperative, unappreciative, or unwilling, unable, or late to pay.

Where Do You Want to Go?

Larger and medium-sized accounting firms have annual retreats to review and update their strategic plans. Individuals and smaller firm owners often lack the time to have similar retreats. The strategic planning for small firms is done in the airplane on the way home from a practice management seminar or most likely not done at all. Accounting professionals need to devote quality time to the effort of planning if their practices are to be molded for future success. Work on your practice, not just in your business.

Practice Management Internal Financial Reporting

- Analyze firm's financial data monthly.
- Set up and monitor budgeting process for:
  1. Billings
  2. Collections
  3. Chargeable hours
  4. Monthly profitability

Having financial targets for the practice will enable you to know the firm's financial position on a monthly basis. It takes time each month to compile and review the data, but knowing where you are financially each month will assist you in reaching your goals. Obviously, you can't do all the work alone. You need a combination of good staff and reliable alliance partners.

Staffing Strategy

Every firm encounters difficulties in finding and retaining a quality staff. The firm's strategy must include a plan for crafting an excellent team. Small firms should also be visible, alongside the Big Five and other large organizations, at the local colleges so they can attract interns and entry-level staff. The small firm must be innovative in dealing with issues such as flexible time arrangements.

Hire the best people you can afford. The successful firms of today and tomorrow must pay and are paying higher salaries. The profitable firm will be in a better position to afford and bill for a team member who commands a higher salary. Too many smaller firms resist paying higher salaries out of a belief that they cannot afford to pay more. This self-defeating policy causes those practitioners to undervalue their work, which in turn leads to lower profitability and an inability to pay better wages to the staff. It is a vicious cycle that takes courage to break.

Alliances

There will be times when your firm needs assistance. This is not a reflection on the qualifications you and your team possess. The firm that is small must have alliances with other firms to meet those specialized needs that will arise. For example, business valuation is a fast-growing specialty and has expanded exponentially as the Internet removes geographic limitations.

Not every practitioner will specialize in the niche discipline, but there should be a relationship with a fellow CPA or accounting practitioner who can assist when the need arises. Similarly, as the new services continue to emerge and evolve, small firms will need to be aligned with providers that will serve their clients in those specialized areas. Conversely, you may develop some specialty practice areas that will be provided in cooperation with other allied firms.

Written Strategic Plans

You must be able to clearly see what you have to do to execute plans into actions and actions into results. Your budgets could be on spreadsheets or databases. Your goals and objectives should be on paper, your computer, or handheld device. The adage "out of sight, out of mind" is very applicable in strategy situations. Put your goals where you will see them every day and can refer to and refine them as necessary.

You are accountable to your partners and perhaps some others for the success or failure of your plan and your practice. Most importantly, you are accountable to yourself. You must accept responsibility to implement your plans based on your goals and objectives and to constantly monitor and respond to the results.

New and Improved Skills (How Do You Get There?)

The marketplace and the Internet are calling on accounting professionals to provide new and more specialized skills. Older skills are being transformed into new areas of expertise. CPAs and other practitioners are becoming certified/accredited business valuation specialists, registered investment advisors, licensed sales representatives of financial service products, and accredited online accounting solution providers. These new opportunities in related fields bring with them new challenges to maintain one's skills. Annual continuing professional education (CPE) units must be carefully planned to include material in your niche areas as well as the core services you provide.

Most of the firms going through this process have core competencies and are working to get to the next or different levels. Rapid growth in the accounting business can be perilous. Accept new clients wisely, keeping alert toward their special requirements and your firm's ability to serve those needs, add value to their business, and do it profitably. As you continue to add clients within your specialty, your learning curve is reduced and your profitability increases. The practitioner who develops an expertise will be able to command higher fees and will attract more clients who seek those specialized skills.

Strategy Process

The strategic planning process never ends. The firm must continue to define and refine its goals and objectives. Evaluate and re-evaluate what worked well and what didn't. Move on from the less successful endeavors. Every service offering will need periodic refinements to remain competitive and provide value to the client.

The legal profession warns that one who represents one's self has a fool for a client. Maybe anyone represented is a fool in that system. As accountants, we are qualified to be our best advisor as well as our own best repeat client.

THE NEW RULES OF ENGAGEMENT

The secret of success is constancy to purpose.
Benjamin Disraeli, Speech
(June 24, 1872)

The new generation of e-business consultants is playing by a different set of rules. These new rules are transforming today's market for digital accounting solutions. Savvy accountants couldn't help but notice a glaring hole in the way integrators provided solutions. Clients went to McKinsey & Company for strategy consulting, IBM or another Big Five company for ERP and supply-chain integration, and Razorfish or Scient for Web services. Hardly any professionals were out in the marketplace with the skills to package it all together.

Wanting to fill that void were the accounting professionals who decided to rewrite the rulebook and build the strengths internally that could turn accounting firms into full service providers (FSPs). That way, the consultancy wouldn't have to partner with other service companies to provide e-solutions, unless the circumstances required it.

FULL SERVICE PROVIDERS (FSPs)

The full service providers saw opportunity to bring vertical-industry solutions together by wrapping strategy with technology components to provide a fully integrated solution. Following is a brief list of strategies, each of which will be expanded upon further on:

1. Look beyond e-business. Provide Web solutions as one part of a larger strategy that includes offline initiatives.
2. Get to know CEOs and others who have a good grasp of their companies' revenue model — not just the CIOs or CFOs.
3. Embrace a healthier client diet. Cut out sugary dot.coms and focus on traditional clients with deeper pockets.
4. Choose engagements that will define new business models, rather than rehash tired, worn-out ones.
5. Don't spread yourself too thin on the tech side. Stick with and leverage a few platforms you know best.
6. Think end-to-end, not piecemeal. Seek out the larger, dynamic projects that use everything you have to offer.

Strategy #1: Move Beyond E

Virtually all leading integrators — from Scient Corportion to Lante Corporation to Sapient Corporation — have already gone to great lengths to establish and differentiate their own "e-methodologies." Other companies, such as Viant Corporation, are spending millions on new branding and advertising campaigns to get the e-word out to clients. So for a smaller consulting firm, it is a little too late to be playing catch-up.

On the client side, it's clear that the worlds of brick-and-mortar and dot.com companies are quickly converging around the Internet, with traditional companies building online initiatives to support their existing businesses and dot.coms finally starting to realize the importance of embracing offline supply-chain, marketing, and call-center processes. Smart integrators have already realized that, as industries ranging from light manufacturing to licensed merchandising to interior design increasingly embrace e-business solutions, individual clients are going to be searching for new ways to differentiate themselves outside of the Web. If your firm can't show them how to do that, they'll look for some firm that can.

This means that it's no longer enough to provide e-business as a be-all, end-all solution for your clients. In this new phase of the marketplace, doing e-commerce is no longer unique on its own. Instead, the new accounting consultants teach their clients to leverage Web solutions as a single part of an overall business strategy that may also include integrated click-and-mortar initiatives such as direct mail, point-of-sales-systems, and — lo and behold — human contact.

What will differentiate accounting firms is their ability to grow revenue and create client relationships across all channels: online and offline. The Internet value chain is one of many channels to the client, but it can't be the only one.

Strategy #2: Avoid the IT and CIO Functions

Clients have a renewed emphasis on business strategy consulting. Today's e-business clients are no longer seeking specific technology fixes. Instead, they want end-to-end solutions that can completely transform their business models so they can compete in tomorrow's digital economy. To better serve their needs, e-business architects are expanding their services way beyond technology to incorporate overall business strategy and industry expertise.

With that new focus in mind, talk to the executive and line of business managers who have their hands on the checkbook and are responsible for driving their customers' revenues. Technology is no long ancillary to business processes, but is instead a critical gear in part of their economic engine.

Old versus New

- **Old Rule**—When selling solutions, always reach out to the CIO first.
- **New Rule**—CEOs and business managers may be the best bet for e-biz.
- **How to Get Beyond It**—Though analysts say the decision-making power of CIOs is dwindling in the face of e-business, be careful not to alienate them, because they still play an important part in selecting solutions.

Strategy #3: Invest What's Necessary

As an accounting services consultant for e-business, you want the best e-minds out there working for you. The problem is that everybody else does, too. If you're not willing to pay top dollar for top talent, one of your competitors will. And that means the money you save today will mean nothing tomorrow once your market share is eaten up by faster, sleeker, and better-equipped firms.

Build your firm with a strong culture based on compensating team members well with salary and benefits. Focus on building the infrastructure internally that will help you attract the best people in the marketplace and allow you to grow organically. It is very important for your firm to keep and develop the people you have. Offer stock options to every single staff member and a very attractive benefits package.

Strategy #4: Choose Your Partners Wisely

Today's clients care a lot less about the name on the business card and a great deal more about whether your firm and the solutions you offer, are fast, reliable, and effective. Your job is to be all three.

Smart accounting firms are picking a handful of vendors whose technology best complements their strengths and are riding them all the way to success. Those firms that spend time and money trying to work with every vendor in every category are steadily falling behind.

Evaluate what you feel are the best-of-breed technologies in each given area, then choose long-term partnerships, and train your consultants in that platform. You need to understand what and where you think your markets are going and try to build your strengths in those areas.

For some accounting firms, sticking to this kind of strategy means occasionally passing up engagement opportunities for the sake of building expertise. Choose not to chase markets that require a very different set of expertise than what you usually do. If a project comes up in those areas, it will be better to walk away instead of spread your firm too thin.

So how do you decide which engagements are the right ones to dig into? A good idea is to concentrate on the ones you know well because they'll ultimately give you the best chance for success. Why not increase your chances for high margins by focusing on the one or two technologies your competitors aren't leveraging? That way you can build a profitable niche in the marketplace.

Strategy #5: A Foot in the Door Isn't Very Important

For years, traditional accounting professionals and consultants lived by the belief that doing the small, thankless jobs for a larger client would ultimately open the door to more strategic and more profitable work. Well, chances are it will—for someone else.

There's plenty of good work out there right now, so it's time to forget the door and throw that tired notion out the window. If a prospective client doesn't want to let you in as a strategic player, then find one who will. Keep doing the small jobs, and it's the small jobs they'll keep giving you.

The general rule to remember when scouting out work is that, as an e-consultant, you're only as good as the solutions you provide. You want to be known by your clients as a strategic asset that can develop and implement fully integrated e-business initiatives.

When client/servers dominated the market, you had the Big Five building all of these vertical strategy practices. But with Internet technology and the range of different applications for things like e-procurement and business intelligence sweeping across all industries, accounting firms have a new lever to move up in the ranks and become a strategic partner.

The strategic relationships you build today are the ones that will shape you for the future. As the Web services space continues to mature and becomes more competitive, there will be a shakeout among consultants. Those who have managed to build a strong vertical expertise and strategic relationships with their clients will be the ones left standing.

Strategy #6: Partner at Your Peril

There's no denying the popularity of partnering for many of today's e-consultants — especially those who are too small or whose resources are too limited to offer clients a full solution. But many leaders of some of the end-to-end strategy firms are starting to give the idea a big thumbs-down. That's because they're spending enormous amounts of money — either through organic growth or acquisition — positioning themselves as full service providers that can give their clients a complete solution. They are loath to bring an outside partner into the fold who in addition to taking a portion of the profit has the potential to ruin the project.

Growth-oriented practices now avoid partnering with other solution providers. The only real partnering that should be on the horizon is with executive management agencies, law firms, or venture capital companies — entities that can provide assistance well beyond the boundaries of end-to-end e-business solutions.

When it comes to the core solution — looking at the business model, the consulting, or the implementation of an e-business infrastructure — do it completely in-house. A major risk in partnerships among providers is that the individual firms learn each other's problem-solving methodologies. Your firm has made a significant investment to ensure that it can bring end-to-end skill sets and services to your clients. You don't want to teach your methodology to someone else who may one day be your competitor.

Remain open to partnering with technology providers when it makes sense, but on the services side, do the majority of work yourself. That allows you to provide quality and speed to your clients.

SUCCESSFUL PRACTICE BUILDING STRATEGIES AND POLICIES

In the long run men hit only what they aim at.
Henry David Thoreau
Walden (1851), 1, Economy

Always, always, always work with a written engagement letter, contract, or agreement. It need not be overly formal or require a gaggle of lawyers to interpret. A simple letter of understanding is often sufficient. Such a document clarifies communications, expectations, and responsibilities and is invaluable should a misunderstanding or dispute ever occur.

When working with partners, associates, or subcontractors, be sure to have a written agreement between the parties. The agreement should include a noncompete/disclosure clause which protects you from their setting up shop on their own and taking your clients with them when they do so. This is something you should not try to do by yourself at home. Get competent professional advice.

Include in every agreement a paragraph that communicates the client's responsibilities and obligations. Include everything that you are depending upon from timely payment of invoices to the provision of data, documents, accessibility, working space, and other support.

Make sure the client realizes your time is as valuable or more valuable than theirs. People have greater respect for and are more willing to do business with those whom they regard as important. One way to have clients view you in this light: Be sure you interview them before they interview you. Controlling the initial meeting is one way to increase the probability of getting the business.

Before the first meeting with a prospective client, be sure to communicate whether there is a charge for this first/initial meeting. It is not recommended that you do charge. But if you do, make sure the client understands the amount and terms of payment.

In the first meeting, with the prospective client, focus on either what they need to do to make their problem go away or how they can take advantage of the opportunity they are confronting. Don't waste the prospect's time providing a verbal resume. If prospects need information on your skills, abilities, and experience, they will certainly ask.

When meeting with a prospective client be sure to answer the five questions which they need to have answered but frequently fail to ask:

1. How will I profit from your advice/services?
2. Why will I profit from working with you?
3. How can you demonstrate that I will profit?
4. To what extent will I profit from your advice?
5. When will these profits/benefits be realized?

Be sure to identify the fears or any misgivings that a prospective client may have about working with you or your firm. It takes some effort, but they will be reluctant to utilize your services until you have identified, discussed, and put their fears to rest.

Always provide the prospective client with a pro forma schedule or time line that identifies when the various components of your work will be completed. The schedule may slip once the work is under way, but it serves to assure the client that you have a healthy concern for one of the client's most important priorities: timely completion of the project.

Schedule a series of meetings (perhaps four to six a year) and invite good clients and prospects to attend without charge. Give each meeting a theme, such as "The Internet and Your Business:Threat or Opportunity?" Bring these people together, under your leadership, to discuss the issue. It will give you the chance to show your stuff and help to identify consulting needs of the participants.

Respond quickly to all e-mails, letters, and telephone calls received from clients, prospects, and others. If possible, return calls and e-mails on the day received and certainly by the next day. If you need more time to give a full answer, at least acknowledge the receipt of their message and communicate by what date you will be able to provide a substantive response.

Spend half a day, at least every quarter, walking around the reference room of a major university library. Pull interesting books, directories, and guides off the shelf and examine them. You will learn about interesting marketing opportunities and new services that you could provide to your clients.

STEP-BY-STEP GUIDE

Take nothing on its looks; take everything on evidence. There's no better rule.

Charles Dickens, Great Expectations
(1860–1861), ch. 40

Appoint a Practice Evangelist

Many successful practitioners believe that one of the biggest challenges they faced in implementation was getting their team on board. An evangelist is someone selected from the team who will act as an effective liaison between the partners and the rest of the team. Look for someone who will be able to do the following:

- Support the need to change
- Have the respect of the team
- Communicate at a partner and a team level
- Have a positive attitude
- Be a driver personality type (refer to Chapter 12 of *Starting and Building Your Own Accounting Business, Third Edition,* by Jack Fox, published by John Wiley & Sons, 2000)

Publish Your Vision

After the firm's vision has been communicated to the entire team, the next step is to articulate it to your clients and to your marketplace.

- Write to your clients. Use a series of letters and e-mails.
- Hold an event to which you invite key clients to announce the future of your firm.
- Establish a Client Advisory Board and publish your vision as part of the feedback from it.
- Write and publish a book about your firm, its vision, partners, team members, and services.

The Accounting Guild, Las Vegas, Nevada has developed an innovative and effective program which provides accounting firms a practice development tool in the form of a Practice Vision book. Utilizing state-of-the-art, print-on-demand techniques, The Accounting Guild works with your firm in writing the content to ensure that it is your book. Print on demand allows you to print only the number of books that you require at any given time. All the material is digitized (stored in digital format) and the printing does not require plates or film. A key benefit is that changes can be made at any time with minimal expense to accommodate changes in the firm's services, partners, and team. New market niches and other specialties can be written into the book. No books are stored in a warehouse to become obsolete. For more information contact The Accounting Guild at http://www.accountingguild.com.

DISCOVERING THE PATH FROM COMPLIANCE TO RELIANCE

The ripest peach is highest on the tree.
> *James Whitcomb Riley,*
> *"The Ripest Peach," st. 1*

For the most part, clients are very well satisfied with the services their accountants are currently providing. At the same time, many of these same accountants are missing out on the greater business requirements of their clients.

The clients have expectations and clearly defined needs that are beyond the scope of what their accountants are addressing. These needs fall into the niches of overall business development, management consulting services, strategic planning, systems analysis, and the development of more meaningful measurement systems. The need is not only for the measurement of traditional financial information, but also productivity and performance indicators within the company that provide clients with a more accurate real-time view of the company's performance.

For many accounting firms, the goal in creating a consulting practice is to shift the focus of the firm from traditional compliance-oriented to reliance-oriented services. The reason is basic: In addition to providing financial information about where the company has been (what may be termed "lagging indicators" or "failing indicators"), companies are asking their accountants to provide "leading indicators." Clients want access to timely, critical information needed to navigate their business with the use of a telescope or at least a windshield, instead of trying to steer their businesses into the future by relying on the rear-view mirror.

REAL-TIME, ONLINE ACCOUNTANTS

Clients want real-time, online accountants. Increasingly, they are abandoning their loyalties to accounting firms and switching from one to the next until they find what they are looking for. This is a critical juncture for both the accountant and the client because of the growing reliance placed on technology by clients, a point which to a great extent is being missed by the accountants.

Clients that use online accounting services often believe they are getting an adequate return on their investment, and that they are receiving all of the data the accountant could have provided. Although the client is getting the data, they are not getting the information that an experienced set of eyes could offer. The clients are missing out on the business acumen and the viewpoint of a professional whose job it is to monitor the external and internal factors that impact how well the client can make decisions.

TECHNOLOGY: BOON OR BANE?

Technology has both helped and hurt the accounting profession. It has improved the level of accuracy and increased the productivity of the firm. However, that same technology has also provided the client with the option of doing the accounting work in-house. This transition has left the accountant much less involved with the day-to-day operations of the client.

In the race to embrace technology, some clients have lost sight of the reason why their numbers were important and the role of technology in organizing those numbers. The accountant's job is not simply to present the numbers, but to improve the quality of decision-making information for clients, to make the information more readily available so that clients can interpret it more accurately and more rapidly than ever before. Ever increasingly, technology will play an enormous role in the process of gathering, analyzing, and producing critical information. Ultimately, the role of the consulting accountant will be to orchestrate the process.

Accounting firms willing to make the investment for education and commitment to support the technology needs of their clients will be further down the path of success, way ahead of those accountants that don't. Firms will be light years ahead if they truly understand the role of technology and service, apply it to improve the quality of information, and thus enable their clients to navigate effectively.

THE ROAD TO SOMEWHERE

First, begin with the end in mind. You must have a clear vision not only of where you wish the firm to be, but where your clients wish the firm to be. Be prepared for the cultural and systems changes that will be necessary. It is not enough just to decide to become a solutions provider and systems integrator. Your business consulting practice is about the application of technology, not just its installation. Your firm must be able to walk the talk. You must get your internal technology act in order first.

Next, you must have a team within the firm who understands the shift in the needs of clients, and has the vision and determination to meet that shift head-on. The goal is not just to provide more information, but to improve the quality of it. You must be willing to invest the resources and time it will take to expand your service mix to include e-business consulting services and apply the appropriate technologies to support the greater needs of the client. It may take the exercise of significant patience to see a return on these investments.

> The return from your work must be the satisfaction which that work brings you and the world's need of that work. With that, life is heaven, or as near as you can get. Without this— with work which you despise, which bores you, and which the world does not need—this life is hell.
>
> *W.E.B. Du Bois, To His Newborn Great-Grandson;*
> *Address on his ninetieth birthday (1958)*

CLIENT FEEDBACK

Client feedback is essential during the building process and throughout all the activities of the firm. Some clients will welcome the firm's new services. Others will be so locked into the traditional roles of the accounting firm that they will have problems seeing the new, expanded relationship. This client feedback will assist in guiding your decision whether to make the new division an integrated part of the firm or a totally separate entity.

CORE COMPETENCIES

The accounting firm will need to insure that the core technologies are in place for the client. At most clients, they are not. The nature of technology is such that there is a baseline level — a foundation — of technology that must be laid before it is possible to begin making better use of information.

Beyond that, many areas of a client's business need this technology foundation. The four key areas that should be considered first are as follows:

1. Finance
2. Operations
3. Management
4. Sales and Marketing

Key Performance Indicators (KPIs)

In each of the above key areas, Key Performance Indicators (KPIs) must be identified and measured. Again, the adage is applicable, what you can measure, you can manage. Accountants are skilled in this evaluation from expertise gained in the financial area. They understand financial KPIs such as cash flow, A/R, A/P, inventory turns, and many other leading indicators measured in financial structures. This same discipline can be applied to measuring the KPIs of other key areas of the business. For some accounting professionals this will require additional education and a reorientation. Some accountants have developed myopia from looking only at finances and have missed the importance of the other three areas. Practice looking for what the clients are looking for.

Computing Technology Competencies

Developing a competence in the full range of computing technologies results in your clients being able to have your firm serve as an outsourced data processing and IT department. That makes your firm cost-effective for the small to medium-sized business. With a sufficient experience base and a cadre of solid clients, your firm can move out of the defensive stage and take a more assertive position in seeking new clients.

A sound consulting practice strategy is to establish consulting teams, working in the accounting software and local area networking marketplace. Build teams that will be tightly integrated into the firm's core client base. Next, extend your focus to include serious business users of powerful software and hardware solutions. These offer opportunities for higher-profit, larger-volume projects that make better use of your expanded consulting capacity and build your reputation as a major consultant.

CREDIBILITY

As an accounting firm or a consulting affiliate of the firm, you carry a level of credibility that conventional consultancies just don't have. The years of experience behind the firm mean that clients don't have to worry about the firm going away one night. At the same time, your firm is a strong consulting business that can open doors to a higher tier for both additional consulting business and other accounting services of the firm.

COMPETITIVE EDGE

Consulting competencies provide a powerful competitive edge over more traditional accounting firms. This will help your firm retain and service the compliance clients. At the same time, the consulting activities provide a model for the firm's compliance professionals to help them improve their individual consulting skills and awareness of client needs. After five years, a profitable consulting practice should comprise approximately 40 percent of the firm's total expanded services base.

CHAPTER 16

Marketing Foundations

Developing an Accounting Firm Brand

MARKETING MISCONCEPTIONS

One of the biggest misconceptions held by accounting firms is thinking that their delivery of quality professional services is all that's required to market themselves. The last decade should have demonstrated that marketing is a high-tech accounting firm's single most important activity. Microsoft Corporation, despite its monopoly powers, maintained a marketing machine that took its place next to Proctor & Gamble (without monopolistic advantages) as the greatest marketing company of the new technology age.

Marketing is one of the most misunderstood business fundamentals — especially when undertaken by professional accounting and consulting firms. The marketing efforts of accounting firms and other accounting solutions providers should drive prospective clients into a sales funnel, where salespeople can evaluate the prospects and initiate the campaign to convert them to clients.

Marketing Ineptness

Professional accounting providers are typically inept at marketing. Basically, many accountants are uncomfortable with selling themselves — a remnant from more protected days when the CPA certificate conveyed a legal license to provide accounting audit, attest, and other services to the exclusion of all persons or organizations that were not certified. In many states, even today, only a Certified Public Accountant can use the words accounting or accounting services in the advertising on their business cards and letterhead.

The attempt by the American Institute of Certified Public Accountants (AICPA) and the politically designated state societies of public accountancy, successfully created a protected business game preserve where only CPAs were allowed the equivalent of a hunting license. Like it or not, those days in the accounting profession are over.

Consistency and Relevance

Many, if not most, accounting services providers fail to devote the consistent time, money, attention, and other essential resources to marketing. That, ultimately, assures an inconsistent return on investment. The explanation for the inconsistency is that not enough importance is placed on this critical activity.

TYPES OF MARKETING

The primary types of accounting professional services marketing are as follows:

- Advertising
- Direct mail
- E-mail campaigns
- Newsletters (Internet)
- Partnering
- Professional sales
- Public relations
- Public speaking
- Seminars
- Telemarketing

For most professional accounting firms, the various types of marketing often fail for several reasons. The sometimes significant expenditures don't result in immediate returns, which prompt the conservative firms to give up before the efforts can bear fruit. Lower cost activities have not been very successful either, though the accounting firms are more comfortable limiting their expenditures. The major reason for ineffective marketing is because marketing is so time-intensive. The firms make the effort only once or twice a year because of the time involved and then prematurely withdraw because the activities aren't immediately productive.

EFFECTIVE PROFESSIONAL ACCOUNTING SERVICES MARKETING

The solution to accounting professional services marketing is to patiently and methodically engage in a consistent variety of both types of marketing activities according to a carefully constructed marketing plan and budget. All activities must present a distinctive, differentiated, professional image of your firm and its capability in meeting the needs of the clients in your designated market niches. Professional accounting services marketing activities include the following:

- **Yellow Pages Advertising.** This is one of the most expensive and ineffective uses of advertising monies. Take only a basic listing that is included in your phone service. Your marketing is proactive and should be directed at the prospective clients you have selected to sell. The phone book advertising is very expensive, you are committed for a year or more, and you are listed in the same place with the competition. The exception would be to participate with your software vendor partners in a "co-op" telephone directory display ad, cutting its cost and making it a continuous form of advertising. Let your fingers (utilizing the Internet) do the walking to reach your targeted market niche.

- **Web Site Marketing.** This is an excellent medium and a requirement for business today. Your firm's site should have information on the services that you sell, firm information, awards won and other recognition, background on the firm's principals, among other features. Have a professional Web designer plan and construct your site to help distinguish you from the competition.

- **E-mail Campaigns.** E-mail can be an effective marketing tool for disseminating information of your firm and its services to a large number of qualified prospective clients. The historical response norms are 1 to 2 percent for traditional postal mail but have been dramatically higher with e-mail. Postal mail can still be used effectively in certain campaigns. A direct e-mail campaign must be tied to a seminar or other event and coupled with tele-marketing. Every prospective client must be telephoned and invited to your seminars or some other "call to action" in your direct mail piece.

- **Turnkey Direct Mail.** Many accounting software vendors are offering a turnkey direct mail program at lower cost, but it may not be a good value. Your software vendor partners buy the lists of prospective clients that more closely fit their profile target in areas like revenue size, SIC (Standard Industry Classification), and employee size. Because they mail the list twice a year, the turnkey program should be relegated to the inconsistent effort category.

- **Seminars.** Many accounting services firms believe that while seminar selling had been all the rage, they now feel that prospective clients are becoming "seminared out." Let your competitors continue with this fallacious thinking, it will make your seminars more productive and profitable. A seminar program is one of the most important components of your marketing program. All advertising and promotion are geared to getting your prospective client into your facility (office or other space) to be sold by your presentations. Overbook your programs to compensate for a 25 percent or more no-show rate.

- **Telemarketing.** Telemarketing is effective when utilized in conjunction with e-mailing and a seminar program. Plan on outsourcing this activity to a professional telemarketing organization. Costs range from $20 to $40 per hour and they may talk to only four to eight prospects per hour. College students and temps are less expensive but will require more recruiting and interview time, additional upfront training, management, and supervision as well as increased overhead.

- **Advertising.** Advertising in the local business journal or newspaper or your state or local CPA journal is a waste of money. It will not build name awareness or result in appointments. Instead offer to write articles about issues relevant to your market niches or other professional specialties. These articles, which include your name, firm name, telephone number, e-mail address, and postal address, are run in the periodical at no cost to you. Moreover, editorial material gets better readership and has much more credibility than paid advertising.

- **Preparation.** Prepare yourself for the onslaught of advertising salespeople. They are very good at what they do. Accept some offers to meet and you may find some excellent candidates for your next professional sales openings.

SELECTING CLIENTS

Smart accounting professionals realize their client list can shape the future of their firms, opening doors for long-term partnerships and future engagements, attracting new clients and staff members, and increasing stature in the marketplace.

It's all about getting someone good on your client roster or being involved at the ground level of a new type of offering or Internet market. You need to know what long-term benefits you will get from the client. During the next few years, professional accounting solutions providers' chances for success will hinge on the strength of their clients.

Successful accounting firms are embracing the Old World clients: companies with deep pockets, established track records, and a strong desire to integrate their existing businesses to the Web. A good mix for an accounting firm would include no more than 30 percent start-up work, with the rest going to established clients.

Show Me the Money

No matter how interesting or challenging a particular client's needs are, if that client can't commit to a concrete reimbursement plan from the start, chances are it's a risky idea. You have to look at the economics of a job, the profitability for your firm. Clients who are constantly trying to beat you down over fees are the ones you should shy away from.

Today's accounting professionals, especially, non-CPA firms or separate firms owned by CPAs, are accepting alternative payment schedules that include an equity stake in a client's business rather than straight payment. This may be an excellent method to share in the benefits of your efforts if the schedules are sanctioned by the applicable governing bodies.

Accounting professionals must look closely at prospective clients' financial resources and business plans to figure out an appropriate course of action. The right approach is to take a balance. If you are too conservative, you will miss opportunities, and if you are too daring, you will get burned.

Good Client/Bad Client

Good Client

1. Financially stable
2. Willing to invest necessary resources
3. Has realistic expectations about e-business
4. Is in it for the long haul

Bad Client

1. Wants immediate solutions, regardless of risks
2. Wants to break rules
3. Treats your team members poorly
4. Can't commit to long-term relationship

COURTING CLIENTS

A successful client courtship begins with listening. Clients require that they be listened to. A direct relationship exists between the amount a prospective client talks and the likelihood that he or she will hire you. The more the client talks, the more comfortable they become. The more comfortable the client becomes, the more you will be trusted. The more you are trusted, the stronger the bond is formed. A stronger bond leads to a commitment.

Establishing trust in a business relationship is based on active and empathetic listening. Determine what the prospective client's emotional needs, wants, and desires surrounding the prospective engagement are in addition to the obvious business considerations. Why does the client really want to buy your products or services? These are a few guidelines to help you sharpen your listening skills as well as develop a closer rapport with your prospective client:

- **Sit back, shut up, and remain in control.** Many accountants think that the talker controls the situation. In actuality, the talker only dominates the conversation. It's the listener or interviewer who directs it. Let your prospective client do the majority of the talking during the sales interview. You should be speaking no more than 40 percent of the time. Tape record a few of your presentations and listen later to make sure you don't spend too much time talking and too little time listening. If your prospect digresses, gets flustered, or runs out of things to say, don't rush in and fill the vacuum with words. Instead, redirect the prospective client with a question.

- **Be curious.** If your prospective client seems a little reticent, warm the prospect up by showing a genuine interest in what the prospect does. Ask questions that don't directly pertain to the sale. This can bring you closer to getting the prospect to commit to your firm because no direct pressure is being made for an immediate decision. The answers might reveal a need for another product or service you offer. Try such open-ended questions as the following:
  ○ How did you start your business?
  ○ What advice would you give to someone who is just starting out in your field?
  ○ What would you do differently if you had the chance?
  ○ What are your biggest challenges?

- **Project the right body language.** What we project physically is just as important as what we say. Your prospective client may even stop talking if they think you're not listening. Nodding your head, maintaining eye contact, or simply smiling will show a potential client that you are paying attention. You can also demonstrate your interest by using such verbal cues as "I hear you" or "I understand what you're saying."

- **Take notes.** Everyone feels important when someone makes the effort to record something they've said. Jotting down notes and questions also shows that you're an organized professional. In addition, these notations can come in handy when discussing details and concerns during the sales interview. Note taking is also a way to ensure that you don't interrupt the prospect's train of thought. Constant writing, however, may distract someone, so limit your notes to crucial information or questions.

- **Hold back on instant solutions.** Refrain from immediately offering solutions to every concern the prospective client brings up. The time to address these issues is after all of the problems are revealed. You won't be able to offer relevant or effective solutions until you get the complete picture.

- **Talk about past successes, not clients.** Don't mention other clients you have worked for in the past or current clients. The prospects will assume that if you are talking about past clients now, they will be the subject of discussion in the future.

- **Leave brochures in your briefcase.** Don't distract the prospective client by presenting a brochure during the sales interview. If you do, they will probably start asking questions about its content. You'll end up talking more about your firm, product, or service than about the client's needs. Instead, mail your brochure along with a handwritten thank-you note after your meeting. It's another opportunity to keep your name fresh in the client's mind.

- **Be yourself.** Some accounting professionals put up a façade during the sales interview. (It may be a matter of self-esteem or innate discomfort or what they think people expect or the way they think professional salespeople are supposed to act. The reasons are outside the parameters of this text to speculate and better left to the psychologists and motivational seminars.) A prospective client eventually finds out the truth. No one likes to be misled. If you're open and honest, prospects are more likely to act the same way with you.

- **Use expanders.** When your prospective client trails off, use such phrases as "Because . . . ?", "Such as . . . ?", and "Why is that . . . ?". Such phrases get the prospect to expand. These phrases will help get the prospective client to the root of the problems in the business and will allow you to offer appropriate solutions at the opportune time.

- **Screen clients before taking on work.** Weed out the potentially problematic client at the initial meeting. Consulting accountants should turn away about one-third of the business that comes their way and focus on the cream of the crop.

- **Cut to the chase.** A simple thing that is second nature to accounting consultants, that they can do to make sure prospective clients are stable and solvent, is to request a look at the business's books. By looking at their general ledger and cash accounts, you can determine if a prospective client qualifies. Accept the ones who have the money. When examining the books, consultants should also check to see if prospective clients have accurate and timely financial statements, what they are currently paying for accounting and consulting services, and the identity of their current providers.

- **Understanding.** Make sure that the client understands the engagement and is aware of potential problems.

COMMUNICATING WITH YOUR PROSPECTIVE CLIENT

No matter what the pop-psychology motivational sales seminar tells you, you will never know what makes your prospective client tick. No matter how experienced a professional you are, you can never really know what a person is thinking. Many times you still don't know what they are thinking even after they tell you what they're thinking.

A time will come in every sales interview when you must open up to the prospective client and prove that you are the best choice for the assignment. Your most persuasive strategy is to remain focused on the specific things the prospective client wants to know. Reinforce the prospect's trust by giving priority to his or her concerns.

Be ready to articulate with conviction when questioned about what can be expected from you in this relationship. You may be asked such things as the following:

- What specific results can I expect if I do business with you?
- Have you ever handled a situation similar to mine? Explain the circumstances.
- What value do businesses receive from doing business with you?
- What type of relationship do you have with your clients?
- How have you helped build your clients' businesses?
- What's the difference between you and your competition?

COMMUNICATING WITH YOUR ACTIVE CLIENTS

More accounting professionals understand the importance of communicating with prospective clients and tend to place communication with their current active clients on a lower priority. Periodically, however, they should step back and evaluate the communication skills they use to get their message across. Here are 10 points CPAs and others need to remember in order to maintain open communication with their clients:

1. **Convey an attitude of trust.** Improving the level of trust between professional and client helps to open the lines of communication. Once trust has been established, ideas and concerns flow more effectively.

2. **Practice intentional listening.** Clients like to be heard. Listen more emphatically. Remember, we have two ears and one mouth, so try to listen twice as much as you speak.

3. **Remain calm.** Maintain your composure in all circumstances. Stay calm, particularly when the client is emotional or even irate. Your composure is critical to fostering a climate that enhances communication. If you get excited, the client will too, and everybody loses.

4. **Accept the reality of personality differences.** If a situation arises where personality clashes may adversely affect communication, accept it as something you cannot change. See the situation from the client's point of view, and avoid showing frustration.

5. **Plan and organize.** When communicating information to a client, particularly with respect to complex issues, it is crucial to do so in an orderly, logical, and organized manner. Present the information in a way that is relevant and meaningful to the client.

6. **Practice a positive attitude.** When a client says something that would tend to put you on the defensive, don't overreact and proffer excuses. Instead, provide sound reasons for the actions you took.

7. **Avoid black or white thinking.** There are shades of gray and not all issues are "either/or" propositions. Don't polarize your thinking. Keep your mind open to new interpretations.

8. **Employ feedback.** Nothing can be more frustrating to a client than not being kept informed. When there is nothing concrete to report, provide clients with an opportunity to ask questions. This will let the clients know they have not been forgotten or, even worse, ignored.

9. **Eliminate information glut.** Don't bury the client with too much information at once. When discussing a complex issue, break the information into easily understood portions. If the client feels overwhelmed, anything you have to say after that point is meaningless.

10. **Do not use jargon.** Always remember whom you are talking
to. If you have to use a term the client is not familiar with, be
sure to define it in words she or he will understand.

CLIENT TURNOFFS

- **Indifference.** Respond to feedback; it shows that you're concerned about how to better serve your clients.
- **Inaccessibility.** Not being able to reach you or not receiving a
prompt response implies no interest. No interest, no work.
- **Not fulfilling the job requirements.** Deliver what was promised and on time. If you can't handle it, don't take it. If possible,
give references. Your honesty and assistance will be appreciated.
- **Being overly eager.** Sounding too hungry for business leaves
prospective clients with the impression that you're not up to
their standards.
- **Excessive hand-holding.** Clients pay for your expertise. You
should be able to pick up the ball and go. They don't want someone who requires continuous directions at every step.
- **Intrusiveness.** It's fine to check in every so often, but don't
become a pest.
- **Looking shoddy.** They don't care what you look like while
you are working at home, but dress according to the client's
environment when on-site, even if you're simply dropping off an
envelope.
- **Surprises.** Discovered an alternate way to proceed? Unless it's
a hands-down improvement, keep it to yourself. If you share your
insights with the client, do so as a suggestion and be willing to
accept rejection without question.
- **Not having the resources or skills to grow with the
clients' needs.** Clients don't want to have to shop around for
a new vendor every time they make a change internally.
Anticipate and meet your client's future needs. Own or have
access to technology that is on the same level as that of your
clients.
- **Nickel and diming.** Be reasonable and flexible. But don't be
cheap. The long-term benefits of occasional perks far outweigh
short-term compensation.

- **Going over budget.** If the difference is small, or if the error is due to your own bad planning, be ready to eat the difference.
- **Pressuring the client for more business.** They admire persistence, but don't turn into a nuisance. If you're good, they'll be back.

THE WAITING GAME

Some accounting professionals get discouraged when they can't consummate an engagement quickly. They worry that time allows the prospective client to come up with more reasons for not retaining the firm. Although you can't preset the length of the sales cycle, you can determine how urgently someone needs your services or how much situational pain the prospect is experiencing. Modify the frequency and intensity of your sales techniques to meet the client's needs.

Keep the Fire Burning

Send your prospective client such tokens of your appreciation as articles and ideas for their business. Meet the people who influence your prospects' business decisions. Keep the lines of communication open. Listen to them and continue to learn more about their companies and concerns. Do all of these activities without becoming a nuisance and you'll have a long-lasting and profitable relationship.

Know the Difference Between "No" and "Not Now"

Just because a prospective client isn't ready to do business with you now doesn't mean the client never will be. You'll never know if you abort communication. Do not presume that everyone who requests information or shows an interest in what you're offering is ready to become a client. People may have innumerable reasons to inquire about your firm. People can have all the problems in the world, but unless they're committed to changing their situations, you'll never make it to third base.

Some relationships aren't meant to be. And we're usually better off without them anyway. When the going gets tough, remember there is always another prospect.

THE CONCEPT OF BRANDING AS A COMPETITIVE ONLINE ADVANTAGE

Note to Reader: For optimum value, use a notebook to record your answers to the following questions.

Your Accounting Services Brand

- Your value proposition:
  1. Types of clients and business partners that you attract
  2. Positioning
  3. Your unique way of doing business
  4. Accounting service/product offerings
  5. Pricing
- The vehicle that drives your strategic business and marketing direction forward.
- What does your brand convey?
  1. How do you feel about your firm?
  2. How do you feel about your clients?
  3. How do you feel about your team?
  4. How do you feel about your accounting/consulting services and products?
  5. What is your potential to offer creative and effective solutions?
  6. What is your level of energy?
  7. How much attention do you pay to detail?
  8. What is your tolerance for risk?
  9. How good is your sense of humor?

Why Brand Your Accounting Firm?

- What you are selling is invisible. It exists only in the virtual dimension.
- You and your firm are the product.
- You must build your perceived value.
- Do not leave interpretation to chance.
- As your practice evolves, you need a vehicle to quickly communicate new messages and opportunities to the marketplace.
- Your brand serves as a defensive measure because your competitors will also employ branding.

What Can You Expect Your Brand to Do?

- Position you in the marketplace
- Differentiate your firm
- Project a dynamic firm culture and identity
- Project quality
- Create a memorable presence
- Look better than any competitor
- Match clients' expectations and perceptions
- Convey strength
- Excite the senses
- Build a platform for integrated marketing

Do You Know You Already Have a Brand?

- Whether you know it or not
- Whether you like it or not
- Whether you define it or not
- Whether it's a strategic tool or not
- Whether you sustain it or let it wither

But What Does Your Brand Mean?

- To your clients?
- To your team members?
- To your competition?
- To the marketplace?

Is Your Brand an Opportunity?

It is if it accomplishes the following:

- Expresses your core competencies and values
- Defines your culture
- Aligns with your clients and prospective clients
- Continuously shows your value
- Helps you stand out from the crowd
- Clearly defines your position
- Demonstrates quality and innovation
- Harnesses the power of your symbol

- Influences how people live and think
- Reaches out to new audiences
- Goes where no one has ever gone before
- Enables you to hire and retain good staff
- Attracts the optimum strategic partners
- Shapes your future

How Do You Stamp a New Brand on Your Firm?

- Work with an expert accounting/consulting marketer.
- Define your practice, business, and marketing goals.
- Create and impart a unique vision for your firm.
- Evaluate and recreate your value proposition.
- Design your brand based on the perceptions of your ideal client.
- Develop beta approaches.
- Get feedback.
- Refine promotion internally and externally.
- Continuously build meaning.
- Innovate and create fresh new ways to deliver your brand to the marketplace.
- Protect your brand.
- Use your brand as a catapult for promoting a dynamic firm culture.

How Do You Promote Your Brand?

- Each point of contact with the client, our team, and the marketplace
- Individuals in the firm
- Client-service level of consultation
- Our Web site (You must have an effective Web site.)
- Advertisements
- Brochures
- Stationery system
- Newsletters
- Firm customized practice vision book
- Building/lobby/signage
- Public relations/media relations
- Strategic alliance partners
- Internal culture

- Innovative marketing campaigns
- Personnel policies
- Personal level of empathy and thoughtfulness

Your Good Brand Is Good Business

- A vehicle for increasing the value of your accounting consulting business
- Higher perceived value = additional business and increased opportunities
  1. Clients
  2. Strategic partners
  3. Markets
  4. Service/products/niches
- Clients select firms that are compatible with their own culture and values = more ideal clients
- Clients pay more to ensure a consistent experience in line with their expectation = a more profitable business

Developing Your Brand

- Identify your firm's assets
  1. Why does a client feel good about working with your firm?
  2. Why do your partners and team choose to have a career with your firm?
  3. Describe what your firm is today.
  4. Describe what you would like your firm to be in the future.
  5. What are your firm's core competencies?
  6. What are your firm's core values?
  7. How does your firm differ from the competition?
  8. Are your services/products superior to those of your competitors? If so, how? If not, why not?
  9. Why do prospective clients select your firm over the competition?
  10. Describe your firm's ideal client.
  11. Describe your firm's most ambitious technology or new services initiatives.
  12. Imagine your firm's ultimate strategic partners. Who would they be and what would it take to attract and align with them?

WINNING PROFITABLE NEW BUSINESS

- Target prospective clients who will truly value your services.
- Determine what services clients really need and want.
- Select and target specific market niches in which you are qualified to excel.
- Introduce your entire array of services to every client.
- Position and brand your firm as a trusted e-business, technological, and financial advisor.
- Deliver knock-your-socks-off service that exceeds all client expectations.
- Price your services based on their value to the client.

MARKETING STRATEGIES

Capability Statements and Brochures
- Prepare a capability statement for each target market you serve. Concentrate on the benefits you provide to each particular type of client. General brochures are not usually sufficiently specific to motivate the desired response.
- When developing capability statements or brochures which describe your services, don't make them too lengthy or exhaustive. A good brochure should raise as many questions as it answers. The purpose of such a marketing piece is to get the prospective client to contact you, not provide a reference work on your services that removes the need for the prospect to obtain more information by talking with you.

Business Cards
- Avoid using your business card as an advertising billboard. Don't list the seven specialty services that you provide to your clients. The more information on the card, the less effective it is. The less said the better. Descriptions of services have a tendency to reduce the number of prospective clients who will have an interest in contacting you.

Resumes
- Never use a resume to promote your services. You may have to develop a resume to satisfy the requirements of an existing client, but it is a disastrous first marketing piece.

Marketing Face Time

- Market on a regular and consistent basis. Devote about 15 to 25 percent of your working hours, each and every week, to marketing and selling. The time to market is not when you have run out of clients or backlog.
- Invest a minimum of 50 percent of your marketing time on activities that will enhance your image and reputation as a knowledgeable resource in your specific fields of expertise. Time spent giving speeches, writing articles, contributing meaningfully to professional and trade organizations, and publishing your own "e-zine" (Internet electronic newsletter) is the most productive marketing you can do.

Public Speaking

- Develop three or more short speeches that you are willing to present to groups that would likely have prospective clients as members. Promote the availability of your services as a speaker to speakers bureaus, associations, and corporation meeting planners.
- When making a speech or presentation, check out and arrange the facilities and equipment in advance of your talk. Checking the sound system and computer presentation equipment, and determining if there is a pitcher and glass of water on the podium are not tasks which should be done after you are introduced. Personally ensure that everything is in order. Don't assume the facility will take care of having everything in order.
- When speaking before a group, avoid setting out a stack of your materials for the audience to pick up and read. Instead, during your talk mention a valuable information item you will be pleased to send to members of the audience if they will give you a business card. This permits you to follow-up personally with each prospective client and to add the person's name to your database for future contact. Just as you are concluding your remarks, remind the audience to leave their business cards if they want the item. As an added/benefit, your host/sponsor will see the group is so motivated by your words that they rush up and surround you when you have finished speaking. This increases the probability you will be asked to speak again.

Prospecting

- The best prospects for your services are existing clients. Devote a minimum of 30 minutes a week (uncompensated) for each client, figuring out what additional ways you could be of benefit to them. Document the thoughts in the form of a mini-proposal such as an e-mail.

Publicity (No Cost Advertising)

- Be listed in all trade and professional directories, printed and online, which reach your target market niches, which you can get into for little or no charge. Many who need your services don't know how to find someone with your expertise. Facilitate connections by being listed in directories. More than half of all directories will allow you to be listed free of charge as a service to their members.

- Get your name and your ideas published in the leading trade magazines/journals that are read by the prospective clients in the market niches you are targeting on a regular basis. Comment on what key people in that market niche are saying. Interpret accounting and technology news for its impact on your clients and prospective clients. The more often your name and your ideas are seen by your prospects, the more likely they will become your clients.

- When sending a press release include a photograph. Doing so increases the probability of your press release being used by about 60 percent.

- If you plan on using a photo of yourself in marketing materials or publicity campaigns use a competent professional photographer who specializes in executive portraiture. This is not the time to save money with inexpensive amateur photography. A poor quality photo can do more harm than good.

Referrals

- Find a professional and comfortable way of letting your clients know that you benefit from and appreciate referrals. Also, show your clients how to make referrals. Improperly handled, referrals are worthless. When done with professional finesse, they are invaluable.

References

- Expect and be prepared to respond to a request for references. If you look surprised and flustered, you will appear as though you lack experience and credibility. Instead, reach effortlessly into your attaché case and extract a long list of references. These should be people who have given you permission to be used as references, but they need not (all) be clients. There are many nonclients who can speak to your credibility, capacity, creativity, and character.
- If prospective clients are constantly asking you for references before deciding to engage your services, you are insufficiently assertive, controlling, and directive.

Networking

- Networking is good for business, but don't spend too much time networking and avoid spending time on unproductive networking. Just standing around with a cocktail glass is not productive. Position yourself to be the leader of the network.

CHAPTER 17

Internet, Database, and Target Niches

Marketing Guide

DATABASE MARKETING

Good Marketing Begins in Your Database

Suppose you knew whom your competitors' clients were, what services they used, what fees were charged by your competitors over the past three to five years, and how satisfied the clients are with your competitors' performance. Wouldn't such information be a gold mine for your firm's marketing and salespeople? Of course it would. But before you start looking for ways to uncover this information on your competitors' clients, put it together on your own clients first.

Very few accounting professionals have a comprehensive client database. If you could mine such a database to target your best clients, what services they purchased, and which prospective clients are in the same SIC (Standard Industry Classification) codes as your best clients, you could make your firm truly client-focused, or at least a lot more marketing savvy.

A reliable client database is the foundation upon which all effective marketing can take place. It can provide in-depth knowledge of your clients and prospective clients and provide you with the resources to communicate with them effectively. You can sell more services and products and provide the kind of client satisfaction that develops client loyalty and excellent referrals. You also can use your database for many types of marketing campaigns.

Database Marketing

Database marketing is about finding prospective clients who are looking for an accounting firm like yours. The potential is exponential sales growth. The downside is that there is a finite number of potential clients and if a competitor implements database marketing faster and better than you, they will get more of the gold.

Some accountants may scoff and say that database marketing is nothing more than common-sense fundamentals. But, for whatever reason, few accounting firms practice it. It might be like their concept of an exercise program: it's good common sense, but just too much trouble. Today, with the Internet, that excuse can no longer be justified. Technology has created new machines to make getting into shape easier and more effective. Like exercise, technology has made database marketing simple and productive with efficient and cost-effective computer hardware and easy-to-use database software.

Definition of Database Marketing

Database marketing is the process of transforming raw data into powerful, accessible, actionable, marketing information systems. In accountants' terminology, database marketing is all of the following:

- Learning everything you can about your clients and prospective clients and their needs
- Storing the gathered data in a central database so it can be turned into informative reports
- Using your expertise to pinpoint prospective clients and meet their needs better than anyone else

For the accountants' bottom line, it is using data-driven marketing decisions to locate and sell to the greatest number of qualified prospective clients at the lowest possible cost. With database marketing you can build your online accounting services business and increase profitability with minimal cost. It is very important to understand that developing a marketing database is an ongoing process. It's a long-term investment in the future of your practice.

Designing Your Database

1. Identify which clients or prospective clients you want to target. The objective of your data is to build a profile of your clients.

This client profile will tell you who and where your best prospective clients are. You cannot know who your best prospects are until you first determine who your best clients are. Generally, there are two types of information you will want to gather:

- Demographics
  SIC (type of business)
  Size (sales volume/number of employees)
  Geographic location
  Source (where did you first learn of them?)
  ○ In-house client files
  ○ Leads from vendor partners
  ○ Mailing lists
  ○ Member lists from industry or professional associations
  ○ Advertising and promotion
  ○ Referrals
  ○ Contacts in billing system
  ○ Marketing contacts

- Psychographics
  Financial capabilities
  Publications read
  Personality of decision maker

   The examples cited are intended to stimulate your thinking. Every practice is unique and must develop its own set of data. Your initial data set will not be complete, but don't let this stop you. Your database will evolve over time and with experience. Plan on expanding your coverage so that over three to five years your database gives you 60 percent to 70 percent of the information you need.

2. Communicate with the clients and prospective clients you've identified via e-mail, telemarketing, newsletters, and Web site promotion. You can invite them to seminars, where you promote new or additional services or targeted market niches.

3. Gather the results of your communications:
   Who responded?
   Who engaged services?
   Which contact names and addresses need to be updated?
   What do they want most?

The first step is to import the information you have in your current client files. This may be little more than names, addresses, e-mail addresses, telephone numbers, and histories of engagements and products purchased. In other cases you may have a significant amount of information that may not be accurate and needs to be updated. From here on, telemarketing will be a key conduit.

Gathering the desired demographic and psychographic data will take place over the phone in the form of qualifying, selling, and servicing contacts and survey respondents. As you capture your data and record it in your database, a profile of your clients begins to emerge. This capture phase gives you a closed-loop way to increase the value of your database and increase the effectiveness of future campaigns.

Relational Database

Consider using a relational database with which you can store profile data on clients and link it to their demographics and responses to your campaigns. A packaged system or one from an ASP (Application Software Provider) is best. Otherwise you will have to spend time and money in programming.

Whatever method you choose, plan to have the activity of your marketing database managed carefully — adding more client records and fields of data, maintaining the structure and contents, and refining the database for incorrect or outdated information. Once you've implemented an effective client database, your marketing plans are off to a good head start.

Building a Better Database

- Compile a comprehensive list of client and prospective client contacts.
- Market directly to each client and prospective client.
- Evaluate individual responses to your marketing campaign.

Client Profiles

- The type and size of clients serviced by your firm
- Which of your marketing efforts is producing engagements
- Who your competitors are and what they are doing better than you
- What is read, watched, or listened to by your clients

Properly designed, your marketing database will constantly be rewarding you in your quest for additional clients and revenue productivity.

DATABASE MARKETPLACE MINING

The amount of marketing data available to most accounting firms is staggering and continuing to grow. This is a result of technology becoming more powerful and relatively inexpensive to use. Powerful microprocessors, inexpensive data storage devices, and increasing amounts of available bandwidth to transmit data, all point to the explosion in the amount of business data available today. Hidden in the gigabytes of stored data is client information that, when uncovered and used, could be of vital strategic importance to an organization.

Your database marketing analysis procedures and techniques must become more sophisticated if your accounting business is to keep up with and use the data now available. Instead of looking at these adjustments as problems to overcome, marketing managers should realize the opportunity now exists to search through mountains of data to find specific information on their clients, client buying patterns, and other valuable information that can have a fundamental impact on revenues and profits.

Accounting Marketplace Data Mining

Accounting marketplace data mining is a concept of searching for, accessing, and manipulating data to produce information useful to an accounting practice. This specialized form of data mining uses new technologies to sift through and analyze data to find meaningful trends, relationships, and correlations among multiple variables.

Database Mining/Marketing Technologies

Data-mining technologies are usually based on a branch of artificial intelligence called machine learning. There are a variety of approaches utilized in machine learning including the following:

- Decision tree induction
- Neural networks
- Case-based reasoning
- Rough sets
- Genetic algorithms

DATABASE MARKETING REQUIREMENTS

A practical accounting practice database marketing system utilizing marketplace data mining requires the following four constructs:

1. Easy access to data
2. Easy manipulation and viewing of data
3. User-friendly analysis
4. Easy use of the results

Easy Access to Data

The mere presence of data does not mean easy access. One of the major constraints facing accounting marketers is being able to obtain timely and usable (e.g., clean) client and marketing data in a suitable format that is accessible from a standards and systems interface point. There may also be a need to obtain supplementary data, such as demographic or socioeconomic data, and apply it to in-house or primary data sources.

Issues regarding data access in smaller to medium-sized accounting businesses include, but are not limited to, the following:

- Poor or nonexistent electronic links to data sources
- Organizational politics inhibiting links
- Inconsistent data
- Incomplete data
- Security
- Lack of sufficiently rich data

Easy Manipulation and Viewing of Data

The second construct is to review and work with the data. For instance, an accounting services marketer may have available 35 or more independent variables on clients and prospective clients from which to choose in creating a client profile. The ability to easily review the variables to determine which may be the most important in the profile is essential.

Thus, providing easy-to-understand information on the data as well as the ability to compare it to a standard index is important. Another important feature is the ability to filter variables to eliminate certain cases.

User-Friendly Analysis

The third construct is to provide an intuitive and easy-to-use analysis tool. This is certainly another challenge. More traditional model and profile building have relied on methods ranging from simple categorization to complex statistical techniques such as multivariate regression. The richness of data now available along with powerful modeling techniques developed suggests the requirement for a sophisticated analysis approach, but without the requisite training.

Data mining has the most to offer accounting practices in the area of data analysis. New approaches in analyzing data sometimes prove to be just as, or more, powerful than traditional approaches, though potentially much easier to use. Another important factor is the ability to integrate an intuitive user interface program with a data-mining algorithm. The interface will have to serve multiple ends. As well as providing an electronic interface to the databases, and simple data viewing, the interface should also enable the user to select and input variables or attributes into a model, choose a simple or more detailed level of analysis, refine the model by adding or deleting attributes, and, electronically use the client profile generated to search for prospective clients in the database.

Easy Use of the Results

The last construct is designed to take the results from the marketplace data mining and integrate them into the firm's marketing operations. An integrated system would be able to search the contact database, extract prospective clients meeting the profile, and save those names and contact information in a separate file. This file would become the e-mail and telemarketing campaign call list.

The marketplace data-mining and marketing system should also be able to use data generated by all of the components in the accounting firm's marketing campaigns. A campaign in progress is a very useful source of additional information for improving the client profile. By analyzing the feedback data, especially those contacts that did not yield an appointment or a sale, the model can be improved or fine-tuned.

REAPING THE REWARDS

Soon you will be ready to make data-driven marketing decisions that not only are cost-effective but also increase revenues from your direct marketing, public relations, and advertising efforts. You can accomplish the following:

- Eliminate marketing efforts that produce too many inquiries from nonqualified prospective clients who waste your selling time
- Duplicate and multiply marketing efforts that produce inquiries from qualified prospective clients

DATABASE MARKETING BUZZWORDS

- **Affinity:** People who are similar in lifestyle.
- **ASCII:** American Standard format for data storage on magnetic tape or disk.
- **Duplication factor:** Percentage of names on one list that are also on another list.
- **Loyalty program:** Special marketing programs that reward clients for repeat business.
- **Market penetration:** Percentage of clients you have, compared to the total businesses in your targeted market niches.
- **Merge/Purge:** Software system used to put different input tapes in varying formats into a common format and eliminate duplications for a mailing.
- **Modeling:** Statistical technique whereby you build a sample of your client from a database of prospective clients identifying similar and dissimilar characteristics.
- **Profile:** Method of describing the prospective client's behavioral characteristics.
- **Recency:** Term for how recently a client has engaged services from your firm.
- **Relationship marketing:** Marketing programs that encourage the client to use the firm's services or products with more frequency; programs that express to the client the appreciation of the accounting firm.

SUCCESS IN THE ACCOUNTING AND CONSULTING PROFESSION

Success in the accounting and consulting profession is a function of effective marketing. Knowing how to sell your services and having the motivation to put this knowledge to work are the keys to making it. As important as specialty, location, contacts, education, and other factors may be, they really don't have as great an impact on your accounting business as marketing does.

Following are marketing strategies for building a successful accounting and consulting practice:

- **Know the market.** Some unsuccessful accountants have an "inventor" mentality. They invest months, even years, creating elegant solutions to respond to assumed needs, never asking the question, "Is this what the market wants and will pay for?" The most successful accounting professionals start with the marketplace. They ask, "What is the market willing to pay for?" Then they respond with a service that clients strongly desire. Successful accounting professionals determine what the marketplace wants by doing basic research. And they read widely. As they read periodicals, they ask themselves several important questions:
  - In what ways will this information have a favorable or unfavorable impact on my clients or prospective clients?
  - What problems will it create?
  - What opportunities have emerged?
  - In what ways can I assist clients and prospective clients take advantage of these opportunities and avoid these problems?

- **Make a commitment to target and niche marketing.** Unsuccessful accountants spend time dreaming about creating the universal service that every client will want to buy. They seek the accounting equivalent to the paper clip. While finding such a service is always a remote possibility, most of us do best by marketing. Divide your markets into segments that can be reached easily and affordably. You can have more than one niche market, but it is almost always best to divide the market before you attempt to conquer it.

- **Make your services cost-effective for the client.** Position your firm so that clients save money by using its services. Target specialized services to the small to medium-sized business segment of the market (smaller fast-growing businesses in a defined geographic area) — that really need, but cannot afford to hire, a full-time controller or chief financial officer.

- **Make your firm's services tangible.** All e-mail and other advertising, brochures given out at speeches, and Web site contents should always include a list of the specific services that a client would receive. Make mention of the fact that all services are provided for a fixed monthly fee.

- **Be a troubleshooter.** Turning prospects into clients requires the ability to translate intangible know-how into tangible outcomes that the prospects can both see and benefit from. Successful accounting professionals convince their clients that they can help solve a problem.

- **Don't limit yourself.** The accountants who find little demand for their services are those who tell prospective clients, "I'm an accountant. Do you have any projects that I can help you with?" This is a vague statement. No one understands the scope of your work as well as you do, and it's up to you to translate an essentially meaningless job title into a list of benefits that a client can relate to.

- **Create an image and a reputation.** Nothing is more important for building a profitable practice than establishing an image and reputation. When you do this, it causes prospective clients to seek you out first, and to ask you to provide your services. If prospective clients don't seek you out, it is in your best interests to have them know who you are when you initiate contact with them.

- **Position yourself as an authority in your field.** Offer to speak at civic and community events. Give seminars, get press coverage, publish your own Internet-based newsletter, write articles or books, network, and join appropriate professional and trade associations. Such techniques let clients know that you mean business before you walk in the door.

- **Keep your name on your clients' lips.** Making contacts will bring you clients. But to achieve success as an accounting professional, it's vital to keep your name on your clients' lips. That way, when they need consulting or accounting services they'll call you, and only you.

WINNING CLIENTS BY ASKING AND ANSWERING VITAL QUESTIONS

A large part of selling your services comes from knowing which questions to ask your prospective clients. Exhibit 17.1 is an excerpt from Jack Fox's Accounting Business e-mail newsletter (available without charge from http://www.accountingguild.com). It lists 20 of the most important

---

During your initial meeting with prospective clients, it's useful to have a number of questions to ask that will help you determine your prospective clients' needs. To guide you in developing questions appropriate for your selling situation, consider this list.

1. What is the major problem this organization faces?
2. Which problems that it faces are shared by the rest of the industry (or similar firms and competitors)?
3. What problems confronting your organization are unique to this geographic area?
4. In what ways has inadequate planning contributed to the problems facing your organization?
5. In what ways have government regulations affected the profitability of your organization?
6. How does this organization rank in the industry in terms of salary, benefits, and employee perks?
7. Is this organization family owned? If so, to what extent does this ownership affect promotions and employee morale?
8. What kind of staff turnover have you experienced? Is this trend up or down from previous years?
9. Have you made any changes in personnel policy based on your assessments of employee satisfaction and productivity?
10. How long have your key management and technical team members been with the organization?
11. How far in advance do you make specific decisions about expansion?
12. What has been the most disappointing area of growth over the past two years?

(Continues)

Exhibit 17.1 Winning Clients with Q & A Interviews

13. In what ways do you ensure that training expenditures will produce results?
14. How do communications work within your organization?
15. How do you identify communication breakdowns in the organization?
16. Who reports to whom in your organization?
17. What is the biggest time bomb in your organization? What steps have been taken, or do you plan to take, to deal with this problem?
18. What impact do you see company problems having on management and staff?
19. What new services do you see as vital within the next five years for this organization to maintain or increase its growth?
20. What is your time frame for implementing new accounting or consulting services?

Source: AccountingBusiness © 2000 by Jack Fox. http://www.accountingguild.com

Exhibit 17.1 *(Continued)*

questions to ask potential clients when you're trying to get their business. The answers can give you information that's essential in meeting your client's needs. Also included are questions that your prospective client might ask you. Be prepared to answer them before you meet with prospects. This will increase your chances of making a sale and securing future business.

Communicating with Prospective Clients

When communicating with prospective clients, avoid asking questions to which you already know the answers. It makes you seem dull and uninterested, as you probably will not pay much attention to your prospect's answers. Do not waste their time. If you have nothing new, creative, and interesting to say or ask, you probably should not be talking to them in the first place.

Don't hesitate to take notes. Reliance on memory can be dangerous and clients are usually flattered that you find their words of sufficient significance that you want to make a record of them. Questions can help you assess the needs and desires of your prospects and clients in order to tailor your services and offer the best and most productive solutions to their problems.

Decision-Making Questions Prospects Ask Themselves

You should anticipate that your prospects will have some of the following questions in mind—even if they don't ask them— when they are deciding whether to retain your services:

- Do I need this service?
- Do I really want this service?
- Can I really afford this service?
- Will I make use of the knowledge I gain?
- Am I being offered a good deal?
- Should I check out the competition?
- Could I get this service for less?
- Is this professional honest, knowledgeable, and reliable?
- Should I decide now or later?
- What will my colleagues think?
- What problems may result if I don't act now?

When you respond honestly, intelligently, and persuasively to these unasked questions, your prospective clients will be favorably impressed with your intuitiveness. Learning and using such strategies, asking perceptive questions, and laying fears to rest should help you turn uncertain prospective clients into solid, profitable clients.

TARGET NICHE MARKETING PLAN

Creating your firm's niche market plan will enable you to concentrate on the benefits of segmenting your markets to increase the practice's popularity. Begin by constructing an overall firm plan, organizing activities along niche lines. If your firm isn't already organized along niche lines, an analysis of the firm's strengths and clients should reveal the niche areas that will provide the most opportunities. The following process is designed to provide guidance in focusing on industry or functional niches:

- Research all prospective niches and their suitability to your firm.
- Assess industry needs within each niche.
- Research the industries that indicate the greatest potential.
- Rate possibilities for increased recognition, business, and profitability.
- Correlate the firm's existing clients with niche findings.

- Match the niche's SICs with the firm's existing clients.
- Analyze the areas the firm has designated as ones it would like to explore.

INVESTIGATE METHODS OF PROMOTING FIRMS' NICHES

Investigate the various methods of strengthening and promoting the firm's niches. This can be accomplished in two phases:

Internal Marketing

Internal marketing consists of motivating the entire team to accept a niche commitment and developing an internal awareness of the firm's presence in the industry. You'll also need to assist the partners and other team members to identify educational opportunities, such as conferences and retreats, where they can acquire the advanced technical expertise needed to advise business owners within the selected specific industries or service areas.

External Marketing

External marketing consists of identifying those methods by which the firm can promote its industry expertise and receive recognition in the marketplace for its contributions within this niche. Joining industry associations and becoming active on committees are two ways of penetrating the network. Speaking at industry conferences and seminars and publishing articles are also very powerful methods because of the implied third-party endorsement. Such endorsements promote the firm's reputation and credibility much more effectively than the firm's own materials or advertising.

Niche marketing is very effective for two major reasons: Clients appreciate the high level of involvement and they have more confidence in an accounting professional who truly understands the particular industry or service area and its unique challenges.

Create a Specific Niche Market Database

Create a database of clients, contacts who represent prospective clients, and referral sources for your niche services. Let them know of your niche focus through specialized niche communications such as e-mails, newsletters, seminars, and reports. Include referral sources (e.g., bankers who serve the same clients) of your firm's niche capabilities.

Individual Partner/Team Member Marketing

A niche focus encourages partners and other team members to concentrate their efforts in an industry or service area that interests them. This should lessen any reluctance to engage in marketing activities. Understand the personality and comfort level of yourself and each partner. Some may be public speakers; others may be writers; others may be fine association officers. Play to each team member's strengths in creating individual plans.

To gain recognition within an industry, encourage partners to write articles for industry publications and to participate in industry conferences or seminars. Ask team members to tell you when something newsworthy occurs in their niche that would be good for a press release. It's important that both industry and business press recognize your expertise in the niche and seek you as a resource. Partners can also expand their reputations by participating in trade associations and using the networking opportunities to meet prospective clients and referral sources. Their professional associations could also be sources of marketing assistance and opportunities.

Speaking Opportunities

Explore the active and popular trade associations and arrange for speaking engagements. Consider a direct mailer to associations, advising them of speaker availability. Good, informative speakers are hard to find, so they should be eager to hear from you.

Niche Marketing Benefits

Adopting a niche-oriented team approach will enrich you and your firm. Working together, the partners and staff provide the technical knowledge that the clients require, while the marketing staff offers the direction, structure, and implementation process for realizing the firm's objectives. Everyone will remain interested and committed to the firm's marketing success.

Exhibit 17.2 lists the prevalent accounting niche (specialty) services at United States accounting firms in the year 2000 in order of utilization.

Exhibit 17.3 shows client industry niches in order of specialization at United States accounting firms in the year 2000.

- Business valuations
- Computer systems/consulting
- Online accounting services
- Applications solutions provider
- Estate planning
- Litigation support
- Accounting systems/software
- Mergers and acquisitions
- Forensics/fraud
- Industry specializations
- Nonprofit organizations
- Business management for wealthy individuals
- Employee benefits
- Personal financial planning
- Strategic planning/business plans
- Compensation/benefit planning
- International tax
- Investment advisors
- Internet/electronic commerce
- Employment search
- Bankruptcy/insolvency
- Financing arrangements
- Software development/training
- Budgetary services: Cash flow
- Payroll services/consulting
- Business management for small business
- Lease versus buy analysis
- E-filing
- Export/import
- Budgeting services: Receivables management

Source: The Accounting Guild, Las Vegas, Nevada, *Annual Accounting Firms' Niche Markets Survey,* 2000

Exhibit 17.2 Accounting Niche (Specialty) Services, Year 2000

- Manufacturing
- Construction
- Real estate
- Nonprofit organizations
- Professional services
- Health care facilities
- Individuals
- Pension plans
- Wholesale distribution
- Retail trade
- Auto dealerships
- Hotels and restaurants
- Insurance agents and brokers
- Banking and thrift companies
- Brokers/securities and commodities dealers
- State/local government
- Dot.com/e-commerce
- Publishing/broadcasting/media
- Entertainment
- Finance companies/mortgage banks
- Franchising
- School districts
- Agriculture/farming/forestry/fishing
- Small business
- Colleges and universities
- Medium-sized business
- Government contractors
- Investment companies and mutual funds

Source: The Accounting Guild, Las Vegas, Nevada, *Annual Accounting Firms' Niche Markets Survey,* 2000

Exhibit 17.3 Accounting Firms' Client Industries Concentration

CHAPTER 18

Partnering: Profiles in Profitability

Accounting Partnership Resources Compendium

PARTNERSHIPS PAVE THE WAY

The Internet economy is dictating new rules of engagement and changing the way many traditional accountants do business. Partnering is shaping up as a key driver for delivering online accounting solutions. Software providers are also listening to the siren call of partnering. As many of them, change their business models, they are adopting partnerships with accounting services providers that were once considered competitors. Partnering allows them to fill the gaps where they lack expertise to deliver certain client solutions and it may be too costly to build or acquire the talent.

In the area of e-commerce solutions, it's critical for the accounting professional to partner. The real question that CPAs are asking is, "How can I make money on e-commerce?" The majority of e-commerce participants have been customers rather than providers of services or products. The key for CPAs and all accounting services providers lies in determining how to use e-commerce to offer new and better services, at a profit, to clients.

Components of E-commerce

1. Technology (This is the most intriguing component, which most accounting professionals don't understand.)
2. Marketing
3. Business expertise

No one would ever consider consulting most CPAs and accounting professionals in the area of marketing. Accountants are perceived as trusted business advisors in the areas of accounting, finance, and business processes. Therefore, they should focus on their strengths and form alliances and partnerships with those who have the marketing and technology skills they lack.

Accounting professionals should focus less on technology and more on business expertise and marketing their services. You don't have to know how to build a toaster oven. You simply have to know how to put two slices of bread with some cheese between them into the oven to make a grilled cheese sandwich.

A new species of technology literate business executive has evolved over the past decade. Unlike technology geeks, these new executives are neither afraid nor enamored of technology. They are practical and realize that technology will play an increasing role in the delivery of goods and services. Pragmatic and profit motivated, they will not accept the mantra "If it's not broke, don't fix it."

They continually desire to make the system run faster and more smoothly. They want to improve or streamline processes. This new breed of executive was termed early adopters or innovators. Many were among the first to embrace personal computers, networking, the Internet, and distributive computing. We all know people who fit this description. There are still a few left in the CPA profession, but most left in the 1990s because accounting was moving too slowly, and there were more lucrative opportunities in other industries.

Technology Gap

A technology gap exists in most organizations, according to my experience and recent accounting industry research by the American Institute of CPAs and The Accounting Guild. The gap is between the business owner, chief executive or chief financial officer, and the technical personnel. Those at the top have a difficult time communicating with the technical personnel.

CPAs should fill this role because of their business knowledge. But practitioners are often too involved in compliance work to even consider clients' technology issues, or clients often haven't perceived the CPA as having technology expertise. Thus, in many organizations, including CPA firms, the technology picture hasn't been pretty. There has been finger pointing, strong opinions, and a great deal of emotional energy released.

It has been a personal observation that those with the strongest opinions tend to have the least amount of knowledge. The more you know, the more tolerant you tend to be of change and alternatives. However, this is rapidly changing and the new executive is far more technology savvy and less tolerant of technology illiteracy.

Firms are quickly learning that the up-front investment is well worth the time and effort. Use the client as common ground. Everyone knows the importance of the client, and some wise firms ask clients what services they desire and want to buy. Once this information is available, an information technology plan and budget will reduce internal battles and gets the firm focused on high-payoff priorities.

Critical Success Factors in E-commerce Services

- Targeting the right clients
- Examining the client relationship from the client's perspective
- Streamlining business processes
- Letting clients help themselves
- Owning the clients' total experience (one-stop shopping)
- Adding value by assisting clients with their jobs
- Personalizing services to your clients
- Developing a community that your clients are proud to be a part of

Stages of E-commerce

1. Brochureware (firm information posted to the Internet)
2. Client support and interaction of the Internet
3. Transactions conducted electronically (e-mail is a start)
4. Personal interaction with the client (requires current profiles)
5. Community

From experience and observation, the majority of accounting professionals and firms are in stage one, and a few are starting to implement stages two, three, and four. In very isolated cases has anyone attempted stage five.

Lack of Vision and Commitment

The e-commerce evolution among accounting professionals has been slow because no one has seen the potential for a return on investment. The more complex issue is that most CPAs haven't had the vision or knowledge.

Without a plan and strategy, it's hard to profit from or take advantage of a situation. Those who have profited from e-commerce haven't just been lucky; they have gone into it with a strategy, a budget, and commitment.

However, most firms have not had the time or resources to devote to e-commerce initiatives. Their plate has been full with personal financial planning and consulting services and with investing in their internal technology infrastructures.

Since accountants haven't led the way with e-commerce, let's benefit from the experience of the Big Five and other large companies. In the accounting industry, the best example would be Intuit. The common element of the Internet successes is that their Web sites are database driven with customer profiles that are maintained by the client. The sites are also interactive and easy to use.

E-COMMERCE IS COMING TO A FIRM NEAR YOU

E-commerce is coming to a firm near you, if not your own firm, within a very short time. There are already major competitors offering tax preparation services over the Internet, led by Intuit. Right behind tax return preparation will be the following services:

- Storage and retrieval of important documents, tax returns, financial statements, agreements, and supporting documents
- Small business financial services, such as payroll and accounting

There is already a growing number of application software providers that allow users to access and use applications software over the Internet.

Action Steps

Who is going to do this and how do I get started? The large firms and consolidators have been doing this and are working to provide ever-increasing solutions. An alternative for the majority of accountants will be to partner with application software providers (ASPs).

Intuit

Intuit is the vendor of Quicken and QuickBooks accounting software. Its Quicken.com program has most of the tools that local practices provide with traditional, as well as emerging, services. Despite the attempt to include accounting professionals in an advisors' program, the actions of Intuit consistently demonstrate a predatory attitude toward accounting professionals.

Bizfinity

Bizfinity sells through CPAs and other accounting professionals to small business clients, which makes perfect sense for firms as well as for Bizfinity. This may be just the solution that the practices that haven't consolidated have been looking for. Think of it as the independent insurance agent. The vendor provides the products and the local agent runs the business as she or he determines. This solves the cultural issues that the consolidators are experiencing. Accountants should look for alliances and partnerships if they want to benefit from e-commerce and survive the onslaught of larger and better-financed competition. Bizfinity offers a service that many need and very few have. This allows accounting professionals to concentrate on what they do best. They can be accessed at www.Bizfinity.com.

E-COMMERCE SPECIALIZED TECHNOLOGY REQUIREMENTS

The e-commerce software is a database developed for a Web platform. High-speed bandwidth is necessary for the volume of users that your Web site should attract. The back office or accounting records must be integrated with the Web site to eliminate redundancy and ensure accuracy and efficiency. To do this, accountants must define and standardize their processes.

As you proceed into e-commerce you should consider the following:

- The skills of your existing team
- The outlook for the hiring of staff in the future
- Current and future client requirements
- The importance of being among the first to market
- Your small inner voice or gut feelings
- With whom you will partner and affiliate

E-COMMERCE PROGNOSIS

Will you make money from e-commerce? Like the lottery, you can't win unless you buy a ticket. You are not obligated to play; however, ignoring the trend in the accounting business will put you at a distinct disadvantage with your competition and will risk your existing client base.

E-commerce is a major undertaking for any size firm. It requires vision, leadership, commitment, budget, discipline, and courage. Only you can decide if it is for you and your firm.

The bottom line is that you must have a strategy and budget, qualified technology personnel (within your firm or with a partner or affiliate), marketing expertise, leadership and vision, a training program, and strategic alliances if you are going to benefit from technology and e-commerce.

PARTNERING COMPATIBILITY

Compatibility and trust are the foremost concerns. Being able to work with your partner has to be at the top of your mind. Look at a potential partner the same way you look at a merger partner. Many times accountants look at partnering as a way to get a particular engagement. That is very short-sighted.

Before you select a partner of your own choice or your client's, make sure it's clear who owns the client relationship. Define areas of responsibility and who owns different portions of it, where the interfaces are and how you handle escalations of issues. Consider, too, how much any potential partner has to gain or lose. You don't want a partner with nothing to lose, because you might be left holding the bag.

MAKE YOURSELF VISIBLE

Get out there. Don't wait for people to come to you. Go to the major conferences, seminars, and symposiums. It's important to be in the places where other people are looking for partners as well. Send your team members for training. If you are looking to beef up your areas of expertise, training your key staffers is a good way for them to meet other people learning about the same technology and possibly establish contacts.

DUE DILIGENCE

Once you've located a potential partner, do your due diligence. Don't rely on what the prospective partners reveals. Talk to the implementers at the partner. Talk to some of their clients to make sure their customers were happy with the work. Get bad references, too. The usual assumption when asking for references is to get happy customers, but no one bats a thousand. There will be misses, problems, and failures in any business, and a company can be more revealing in failure than success. The way you deal with adversity will say more about how well you work than what you do when things are going well.

ONLINE ACCOUNTING PROFITABILITY PARTNERSHIPS

Virtual Growth

Virtual Accountant software is a Web-based, accounting and bookkeeping service that combines the power of the Internet with a dedicated team of accounting professionals. The accountant gets clean, accurate numbers, clear financial reports, anytime, anywhere. Accountants can get the services privately branded so they can provide clients with world-class accounting without the hassle and expense of an in-house department. Your virtual accounting practice will not require a staff and equipment investment, which is perfect for situations that cannot support a full-time operation. The software can be accessed at www.virtualgrowth.com.

BECOMING AN ONLINE ACCOUNTING SUCCESS STORY

A profitable Web-based accounting practice requires an entirely new business model. Even the largest and most savvy accounting firms may flounder in the race to get their online practice right while many small-budget accounting practitioners jump in and start making money their very first month.

So what is the essence of planning, researching, evaluating, launching, and building a successful online accounting business? What does it take to bring in clients, generate leads, cut costs, build client and staff loyalty, or achieve your firm's unique goals and objectives?

It's not any one thing. It is not doing things 1,000 percent better. It's more like doing 1,000 things, one percent better. What most successful online accounting businesses have in common is a precise and unique blend of techniques, strategies, skills, and methods.

Individually, none of these things are difficult to develop or practice, but finding the specific blend that works right for you could take months—even years—of expensive experimentation. And every day that you're not up and running online at top speed translates to missed opportunities. Your competitors may steal away your hard-won clients and market share and countless dollars may slip through your fingers.

TECHNOLOGY AS A STRATEGIC ASSET

The CPA, independent accountant, bookkeeper, computer consultant, and accounting software trainer who are not already engaged in a cyber-based online accounting practice must adopt the attitude of technology as a strategic asset. The major difference between those accountants who leverage technology and those who don't is increased profitability. The great lesson to be learned here for marketing accounting services: Make certain that you know your client. The key to success is being the right thing to the right people.

The Internet is drastically altering the way business is conducted. Your client's perception and experience with using the Web has changed the products and services that your firm provides. Transforming your accounting business to tap into the Internet requires integrating your entire professional practice into one cohesive entity. Now there is a once-in-a millennium opportunity for technology, business financial services, marketing, and demand to place your clients at the center of your e-professional strategy.

Accountants with an attitude based on technology and marketing have the daring option of leaving legacy technology behind and adapting an architecture that enables service-enriched access to dynamic Internet-based possibilities. The good news is that the accountant has a choice; the bad news is that the accountant must make that choice. The noted pundit George Gilder may have it right when he says, "Don't solve problems. You'll just achieve costly mediocrity. Pursue opportunities instead."

An effective accounting professional must be able to have instant information about his or her client's financial transactions and be capable of accessing the client's previous decisions. Changes between forecasts and actual results must be instantly available. Now you can get what you need, when you need it, and wherever you need it.

SMALL BUSINESS CLIENT ACCOUNTING PRACTICE

It is false economy to retain the wrong foundation for a new structure rather than scrapping it and starting anew. Most accountants with a small business client practice produce knowledge products from information provided by clients who either use QuickBooks, Peachtree, MYOB, or one of the other low-end accounting software programs. Clients who use such software are missing many of the benefits that online computerized accounting applications can provide.

The Internet has fundamentally altered the potential for the practice of small business public accounting. GAAP and tax compliance have remained essentially unchanged. The environment for collecting data efficiently and accurately has been transformed dramatically with the advent of online accounting software providers' Web-based accounting solutions for small business.

ONLINE ACCOUNTING SOFTWARE

Online accounting software is a new generation of software—one that is never a product but only a service. Accountants must understand this new model, because it will have a profound impact on accounting services delivery and management in the near and long term. Accounting professionals have now been provided another option for delivering functionality to their clients.

Interested accountants are trying to select the best accounting applications, the ones that best fit their clients' business needs, and then determine how to actually implement those applications. The primary reasons for an accountant to select an online accounting service are based on cost, resources, and service levels.

The accountants' clients can now receive their most pressing business information needs from, and with the guidance and assistance of, their accountant. The accounting professional will empower the client's sales, support, and service deliverables through automation. Clients will experience enhanced effectiveness and efficiency throughout their entire operations. Clients and accountants will be able to securely access any information, any time, anywhere. Clients may engage their customers, suppliers, and partners through electronic value chains.

Accounting professionals' and clients' utilization of superior integration of critical information systems allows each to seize the future with confidence. The online accounting software model has evolved rapidly into a stratification of the accounting industry in a number of interlocking areas.

Many vendors are entering the market as followers without realizing that they possess core competencies in perhaps only one or two of the layers. Often, a vendor partners or subcontracts with another vendor to provide services in another layer.

The Online Accounting Software Value Chain

The new and unfamiliar dynamics of the burgeoning online accounting software services marketplace have contributed to the marketplace's unawareness of what such services really do. Accounting has rapidly moved from the quill pen and parchment era to computer bits and bytes on the Web. Online accounting software creates an application service chain that includes the following:

- Consulting
- Configuration and implementation
- Data Center infrastructure and hosting
- Accounting applications management
- Service delivery and management
- Business process services

Small businesses gain special benefits from cost savings. Historically, smaller businesses have been the last to upgrade applications. They have been reluctant to retrain employees and reconfigure desktops because they are afraid the upgrade cycles will continue ceaselessly and the data will be incompatible. As soon as the accounting professional starts discussing software deployment over the Internet to these people, the whole notion of Total Cost of Ownership (TCO) plummets dramatically.

Small Business Internet Accounting Software Issues

Small business owners are used to buying a piece of accounting software, training people to use it, performing maintenance, and then doing it over again every time an upgrade is necessary. Now they can predict the cost of accounting software for the entire year. Expenses are controlled, projected, and determined by the client and their accountant. Hidden costs are identified and eliminated.

Online Accounting Value Proposition

For small businesses the online value proposition includes the following:

- Faster implementation time
- Software rental rather than purchase
- No up-front capital cost and lower ongoing total cost of ownership
- Full life-cycle application services
- Simplified pricing
- Limited customization
- Industry-specific implementation
- The ability to leapfrog to top-tier applications

ACCOUNTANT AFFILIATION PROGRAMS

An accountant affiliation program provides for a collaboration of industry-specific domain expertise and templates that is made possible through the cooperation of accounting professionals who target clients in selected industries and a facilitating organization such as The Accounting Guild (http://www.accountingguild.com). That approach empowers accountants affiliated with The Accounting Guild to more easily provide an end-to-end service offering encompassing the implementation, customization, and ongoing operation and support of applications (e.g., Internet-packaged accounting software application with the infrastructure delivered to clients for a flat monthly fee) for specific industries and types of business activities.

ONLINE ACCOUNTING SERVICES BUSINESS MODELS

The online accounting software services model is not exactly outsourcing, although in many respects it appears to closely resemble an outsourced accounting application service. Each of the many new vendors entering the marketplace seems to add a degree of hype, making it quite reminiscent of the older service bureaus and time-sharing models. This time, the new hype does not present the same old story. Online accounting services encompass a business philosophy that relies not only on technology, but also on a new way of thinking about client services practices, client and accountant financial skills, performance measurement, and management theories.

The Accounting Guild business model differs from traditional outsourcing business models in several important ways. The major differences between today's application outsourcing services and the innovative Accounting Guild model are as follows:

1. Delivery over the Internet
2. Shared operations (server-based processing and hosting)
3. Full life-cycle application services versus outsourcing only
4. Simplified pricing and billing
5. Limited customization versus anything goes
6. Rapid implementation
7. Complexity screened from the end user

ACCOUNTING PROFESSIONALS' STRATEGIES

Many accounting professionals are finding it difficult to make sense of the fast-changing online accounting software market and the various vendors that are in the market. Therefore, it is helpful to view the vendors in light of an individual vendor's go-to-market strategy, which will vary based on at least three categories:

- **Customer Focus.** Target clients are often small, innovative companies with no established infrastructure and an uncertain growth trajectory. The complexity of the business varies and may include many targeted market niches.

- **Breadth of Solutions.** The breadth and depth of the accounting applications offered by each vendor vary widely. Many providers are struggling with whether they should concentrate on a few select packages (e.g., time and billing) or eventually offer expertise on a wide variety of packages.

- **Range of Services.** A very wide range of services is provided, either directly by the vendor or through partnerships. Some online providers may provide all required services, while others will establish partnerships with a variety of vendors.

Evaluation Criteria

The accounting professional must consider each vendor's strategy and determine whether the strategy makes that vendor a valuable partner and viable contender over the long term. Because of the previously discussed hype that is unfortunately surrounding the accounting software market, it is quite important that accountants have a useful set of evaluation criteria. Vendors will vary in their approach to issues such as pricing and the various services the vendor is willing to provide.

The online accounting services market has evolved significantly in response to the market need for cost-effective application service solutions for the small business market. "Pure play" providers deliver accounting package applications over the Internet on a subscription basis. Sometimes, some vendors will partner with selected external service providers that have an established outsourcing business (e.g., Virtual Growth [Virtual Accountant], ADP, Paychex, and OneCore.com) or with niche vendors that offer specific industry experience.

ACCOUNTANTS' PROFESSIONAL IMPLICATIONS

Why should this nascent market warrant such attention from the accounting profession? The answer is that the market sits at the intersection of three paradigm shifts that are shaping today's business:

1. Outsourcing
2. Packaged-application business strategies
3. The Internet

Since late 1998, the largest and most powerful vendors in the information technology industry have launched a succession of products and services directly at the emerging online accounting software marketplace. This is in direct contrast to the majority of traditional accounting software vendors who had still been trying to migrate accountants from DOS to Windows, akin to rearranging deck chairs on the Titanic. The future trend for application delivery is pre-partnered, repeatable solutions, in which multiple providers (e.g., accounting professionals, system integrators, consultants, and other application providers) affiliate in formal partnerships to deliver the full spectrum of accounting application services.

ACCOUNTING—THE LANGUAGE OF BUSINESS

Accounting has long been called the language of business. Throughout our early education we learned the vocabulary and other basic elements of the English language, or another native tongue, so that we would be able to communicate effectively. The purpose is the same for accounting. Your clients have no wish to become accountants. For small business clients to be able to understand and use accounting information most effectively, an accounting professional must provide them with a solid grounding in its fundamentals.

Rather than having your clients suffer the rigors of college Accounting 101 and Accounting 102 courses, which they will not do, instead, act as their accounting mentor and impart the basics of accounting with turn-key materials available from the accounting professionals' affiliation program— The Accounting Guild, Las Vegas, Nevada (http://www.accountingguild.com).

There was a time when knowing how a car worked made a difference. Now, only mechanics really need to know how cars work. New cars perform reliably and come with support services to insulate the driver from the need to know how to repair mechanical problems. Few business clients understand the most basic accounting concepts and how the Internet works, but most business people need to have such an understanding if they want to make informed decisions. The reality for the businessperson is that selecting an accounting firm requires a far more sophisticated understanding of the integration of technology and business processes than the computing equivalent of roadside assistance.

Your clients do not need to understand the finer points of accounting that they will probably never encounter in their business transactions. They do require the essential knowledge necessary to read important financial statements and to effectively use an online Web-based accounting system. Offering and operating a two-day, **"Accounting Basic Concepts"**™ program for clients, bookkeepers, and the general business public (prospective clients) will bring in new profits and clients for your practice (info@accountingguild.com).

ACCOUNTANTS' CLIENT TRAINING COURSES

The ABC's course enables your clients to gain a greater understanding and knowledge to prosper their businesses and you in turn will have more viable clients and the commensurate higher income. The online accounting market represents a dramatic change in accounting services delivery. In the short- and long-term, your practice will deliver accounting services in a very different and dynamic way. Your client write-up work will be transformed from a low-profit, commodity compliance chore into a high-profit reliance service. The Accounting Guild has developed a comprehensive marketing training program to ease the transition and guide you towards a more profitable future.

ACCOUNTANTS' CLIENT/CUSTOMER RELATIONSHIP EQUATION

As a trusted professional accounting advisor/consultant, you are a key stakeholder in the overall client/customer relationship. By partnering with vendors who offer the same degree of excellence, you can deliver seamlessly integrated business applications that combine enterprise performance and reliability with unprecedented ease of use and low prices. Be certain that every service you provide will nurture your professional accountant/client relationships and never permit anything to subvert that relationship.

Accounting Partnership Resources Compendium

ABS Systems
Lake Mary, FL
www.mrasystems.com

Accountant's Advanced Marketing Network
Williamstown, NJ
www.afdcenter.com

Accounting Guild
Las Vegas, NV
www.accountingguild.com

ACCPAC International
Pleasanton, CA
www.accpac.com

ADP (Automatic Data Processing)
Roseland, NJ
www.adp.com

Affiliated Conference of Practicing Accountants International
www.acpaintl.org

American Accounting Association
www.rutgers.edu/Accounting/raw/aaa

Association for Accounting Marketing
www.accountingmarketing.org

Association for Computers and Taxation
www.taxact.org

ATX
Caribou, ME
www.atxforms.com

Bizfinity
Cupertino, CA
www.Bizfinity.com

Citrix Systems Inc.
Fort Lauderdale, FL
www.citrix.com

Datair Employee Benefits Systems, Inc.
Westmont, IL
www.datair.com
  Large, comprehensive vendor of Pension and Cafeteria/Section 125
  plan software.

Forensic Accountants Society of North America
www.fasna.org

Greatland Corporation
Grand Rapids, MI
www.greatland.com
  Foremost producer of check-writing software and supplies, tax preparation forms, and many more accounting practice necessities. Laser
  print professional looking forms or use their preprinted forms.

Great Plains Software
Fargo, ND
www.greatplains.com

Howell Client Accounting Software
Lake Mary, FL
www.mrasystems.com

IBM Corporation
Armonk, NY
www.ibm.com/software/partnerweb

Institute of Management Accountants
Montvale, NJ
www.rutgers.edu/Accounting/raw/ima
  Publisher of Strategic Finance and Management Accounting magazines.
  Excellent organization for accountants in the private sector and those
  considering a private practice.

Intacc Accounting Systems Inc.
Longueuil, Quebec, Canada
www.jbmlogic.com

Microsoft Corporation
Redmond, WA
www.microsoft.com

National Association of Enrolled Agents
www.naea.org

National Association of Tax Practitioners
Appleton, WI
www.natptax.com

National Society of Accountants
Alexandria, VA
www.nsacct.org

National Tax Association
www.cob.asu.edu/nsa

NetLedger, Inc.
San Mateo, CA
www.netledger.com

OneCore Financial Network, Inc
Bedford, MA
www.onecore.com

Oracle Corporation
Redwood Shores, CA
www.oracle.com

Paychex
Rochester, NY
www.paychex.com

Red Wing Software
Red Wing, MN
www.redwingsoftware.com

Sage Software Inc.
Irvine, CA
www.sage.com

Scient Corporation
San Francisco, CA
www.scient.com

Solomon Software Inc.
Findlay, OH
www.solomon.com (Now owned by Great Plains)

Syspro Impact Software
Costa Mesa, CA
www.sysprousa.com

Tax and Accounting Software
Tulsa, OK
www.taascforce.com

UniLink
Jackson, WY
www.unilink-inc.com

Virtual Growth
New York, NY
www.virtualgrowth.com
  Virtual Accountant is an outsourced, online bookkeeping and accounting service that provides cost-effective, comprehensive services that an
  accountant can private label and offer as its own.

Visual Practice Management
Pensacola, FL
www.cpasoftware.com

CHAPTER 19

Team Building and Retreats

VISION AND MISSION

The firm's vision and mission must be articulated in a statement that meets the following criteria:

1. **Imaginable.** Conveys what the abstract accounting and/or consulting business will look like in the physical dimension
2. **Desirable.** Appeals to the long-term interests of all the stakeholders — owners, team, and clients
3. **Challenging but Feasible.** Are the statements realistic and achievable?
4. **Measurable.** According to the principle that what you can measure, you can manage
5. **Focused.** A lighthouse to be used to guide decisions
6. **Flexible.** Enables individual interpretation and initiative but is always subject to an overall code of guiding principles
7. **Communicable.** Easily explained and understood by everyone irrespective of position and intellectual capacity
8. **Strategic Integrity.** Makes strategic sense. Its various elements, particularly as they relate to the stakeholders, must possess internal integrity to avoid ambiguity and dysfunction in operation.

BUILDING A WINNING TEAM

Team Members

- Only the best candidates are hired.
- Members are proud and happy to be working for the firm.

- Compensation is above average.
- The working environment is enjoyable and comfortable.
- Professional advancement is attainable and encouraged.
- Achievement of personal growth is a priority of the firm.
- Members play a meaningful role in the decision-making process.
- Members trust and respect all other team members, partners, and clients.
- Members understand and support the firm's vision and mission.

The Partners

- Put the welfare of the clients, team, and firm above their own self-interests
- Expect to receive equitable compensation

Services

- Innovative
- Clearly defined, highly structured, and priced according to their value

The Accounting or Consulting Firm

- Increases the net financial worth of its clients
- Maintains an aggressive, totally professional, and focused marketing posture
- Maintains the highest standards of ethical conduct
- Becomes the preeminent practice in its chosen niches

IMPLEMENTATION

Increase the Net Financial Worth of Its Clients

1. Select clients with the greatest potential for growth.
2. Do Client Business valuation services every other year.
3. Measure performance by the yearly client growth achieved.
4. Create value-added system applications.

Aggressive, Professional, and Focused Marketing Posture

1. Aim for 25 percent annual fee growth.
2. Target market niches in small to medium-sized marketplace segments.
3. Maintain and follow a written Marketing Plan that is totally consistent with the firm's primary mission.
4. Employ timelines and milestones for the marketing initiatives.
5. Use Internet-based marketing: e-mails, seminars, and newsletters.
6. Have a structured and systematized referral system.

Maintain the Highest Standards of Ethical Conduct

- Conform to both the spirit and letter of the profession's ethical precepts.
- Practice the highest level of professional and personal integrity.

Become the Preeminent Practice in Its Chosen Niches

- Use an independent research organization to monitor the firm's business niche marketplace share, awareness, and perception.
- Cite references to the firm in local and national press.
- Maintain targeted growth rate.

TEAM MEMBER IMPLEMENTATION

- The candidate's overall quality takes precedence over the availability of work.
- The number and caliber of people will enable the firm to accomplish its goals.
- Team members receive feedback on a monthly basis.
- Monitoring and exit interviews determine true reasons for resignations.
- Salaries and benefits are at least 15 percent above those paid by competitive firms of equivalent standing in the community.
- Team members' accommodations have appropriate privacy, lighting, comfort, and refreshments.

- Staff has suitable technology and tools to do the job expected.
- Fun breaks, birthday parties, pizza, sandwich and appreciation days occur during work hours.
- The firm participates in team sports and events.
- Innovation and excellent client service are recognized and rewarded frequently, vocally, and financially.

Professional Advancement

- Budget and spend five times more than industry standards for training that is consistent with the skills development requirements of the firm.
- Create a learning division and make it a policy to delegate work whenever possible to give team members at lower levels the opportunity to stretch themselves and to give their immediate supervisors the opportunity to train and mentor.
- Schedule significant amounts of client contact.
- Reward team members for the productivity levels of those who report to them rather than for their own levels of productivity.

Personal Growth

- Conduct career counseling and evaluation sessions annually and performance reviews every six months.
- Allow the training budget to be used for personal as well as professional development.

Involvement in Decision Making

- Invite all team members to an annual strategic planning retreat.
- Employ small teams to deal with operational problems and systems design.
- Appoint team members on a core drill-down basis from all levels to the firm's Advisory Board.
- Formally deliver critical decisions made by the Management Board to all team members.
- Provide team members with regular and relevant feedback on the firm's financial results.

Trust and Mutual Respect

- Practice the Golden Rule.
- Treat people courteously.
- Ensure an open, communicative environment.
- Be honest and give people immediate and impartial feedback.

Team Members to Understand and Support Firm's Vision and Mission

- All new team members receive a copy of the Vision Statement and are evaluated on their understanding of its fundamental meaning, the way it affects the work they do, and the success of the firm.
- All managers refer to the Vision Statement when discussing issues with team members where judgment must be exercised.

Team Member's Role

- All individuals understand the parts they play in the firm and how they contribute to the firm's success.
- Ask team members who do not want to contribute fully into the vision and mission of the firm to leave the firm.

PARTNERSHIP ISSUES

- The Partnership Agreement reflects the expectations of the individual partners, their responsibilities to the firm, and their obligations to those who follow them.
- Partners must detach ownership from operations. They must understand that they hold a stewardship role as well as an equity share in the firm.
- Partners can expect to be compensated at a level that reflects the profitability of the firm.
- Compensation for operational work will be on the basis of salaries and benefits that would apply to an equally qualified team member who does not have an ownership share of the firm.

- Partners' billable time expectations reflect the nature of their contribution to the firm as a whole.
- Each partner presents an annual personal business plan to the Managing Board, which forms the basis of the partner's performance evaluation.
- Return on equity for partners is based on their share of the imputed yield from the goodwill and retained earnings of the firm.
- The Managing Board values goodwill each year by reference to the firm's "hard core" earnings after partner salaries and capitalized at a rate that is determined from time to time.
- If a partner no longer wants to abide by the firm's vision and mission statements, that partner is expected to voluntarily resign.

SERVICES

- The firm is continually alert to new developments in both content and process of service delivery.
- The firm establishes a planning target of revenue growth to come from the introduction of new or extended services to existing and new clients.
- Deliverable services are to be systematized to the finest detail, and there is a logical extension of services to meet the emerging needs of individual clients.
- Fees are communicated clearly to clients in advance of all engagements and are changed only after consultation with the client.
- Fees are determined according to their estimated value and are written down only when the firm fails to meet the client's expectations.

RETREATS

Partner Retreats

During the course of a typical year, accounting and consulting firm partners are simply too busy to do much forward thinking, challenge existing practice models, and focus on the business rather than on the clients. However, once a year or more frequently, many firms find it valuable to escape the office and invest a few days in strategic discussions and strengthening personal bonds.

Often, a retreat is dedicated to questioning the existing ways of doing things. Questions such as the following are asked :

- Are we satisfied with the firm's growth and profitability?
- Are we providing services that clients want and need?
- What kind of a firm do we want to be in five years?

A retreat provides an environment in which partners can openly and deeply communicate their feelings on the firm, their roles, and whatever else is on their minds. It can solve problems and allows for general planning.

Unsuccessful Retreats

Most unsuccessful retreats follow the above pattern. Gut issues are addressed, open and frank discussions are held, and a number of ideas are generated from those discussions. Participants feel the retreat is worthwhile. But as soon as everyone gets back to the office, it's business as usual. None of the ideas generated at the retreat are ever enacted.

Retreats Must Lead to Action

A retreat must lead to action afterwards. There are ways to ensure this. Announce the retreat well in advance and agree on agenda topics early so participants can do some preparation. Make sure the retreat follows that agenda. A structured meeting will lead to focused discussions, which facilitate the formation of action plans. You also must make sure detailed minutes are kept. The ideal way is to invite a secretary who can keep confidences. Otherwise, one of the participants or the facilitator can take notes.

It is a good idea to use a facilitator from outside the firm to run the retreat. If the facilitator is good, he or she will be tenacious in making sure that action items result from every discussion.

At the conclusion of each topic, you should make sure the group discusses how to address the issue. Make the recommendations as specific as possible, and assign responsibility for implementing each recommendation together with a deadline, which should be incorporated in a prioritized "to do" list. The question "What will it take to make us do this?" should be answered, and there must be agreed-on dates for future meetings to review the progress.

Finally, there should be accountability for carrying out the retreat recommendations. If there are no consequences, then it is unlikely there will be a follow-through.

Varieties of Retreats

It is easy for a firm to fall into a rut when their retreats are the same every year. Same topics, same dominating managing partner who leads the same discussions, same location, and same everything else. The best way to avoid this is to vary the retreats from year to year, have a pre-set agenda, and use different locations, alternate times of year, and outside facilitators. Retreats can be structured in many ways.

Retreat Structures

- **Focused Topic Retreat.** The most common type of retreat is one that focuses on specific topics. Firms identify a limited number of topics to cover and generally devote one to four hours to each.

- **Planning Retreat.** Virtually the entire retreat focuses on the development of a strategic plan, a marketing plan, or even both.

- **Associate Issues Retreat.** Retaining and developing associates is one of the most important issues facing an accounting or consulting firm. The best way to make your firm a fantastic place to work is to start with an associate survey, to be administered before the retreat itself. At the retreat, the results are discussed and action items are developed to address the key issues.

- **Practice Management Review Retreat.** An accounting practice development consultant is retained to conduct a practice management review before the retreat. The focal point of the retreat is the consultant's presentation of the results and a brainstorming session to discuss the consultant's findings and recommendations.

- **New Services and Niches Retreat.** The pace of change of the accounting industry is rapid. With professional services, a retreat can focus on specialization — what services are needed to provide clients with one-stop shopping. Determining what specialty area(s) to get into and how to enter it requires a market analysis before the retreat and structured discussions during the retreat.

- **Client Satisfaction Retreat.** The focal point of the retreat is a brainstorming session to discuss what can be done to address the issues arising from a client survey. A good survey identifies three things:
  1. How to improve service quality.
  2. How to get more business from clients.
  3. What new services the firm should be providing in the future.

- **Single Practitioner Retreats.** Retreats work out well for multipartner firms because they allow the partners to focus on the major issues facing the firm, to interact, and to develop a plan of action. Single owners aren't so fortunate unless they can meet with others similarly situated and from different locations.

The author's firm, The Accounting Guild, conducts sole practitioner retreats on a regular basis in various parts of the nation and Canada. The retreats become a strategic meeting for a virtual firm of 50 to 70 partners. They are structured as roundtable workshops to determine the critical issues facing a sole practitioner. Many would think that the issues would center around staffing, creating alliances, or moving into new product and practice areas. However, we found the major concern boiled down to life balance.

It is not so surprising when you really think about it, since life balance is one of the major reasons small firms exist. Most sole practitioners set their target at earning a comfortable livelihood and are satisfied if they reach it, thereby leaving time to do the things they really care about.

This doesn't mean that the other concerns fail to tie into the desire for balance. At one such retreat, an accountant said, "They are all subsets. Get your staffing, your alliances, and new profitable niches in order, then your life falls into place."

Partner Relations, Problems, and Solutions

Most retreats restrict participants to partners because of the confidential nature of the discussions. However, on occasion, it makes sense to invite some or all of the nonpartners. Some firms invite all personnel to the entire retreat, while others designate a portion of the meeting for partners only and the remainder for some team members.

About two thirds of accounting and consulting firms suffer from a serious degree of partner relations or communications difficulties. They range between two extremes. One extreme is the overt kind, tantamount to an undeclared war. One or more partners are actively engaged in open conflict and essentially don't talk to each other. Partners frequently talk about splitting up the firm, and staff morale is negatively impacted as a result of the openness of the disputes.

The other extreme, which is more common, is also subtler. Partners are civil to each other, but they really don't communicate and they certainly don't share clients, knowledge, and referrals. There is little teamwork, and partner meetings are generally only convened for emergencies. These firms are really functioning as groups of solos practicing under one roof, sharing overhead and associates.

In addressing both extremes, and those that are somewhere in between, it's important to achieve a blend of the following. On the one hand, be constructive and respectful in your remarks. Don't attack. But on the other hand, don't be overly concerned about this. Some partners make the mistake of being too nice to each other, avoiding any semblance of a disagreement.

When partners get along with each other and communicate effectively, the firm can grow and prosper. Effective partner relations are no guarantee that the firm will be successful, but they sure help.

Retreats Should Provide Opportunities for Partners to Be Open and Honest

Use the retreat to address partner relations and communications issues. Retreats should provide opportunities for the partners to air differences, address conflicts, and be open and honest with each other about their feelings.

The Outside Facilitator

Using an outside facilitator has certain advantages. It is very difficult for partner groups to run an effective retreat on their own without outside assistance. The dynamics of a partner group are well established. The partners usually sit at the same seat around the conference table.

Partners get tired of saying the same things over and over again, so they stop talking.

Under these conditions, which are quite common at firms, the openness and honesty that are required for a successful retreat are impossible to attain without the help of an expert outside advisor/facilitator.

When an outside facilitator runs the meeting, there is a new set of dynamics established. Good facilitators prevent individuals from dominating and get the reticent ones to speak up. As a result, fresh ideas and views bubble to the surface and are expressed.

Another advantage is that the presence of a facilitator allows the managing partner to be a participant rather than the retreat leader. The facilitator should always have experience with accountants. In that way the firm also benefits from the collective knowledge of a consultant who will benchmark your firm.

What to Look for in a Facilitator

You want someone who does their homework and reviews important firm documents—perhaps even conducts interviews before the retreat begins. The facilitator should always have an eye on your firm's profitability and knowledge of the trends and hot issues in accounting and consulting. The facilitator must be able to tell it like it is in a constructive manner without arrogance or insensitivity.

Finally, the facilitator should be concerned with the implementation. Follow-up should be something you can count on from the facilitator as well as a comprehensive report shortly after the end of the retreat.

Retreat Bottom Line

Spend the most time talking about what you want to accomplish. Accounting and consulting firms should only consider the agenda after answering the following questions:

- What changes do we want to occur as a result of the retreat?
- How will we measure if it is a success?

There are two main things that should happen at a retreat. First, the agenda and the related nuances should be discussed. Second, the group should decide how they will implement the ideas generated and what are the potential obstacles. In many cases virtually all of the time at

	Retreats	**Partner Meetings**
Topics	Strategic	Operational
Focus	Future	Past and present
Location	Outside the office	At the office
Leader	Usually an outside facilitator	Managing partner
Administrative	None	Varies from little to much content
Duration	One to two days	Usually a few hours
Attendance	100 percent mandatory	Short of mandatory
Goal	Change, improvement	Survive the meeting

Source: The Accounting Guild, Las Vegas, Nevada © 2000

Exhibit 19.1 Retreats Compared to Partner Meetings

retreats is spent addressing the agenda. More time should be invested talking about implementation. Exhibit 19.1 compares retreats to partner meetings.

APPENDIX

The Accounting Guild and e@ccounting™

Seminars, Consortium, Training, and Consulting

RETREAT FACILITATION

Jack Fox, MBA, author of this book and six others, including *Starting and Building Your Own Accounting Business, Third Edition,* published in 2000 by John Wiley & Sons, is a management and marketing consultant to CPA, accounting, and consulting firms. His firm, The Accounting Guild, based in Las Vegas, Nevada, assists firms in retreat facilitating, sole practitioner retreats, profitability enhancement, practice management reviews and development, strategic planning, partner compensation, partner conflict resolution, associate development, mergers and acquisitions, and Internet-based marketing.

Contact The Accounting Guild at info@accountingguild.com or its Web site http://www.accountingguild.com for available dates and fee information.

CONTINUING PROFESSIONAL PRACTICE DEVELOPMENT

Jack Fox, author of *Building a Profitable Online Accounting Practice,* is one of the most sought-after accounting practice development authors, consultants, speakers, and accounting firm retreat facilitators on the Internet accounting practice circuit.

Call Jack Fox today to find out how he and The Accounting Guild can train your staff, help your practice present prospective client seminars, or facilitate your next retreat. You can join one of his effective single practitioner retreats, which recognize that you are in business for yourself, but not necessarily by yourself. Send e-mail for services to info@accounting-guild.com. Send questions or comments about this book and its relation to your practice to jfox1961@aol.com or call 702-242-8725 Las Vegas, Nevada (Pacific Time) during normal business hours.

THE ACCOUNTING GUILD

The Accounting Guild (8713 Short Putt Drive, Las Vegas, Nevada 89134 http://www.accountingguild.com) is an international, Internet-based organization providing effective marketing programs to professional accountants and consultants. These include professionally prepared direct e-mail campaigns, advertising, promotional materials, seminars-in-a-box kits for various market niches, and initial and ongoing consultation.

The Accounting Guild offers a unique strategic alliance between affiliated accounting professionals, CPAs, accounting firms, accountant/VARs, consultants, accounting software publishers, and accounting application software providers. The guild's programs include focused research and publishing that concentrate on the creation and operation of a profitable Internet-based accounting business.

e@ccounting Client Acquisition Marketing Seminars™

Designed for the new practice or accounting businesses that are transitioning from compliance to reliance and traditional accounting to an Internet-based practice. This two-day seminar program will differentiate your practice from your competitors in the marketplace. The process of developing and growing a state-of-the art, Internet-based e@ccounting™ business in today's marketplace begins with this invaluable seminar.

e@ccounting Marketing Alliance Consortium™

Utilize the world's most powerful Internet-based accounting system, recruit the finest team of professionals, have the capacity to support traditional and e-commerce business models, and stand ready to deliver the efficiencies and savings that come from a robust practice. All of these without clients means you don't have a business. You only have potential. Potential without actualization nets a bottom line of nothing.

At the heart of the e@ccounting Marketing Alliance Consortium™ is the industry's most advanced and effective marketing system. The system functions seamlessly with your practice's activities and interacts with every prospective client, present client, and all networking activities. If your practice is like most professional accounting organizations, you are faced with the severe challenge of attracting and retaining profitable clients for your accounting services. Wouldn't it be wonderful if you have your own Internet-based marketing and sales department? Wouldn't it be great to have clients perceive your practice as a state-of-the-art organization that stands ready and able to guide them through the New Economy?

Focus on what you do best and enjoy the benefits of outsourcing the marketing operational issues of managing lead development, production of collateral materials, personalized client newsletter programs, networking campaigns, seminar development, sales training and management of your outside sales force. You're free to focus on what you do best: providing your clients with the finest professional accounting and consulting services.

The comprehensive e@ccounting Marketing Alliance Consortium™ is available for licensing in limited selected areas. Further details including participation, pricing, warranties and restrictions are available by emailing info@accountingguild.com.

e@ccounting TeleSeminars™

First presented in 1999, in response to numerous requests from readers of *Starting and Building Your Own Accounting Business* (first edition published in 1984, second edition in 1991, and the all new third edition published in 2000 by John Wiley & Sons). Now conducted live by the author on a regular basis, the professional accountant learns how to acquire clients, without which there is no business.

The TeleSeminar is composed of four segments held over a special conference line. You simply call into a conference telephone number at the prescribed time and join the others. No special phone equipment or computer is required. Course materials will be sent to you in advance and will cover each specific area that Mr. Fox will build upon as all the segments unfold. At the completion of all four segments, you may schedule a 15-minute no-fee private consultation with Jack Fox himself for guidance on using the seminar knowledge to build and grow your firm.

The TeleSeminars are about differentiation, service, and the knowledge and tools to be able to market your differences. Any sense of professional isolation you have will diminish when you let Jack Fox and the other TeleSeminar participants accompany you on your entrepreneurial career path.

TeleSeminar Class Agenda

Introduction
- How to succeed in an Internet-based new Millennium accounting business
- Why do I need practice development?
- Building the business plan and charting your course
- Defining your practice and firm

You Don't Have a Business without Clients
- Analyzing present and prospective clients' needs
- Providing the basic services to meet clients' needs
- Internet-based business services
- Effectively positioning and marketing your services

Fundamentals of e@ccounting ABCs' (Accounting Basic Concepts™) Training
- Discussion of how any qualified accountant can operate a training center
- Client building process inherent in accounting training courses
- Profitablity opportunities from teaching client's staff
- Providing a menu of services

Steps to Transformation
- Blueprint for management
- Growth, profitability, and survival
- Steps to transformation
- Complimentary 15-minute consultation call with the author/moderator.

e@ccounting ABC's Accounting Basic Concepts™ Training Centers

The Accounting Guild has published, copyrighted, and protected the trademark on course materials that enable affiliated accounting professionals and firms to teach clients, prospective clients' staff, and the general public the basic accounting concepts necessary to capably use any accounting software. Using a uniform content and professionally prepared materials for presentation as well as student work/notebooks, your students will be able to achieve in two days a level of competence that community colleges take two semesters to impart.

The purpose of these courses is to provide a source of new clients in addition to being a significant profit center. This innovative program is applicable to all accounting software programs including NetLedger, Bizfinity, and QuickBooks. The common complaint with previous programs has been that clients can perform operations with accounting software but lack any real understanding of the accounting concepts that are the foundation of their entries. An educated client is a boon to the accountant.

Accounting Practices Assessment Tools

The Accounting Practices Assessment Tools (APAT) are being developed to measure valuable feedback about individual practitioners from within an organization, active and prospective clients, and characteristics from target market niches. It is based on real-time, nonfinancial performance to assist the accounting professionals in measuring and improving their performance.

Readers of this book are encouraged to participate in the studies without any cost or obligation. The Accounting Guild is developing the tools with Success Profiles that are designed to identify the critical performance issues facing accounting professionals. Once the assessments are completed and collected, the data is scanned, verified, and complied using state-of-the-art computer hardware and software technology. After the data has been analyzed, it is converted into a user-friendly, graphical format and shared on a confidential basis with each participant.

Our primary goal is to provide accounting professionals with "Actionable Knowledge," no just raw data. Understanding the key messages from the assessment tools are the primary steps to helping the professional make positive improvements. Your performance will be compared to the "Best of the Best."

Contacting The Accounting Guild

The Accounting Guild
8713 Short Putt Drive
Las Vegas, NV 89134
http://www.accountingguild.com
info@accountingguild.com
702-242-8725

The Guild encourages its affiliates to work together whenever appropriate. This allows all to benefit from the input provided by each member of its growing network. Affiliate vendor providers offer software, application solutions, and other products for your practice and for resale to your clients at special discount pricing available only to members of the Guild.

Glossary

@: What goes between a user's name and the domain name in an e-mail address. For example, jackfox@accountingguild.com

Applets: Client-server programs that can be imported and recompiled across a wide range of system applications. They can be downloaded from the Internet to perform specific tasks.

Application: A shorter but less descriptive way of saying software program.

Application Software Provider (ASP): An application software provider owns the offsite computer on which the user's software is housed. That software can include accounting and tax preparation. The ASP is like a landlord who rents space to a tenant. ASPs provide much of the infrastructure (cabling, backup, technical support) but they don't run the software or perform professional services such as write-up or tax preparation.

Applied information economics: Uses scientific and mathematical methods to evaluate the information technology investment.

ARCHIE: A utility to find files stored on FTP servers.

Auction: The process of bidding on a contract or RFP (request for proposal) via an Internet exchange.

Authentication: Making sure users are who they say they are, using passwords, smart cards, biometrics, or other means.

Balanced scorecard: Integrates traditional financial measures with three other key performance indicators: customer perspectives, internal business processes, and organizational growth.

Bandwidth: Used in practice to describe the amount of data that can be transferred over a network connection, or "how big the pipe is."

Baud: The speed at which modems transfer data. The speed is listed in BPS, or bits per second.

Bookmark: Also known as Favorites, a shortcut to return to a resource you plan to refer to often.

BIT: Short for "binary digit," the smallest unit of information stored in a computer, corresponding either to 0 or 1, false or true, off or on. Eight bits equal a byte.

Browser: The software program that allows users to read pages on the World Wide Web.

Buy-side participants: Businesses that need products and services as well as cash.

Cache: The use of memory (most often the hard drive) to store the information used by your browser. This saves time when you return to the same site in a session, as the speed of retrieving information from your memory is much faster than over the communications line. Cache tends to take up a lot of storage.

Cookies: A method of storing data on your computer for several purposes including tracking.

Data warehousing: A method of accessing the potential of numerical accounting data and harnessing its power in a single query-oriented database to provide decision support and business management functions.

Domain name: A mnemonic device that makes it easier to use resources on the Internet than trying to remember a string of 32 bits.

Download: Retrieve files from the host to your computer.

Drill across: The ability to compare data from different sectors of corporate activity at the same scale of detail.

Drill down: The ability to pursue a database query through successively finer-scale views, from a general overview to a specific item or cell.

Economic value added: Calculates the "true" economic profit by subtracting the cost of all capital invested in an enterprise—including technology—from net operating profit.

Economic value sourced: Quantifies the dollar values of risk and time and adds these into the valuation equation.

E-mail: A system of exchanging messages through computer networks using computerized mailboxes and mail servers to handle the flow.

Encryption: Temporarily changing data so it is unreadable unless you have the tools to read that data.

FAQ: Frequently asked questions, a list of basic queries to help newcomers get answers and reduce redundant postings.

File Transfer Protocol (FTP): A method for sending and retrieving files from the Internet.

Firewall: Hardware and software used to guard an internal network from unauthorized access from the outside and sometimes to limit the internal use of outside resources.

Flame: To post really nasty messages to someone else on the Internet.

Gateway: An intermediary device between disparate networks.

GIF: Pronounced like the well-known peanut butter, a graphical format standard on the Internet.

Granule or module: Units of system functionality in accounting software. Where a given accounting task (for example, inventory, job costing, invoicing) might have been handled by a module of software, increasingly, they are being broken down into granules to allow for even finer-scale customization.

Graphical User Interface (GUI): A program used to assist (and limit) the user when interacting with a computer through the use of windows, icons, menus, and pointing devices.

Hosting: Hosted software is simply software that runs on a computer other than the one at the user's desk. Most PC users have their application software on their hard drives. In hosting, the software is somewhere else, often in a data center outside the user's location. Users access the software by an Internet browser like Microsoft Internet Explorer or Netscape Navigator. The user also buys or rents the software and has the licensing rights and responsibilities.

Hot-swappable drives: Hard drives that can be plugged or unplugged without turning off the power to a server.

HTML: The Hypertext Markup Language provides hypertext links from a World Wide Web document to different types of data.

Hypertext: A system where documents scattered across many sites are directly linked.

Information superhighway: The descriptor for a worldwide system for the exchange of ideas and information in multimedia format. Not synonymous with the Internet, but encompassing it.

Internet: The world's largest network of networks.

Internet accounting: Distributed access, using custom applets appended to users' Web browsers, permitting use of core accounting software from remote locations. This enables reports to be written as HTML pages and data files to be transmitted via e-mail or FTP over the Web. A way of exploding the traditional corporate accounting department in time and space.

Internet server: Manages the connection of Internet users to the accounting database and process servers.

IP address: A 32-character number (in the format xxx.xxx.xxx.xxx.xxx, where xxx <256) that uniquely identifies a location on the Internet. The next generation of IP (IP version 6) will be much larger.

ISP (Internet Service Provider): Some entity that lets you share connection to the Internet.

Legacy data: Historical information, usually from many sources within the organization, that goes into building multidimensional databases.

Link: An area that can be clicked to jump to another Web page or access another resource on the Internet.

Low end: Refers to accounting software costing less than $300 and built for small businesses with fewer than 50 employees and typically less than $1 million in revenue.

Lurking: Reading messages in a forum or newsgroup without adding comments or participating.

Metric: One dimension or type of measurement within a multidimensional database.

Middleware: Software providing a link between applications that do not use the same programming language.

Mid-range: Accounting programs costing more than $1,000, usually sold by the module and developed for medium-sized businesses with more than $1 million in revenue and with 50 to 100 employees.

Mirrored drives: A technique using a RAID system where a copy of everything written to one drive is copied onto another simultaneously. If the first drive develops problems, then the server management software can automatically switch to the backup drive.

Modem: A device that connects a computer to a phone line and enables users to transmit data between computers.

Module: The components of an accounting software program that address separate financial departments. Some programs offer several main modules as a bundle and then additional modules at extra cost. The main modules for mid-range accounting programs are system manager, general ledger, accounts receivable, and accounts payable.

MRO: Goods for maintenance, repair, and operations, sourced indirectly.

Multidimensional database (MDD): Also called "data cube," a database that organizes data across many dimensions (e.g., region, products, costs, and sales volume).

Needs analysis: Listening to clients talk about their needs and goals before presenting a product or service.

Netiquette: The etiquette or rules of the road to behave properly on the Internet.

Net market-maker: Vendor responsible for overseeing an Internet exchange.

Network: Computers communicating with computers.

Newbies: Newcomers to the Internet.

Off line: Not connected to the Internet; not running.

On line: Connected to the Internet; running.

Online analytical processing (OLAP): Business intelligence using multidimensional analysis; builds a multidimensional data cube from information stores in relational and other two-dimensional databases.

Outsourcing: Outsourcing is sometime confused with hosting. Outsourcing simply means hiring somebody else to provide a service that a client might perform in-house, such as payroll. A provider of out-sourced bookkeeping services performs the actual bookkeeping and uses its own software. The end user may or may not own or rent the software.

Packet: A chunk of data.

Posting: Sending messages to a discussion or newsgroup.

POTS (Plain old telephone service): Normal phone lines.

Prescriptive selling: Offering clients a product or service solution that cures a particular problem, without first listening to the clients to determine the true problem.

Procurement: The act of attaining direct and indirect — MRO and commodity — supplies.

Protocol: A set of standards that describes ways to operate and ensures compatibility between systems.

RAID (Redundant Array of Independent Disks): A group of hard disks that are managed as a unit to provide increased performance and various levels of error recovery.

RAM (Random Access Memory): The working memory of the computer. The "random" means that the contents of each byte can be directly accessed without regard to the bytes before or after it. Ram chips require power to maintain their content, which is why you must save your data on disk before you turn the computer off.

Redundant power supply: Typically an additional power supply plugged into a server that activates automatically should the main power supply have problems or shut down.

Scalability: If a system is built so that additional components may be easily added, it is known as scalable. Scalability also refers to the system's adaptability to increased demands.

Scanner: A device that can convert printed pages and color pictures into editable, usable, computer files. With optical character recognition (OCR) software, the scanner can convert printed pages and forms into word processing text.

Sell-side suppliers: Businesses that offer products and/or services via an exchange.

Server: A computer or program that provides information or shared resources in response to external requests. For example, a file server stores on its hard disks the programs and data files for all the workstations in a local area network (LAN).

Service provider: A utility that provides connections to the Internet.

Signature or **sig:** A personalized address at the bottom of a message often containing contact information and a short commercial description.

SLIP and **PPP (Serial Line Internet Protocol** and **Point-to-Point Protocol):** Two common types of connections that allow your computer to communicate with the Internet.

Smileys and **emoticons:** Typographical versions of faces that display emotions in text messages.

Snail mail: Mail sent through the United States Postal Service, so named because of the relative speed of delivery of e-mail.

Spamming: Posting or mailing unwanted material to many recipients. A flagrant violation of Netiquette.

Spider: Tool that searches Web sites and creates an index from the sites it finds. It is a spider because it crawls over the Web. Also known as webcrawler.

System manager: The accounting software module that maintains the whole system's options, such as company name, address, tax ID, other general client information, user Ids and passwords, and various other options that are the foundation of each module.

Tacit knowledge: Unspoken language manifested in individual skills, routines, and experience.

Target market: The most likely group, based on any number of criteria, determined to have the highest potential to buy a product or service.

TCP/IP (Transmission Control Protocol/Internet Protocol): The standardized sets of computer guidelines that allow different machines to talk to each other on the Internet.

Trade association: An organization formed to benefit members of the same trade or industry by informing them of issues and developments that could affect their operations or sales.

Trading network: A business-to-business, many-to-many Internet-based commerce environment.

Uninterruptible power supply (UPS): Backup power used when the electrical power fails or drops to an unacceptable voltage level. A UPS system can be connected to a file server so that, in the event of a problem, all network users can be alerted to save files and shut down immediately.

Upload: To send a file from your computer to another.

Uniform Resource Locator (URL): A type of address that points to a specific document or site on the World Wide Web.

Value-added reseller (VAR): The professional or company from which mid-range accounting programs are purchased. The VAR often has access to the source code in which the accounting software was written. By knowing how the software was built, they can customize it to better fit a client's needs. The VAR will usually be certified to install the software on the system and to train the client's staff to use it.

Virus: A self-replicating program that runs on your computer without your permission. It may do nothing but reproduce and spread to other computers, it may do some slightly vexing things, or it can destroy your data.

Wide Area Information System (WAIS): A system that allows users to search by keyword through the full text contained on many databases.

WWW: World Wide Web: A graphic, hypertext-based system of documents that may include text, graphics, photographs, sound, video, and links to other documents and services.

XML (eXtensible Markup Language): A way to add tags to text files to create self-describing, cross-platform, machine-readable files that offer new searching and computing capabilities.

Index

Accountants, primary
 issues, 2
Accounting
 associations, 72–73
 Big Five, 19–20
 business questionnaire,
  145–147
 client/accountant IT
  consulting brokerage,
  191–192
 client concerns, 8–9
 client training courses,
  302–303
 Internet-related services,
  18
 language of business, 2,
  302
 mission-critical
  application, 113
 opportunities, 18, 170
 professional growth areas, 8
 professional implications,
  301
 professional
  prognostications, 55
 publications, 33–35
 services, market
  opportunity, 15
 software vendors, 119-121
 solution providers, 13
 start-up, 209–213
 strategies, 18
 structure, 53
Accounting Business,
  281–282
Accounting Guild (The), 19,
  303, 320
 ABC's accounting basic
  concepts training
  centers, 323

accounting market
 characteristics study,
 59–60
accounting solutions
 provider study, 134
annual accounting firms'
 niche markets survey,
 286–287
business plan assistance,
 51, 217–219
CEO study, 22
client acquisition
 marketing seminars, 320
contacting The
 Accounting Guild, 323
e@ccounting strategy
 symposium, 145–147
Internet challenges, 71
Linux server study, 108
marketing alliance
 consortium, 320
mission statement, 222
practice vision book,
 244–245
retreats compared to
 partner meetings, 318
TeleSeminars, 321
Accounting Today, 17
ACCPAC International, 17,
 119, 303
Adaptive style leadership
 attributes, 2
Adaptive success skills, 1
 first law of adapting, 7
ADP.com, 12, 61, 63, 125,
 303
Advertising, 44
Aggregators, 140–142
Alliances, 235–236
Amazon.com, 12

American Institute of
 Certified Public
 Accountants (AICPA),
 73
Analysis
 client, 43
 online analytical
  processing (OLAP),
  192–193
 SWOT, 46
 timetables and
  benchmarks, 47
Applications
 adoption preferences,
  108–110
 mission-critical, 113–114
 targeted, 187–188
Application software
 provider (ASP), 21,
 121–122, 131–136,
 138–140
Associations, 72–73

Bandwidth, 78–79
Bizfinity.com, 12, 18, 58, 119,
 121, 293, 304
Branding, 263–266
Business intelligence, 176,
 189
Business plans
 adapting to change,
  214–215
 advice and considerations,
  47–48
 appendices and exhibits,
  47
 assistance, 51
 background, 39
 confidentiality
  considerations, 49

Business plans *(continued)*
 definition, 37
 description and analysis of
  accounting practice,
  39–40
 model online accounting
  practice, 215
 narrative, 37–38
 next steps, 230–231
 objective review, 50
 optimum fit, 217–218
 organization, 48
 resources, 219–220
 software tools, 218–219
 suggested table of
  contents, 38
 summary, 38–39
 trends, 213–215
 writing, 48

Cable, 82, 91
Cisco Systems, Inc., 97
Clients
 accounting concerns, 8–9
 analysis, 43
 business client pre-e-
  business creation
  questionnaire, 26–27
 choosing to use an ASP,
  135
 communications,
  259–262, 282
 feedback, 247
 goals, 150
 hopes and fears, 171
 information technology
  functions, 190–191
 perceptions, 150–151
 potential, 40
 probing questions, 229
 profiles, 274–275
 prospective client wants,
  148–149
 small business accounting
  practice, 296–297
 turnoffs, 261–262
Client/server, 116
Communication, 231–232,
 259–261, 282
Compensation, 42
Competition, 40, 43
Compliance
 services, 57
 transition, 245

Computer Associates, 17
Confidentiality, 49
Connectivity
 information sources, 90–91
 jargon, 87–90
Consulting, 44, 205–207,
 224, 231
Costs
 start-up, 84–85
 total cost of, 186–187

Data
 enterprise reporting,
  179–180
 marts, 170–171
 mining, 173–176, 201
 modeling, 169
 warehouses, 167–169
Databases
 analyses, 165–166
 background, 159
 choice, 164
 definitions, 160–162
 design, 272–274
 foundational popularity, 116
 knowledge, 163–164
 marketing, 271–274
 multidimensional, 201
 privacy issues, 167
 relational, 274
 uses, 165
Datair Employee Benefit
 Systems, Inc., 68, 122,
 304
Demographics
 client study, 234
 consulting market, 224
Dial-up, 79
Digital subscriber line (DSL),
 80, 88
Document management,
 176–179
Dun & Bradstreet, 30

e@ccounting™
 e-commerce accounting
  process methodology,
  227
 online virtual
  e@ccounting, 1
 server choice, 77
 specialized areas of
  expertise, 60
 Web site, 76–77

E-commerce
 evolution, 27
 key process issues, 25
 misconceptions Q & A,
  23–24
 partnering, 289–292
 transitional factors, 25, 28
Electronic data interchange
 (EDI), evolution, 151–152
Employee benefits
 consulting, 66
 Internet implications, 68–69
 market niche, 67–68
End-to-end management,
 97–98
Enterprise resource planning
 (ERP), 152–155
Entrepreneurship, 205
Expertise
 importance, 148
 specialized areas, 69–73
Extensible business
 reporting language
 (XBRL), 157
Extensible markup language
 (XML), 155–157

Financial
 information, 45–46
 invest what's necessary,
  239–240
 personal finances, 208
 protecting future
  investment, 218
Financial planning
 Internet market
  implications, 10, 65
 services, 59
 software, 65–66
Fixed assets
 management, 61
 resources, 61
Full service providers (FSP),
 237–238

Goals, 55–56, 69–73,
 221–223
Greatland Corporation, 72,
 122, 304
Great Plains Software, 17, 72,
 119, 304

Hewlett-Packard
 Corporation, 17, 98

Human element, 85–86

IBM, 15, 17, 305
Imaging, 186
Information technology
  demands, 84
  strategy, 143–144
Institute of Management
  Accountants, 305
Integrated services digital
  network (ISDN), 80
Internet
  accounting implications, 1
  accounting-related
    newcomers, 12
  change, 75
  connections, 78
  definition, 75
  financial planning market
    implications, 10–11
  infrastructure, 75
  time, 144–145
Internet Service Provider
  (ISP), 19, 22, 78–79, 87,
  89
Intuit, 292–293
  QuickBooks, 16

Jargon
  ASPs from A to Z,
    138–140
  connectivity, 88–90
  databases, 160–162
  marketing buzzwords, 278
  professional, 48–49
  relational, 162–163
J. D. Edwards Corporation, 17

Knowledge
  databases, 163–164
  management, 195–198

Linux, 108

Marketing
  branding, 263–266
  client selection, 255–256,
    281–282
  consistency and
    relevance, 252
  database, 271–274
  database marketplace
    mining, 275–278
  ineptness, 251–252

misconceptions, 251–252
  strategy, 42, 267–270
  target niche plan, 283–285
  types, 252–255
Markets
  accounting niche
    (specialty) services, 286
  changing conditions, 9
  client analysis, 43
  overview, 15–19
  size and trends, 40
  small to medium-sized
    accounting services
    market opportunity, 15
  target markets, 42
Microsoft Corporation,
  96–97, 305
Middleware, 99–103
Mission statement, 221
Motivation, 55

NetLedger.com, 18, 120–121,
  305
Networks
  change, 95
  integration, 93–94
  storage, 184–186
Niches, 69–72, 194–195, 198,
  283–287

OneCore.com, 18, 59, 62,
  305
Online accounting
  basic preparation,
    203–204
  business models, 299–300
  components, 57
  consulting market
    demographics, 224
  failure factors, 209–210
  focus, 211
  marketing and selling,
    211–212
  menu of services, 57
  real-time, 246
  specialized areas of
    expertise, 60
  strategic planning,
    233–237, 300–301
  success factors, 211–213
  technology, 246–247
  value proposition, 299
Online analytical processing
  (OLAP), 192–194

Open source, 104–107,
  110–111
Opportunities, 209
Oracle Corporation, 17,
  95–96, 305
Outsourcing, storage, 188
Ownership, 42
  total cost, 186–187

Partnering
  affiliation programs, 299
  alliances, 235–236
  application hosting, 118
  choose your partners
    wisely, 240–242
  compatibility, 294
  database vendors,
    168–169
  e-commerce, 289–292
  negotiating an ASP deal,
    135–138
  profitability, 295
  options, 227–228
  resources compendium,
    303–306
  rules for dealing with
    vendor propaganda,
    183–184
Partnership
  issues, 311–312
  relations, problems and
    solutions, 315–316
  retreats, 312–315
  services, 312
Part-time consulting,
  205–207
Paychex.com, 61, 63, 125,
  305
Payroll processing
  service bureaus, 63
  software and service
    provider resources, 63,
    125–126
  Web-based, 61–64
Platforms, 84, 110, 199–200
Practice, accounting
  business structure,
    223–224
  competitive edge, 249
  compliance to reliance,
    245
  computing technology
    competencies, 248–249
  core competencies, 248

Practice, accounting
    (continued)
    credibility, 249
    development, 244-245
    goals, identification,
        222-223
    goals, strategic, 221
    internal financial
        reporting, 235
    key performance
        indicators (KPIs), 248
    leadership, 244
    lifeblood, 226
    management, 118,
        126-127
    mission statement, 221
    new rules of engagement,
        237
    prospectus, 221
    skills, 236-237
    small business client
        accounting, 296-297
    staffing strategy, 235
    strategies and policies,
        242-245, 300-301
    transition, 228-229
    vision, 244
PricewaterhouseCoopers
    (PwC), 17, 20
Pricing, 44, 148
Pro2Net.com, 124
Professional
    asset protection, 207
    balancing with personal
        life, 204
    growth areas, 8
    overcoming obstacles, 209
Profit, 55
Promotion, 44
Publications, 32-35

Relational databases,
    162-163, 200-201,
    274
Report management, 180
Retreats
    bottom line, 317
    facilitators, 316-317, 319
    partner, 312-314
    structures, 314-315
Risk, factors and rewards, 46

Satellite, 82, 91
Satisfaction, 53-54
Servers
    choice, 77
    cost considerations, 78
    function, 78
    performance, 77
    reliability, 77
Services
    basic core accounting,
        57-58
    compliance, 57
    menu, 57
Small business
    client accounting practice,
        296-297
    market, 12-13, 16
    overview, 15
Small Business
    Administration (US), 16,
        30, 219
Software
    accounting categories,
        114-116
    accounting resources,
        58-59
    client/server, 116
    financial planning, 65-66
    fixed asset management
        resources, 61
    high-end accounting, 117
    mid-range accounting, 117
    online accounting, 297-299
    other software resources,
        122-130
    payroll, 63
    tax return preparation,
        64-65
    vendors, 119-121
    web-enabling, 95
    write-up resources, 59,
        129-130
Staffing
    compensation and
        ownership, 42
    key managers, 41-42
    organization, 41
    strategies and issues, 5-6,
        235
    team building, 307-311
    training, 86-87

Storage, 180-183, 188
Strategy, 42, 54, 221-223,
    236-245, 267-270,
    300-301
Structure, 53, 223-224
Success in accounting and
    consulting, 278-280
Success skills, 1, 211-213
Sun Microsystems, Inc., 96

T1, 81
Talent, 94
Tape, magnetic, 187
Tax preparation, 64-65,
    128-129
Teams
    implementation, 308-311
    vision and mission, 307
Technology
    boon or bane?, 246-247
    Fox's Law, 10
    gap, 290-291
    solution providers, 13-14
    strategic asset, 296
    transitional factors, 25
    value proposition, 79
    vendor concerns, 7
    vendors' issues, 6
Telcos, 87, 90

United States Government
    Department of Labor, 30
    resources for building a
        small to medium-sized
        business presence, 32
    Small Business
        Administration, 16, 30,
        219

Vendors
    concerns, 7
    rules for dealing with
        propaganda, 183-184
    technology issues, 6
Virtual Growth (Virtual
    Accountant), 122, 295,
    306
Virtual opportunities, 209
Vision, 291-292

Write-up, 59, 129-130

About the Author

Jack Fox is an expert advisor and author who offers hands-on, nononsense guidance on the real world specifics of creating and marketing an Internet-based accounting business.

Mr. Fox is the Founder and Executive Director of The Accounting Guild, http://www.accountingguild.com. This unique Internet-based organization assists accounting and consulting professionals in establishing and developing Internet-driven accounting and consulting practices. The Guild networks practitioners in a strategic alliance with other professionals, integrators, application software providers, and accounting solution providers.

As an unforgettable speaker, retreat facilitator, and practice development consultant, Jack Fox has shared his extensive knowledge and experience in assisting many accounting and consulting professionals start, build, and prosper in the accounting business. His other books include *Starting and Building Your Own Accounting Business, Third Edition,* and *Accounting and Recordkeeping Made Easy for the Self-Employed,* both published by Wiley; *Accountants' Guide to Budgetary Automation; GOD's Business Gamebook and Business Planning Guide,* a book on the Christian perspective of business published by The Accounting Guild; and *How To Obtain Your Own SBA Loan.*

All communications from readers are welcome and acknowledged. Personal experiences about your own accounting and consulting business hurdles and successes are particularly encouraged. For any and all comments, questions, plaudits, information requests, and seminar, retreat, or consultation inquiries, please e-mail the author at jfox1961@aol.com or jackfox@accountingguild.com.